Also by Mark Binelli

Sacco and Vanzetti Must Die!

DETROIT CITY
IS THE
PLACE TO BE

DETROIT CITY
IS THE
PLACE TO BE

The Afterlife of
an American Metropolis

Mark Binelli

Metropolitan Books
Henry Holt and Company
New York

Metropolitan Books
Henry Holt and Company, LLC
Publishers since 1866
175 Fifth Avenue
New York, New York 10010
www.henryholt.com

Metropolitan Books® and ▥® are registered trademarks of
Henry Holt and Company, LLC.

Library of Congress Cataloging-in-Publication data

Binelli, Mark.
    Detroit City is the place to be : the afterlife of an American metropolis / Mark
Binelli.
        p. cm.
    Includes index.
    ISBN 978-0-8050-9229-5 (hardback)
    1. City planning—Michigan—Detroit.   2. Cities and towns—Michigan—
Detroit.   I. Title.
    HT168.D45B56 2012
    307.1'2160977434—dc23

                                    2012016123

Henry Holt books are available for special promotions and premiums.
For details contact: Director, Special Markets.

First Edition 2012

Designed by Meryl Sussman Levavi
Printed in the United States of America
10 9 8 7 6 5 4

For Lydia and Evan, with much love

"And Marco answered: 'While, at a sign from you, sire, the unique and final city raises its stainless walls, I am collecting the ashes of the other possible cities that vanish to make room for it, cities that can never be rebuilt or remembered. When you know at last the residue of unhappiness for which no precious stone can compensate, you will be able to calculate the exact number of carats toward which that final diamond must strive. Otherwise, your calculations will be mistaken from the very start.'"

Italo Calvino, *Invisible Cities*

CONTENTS

DETROIT CITY

IS THE

PLACE TO BE

DET

SPIR

NOT TO SCALE   UPPER LEGEND: NEIGHBORHOODS   LOWER LEGEND: ∘∘ POINTS OF INTEREST

MAP BY: RODGER BINYONE (PEACEFUL TRAVELER / WICKED WANDERER) 2010

INTRODUCTION

BACK WHEN I WAS a boy, growing up just outside of Detroit, my friends and I beheld any mention of the city in popular culture with a special thrill. We loved how Detroit was deemed terrifying enough to be chosen as the dystopian locale of *RoboCop*, the science fiction film set in a coyly undated "near future," when Detroit had become so dangerous that the outsourcing of law enforcement to an armored, heavily weaponized cyborg would seem a prudent and necessary move. And when the producers of *Beverly Hills Cop* decided to make the hometown of Eddie Murphy's fish-out-of-water detective our own—because, after all, what could be more antipodal to Rodeo Drive than Woodward Avenue, what more alien presence to the Beverly Palms Hotel than a black dude from Detroit in a Mumford High T-shirt?—we delighted in that, too. We certainly tested the speakers of our American-made Dodge hatchbacks whenever a Detroit song found itself played on one of the competing local rock stations. Who would be churlish enough to flag these songs as relics of an earlier era or point out how the lyrics pivoted off the city's reputation for chaos, riotousness, destruction to such a degree the very *titles*—"Panic in Detroit" (Bowie, 1973), "Detroit Breakdown" (J. Geils Band, 1974), "Motor City Madhouse" (Nugent, 1975)—could be mistaken for headlines from July 1967? To this day, when the plangent opening piano chords of Journey's "Don't Stop Believin'" blare from a dive bar jukebox, who among us begrudges even this most overplayed of power ballads a respectful split-second cock of the head and perhaps a secret inner smile as well, all because the protagonist of the song was "born and raised in South Detroit"—no matter that there wasn't really a neighborhood called South Detroit or that the person living there wanted so badly to get the hell out he took a midnight train goin' anywhere.

My parents subscribed to *Time*, and I can remember excitedly reading a story, at the height of the tension between Ronald Reagan and the Soviet Union, detailing the effects of a single nuclear bomb dropped on a major American city. This city, the editors explained, had been chosen entirely at random—but of course it was Detroit, a choice that by 1982 probably came across to most locals as an ungallant case of piling on. Still, at twelve years old, I devoured the shout-out as if the city had won some national lottery.

The article began, "Say it is late April, a cloudless Thursday evening in Detroit. Assume further that there is no advance warning."

Beginning at ground zero of the blast and expanding concentrically, the story proceeded to describe, in gruesome detail, the fate of Detroit and its residents. If you happened to be watching a baseball game at the old Tiger Stadium, for example, you would immediately go blind. Then you would burst into flame. "But," the writer continued, unhelpfully, "the pain ends quickly: the explosion's blast wave, like a super-hardened wall of air moving faster than sound, crushes the stands and the spectators into a heap of rubble."

Skyscrapers topple. Commuters melt inside their cars. Even Canadians in neighboring Windsor—this I found particularly satisfying—would be fatally pelted with fragments of the Renaissance Center, "hurled across the river by 160-m.p.h. winds." Following the geography of the article to my family's own suburb, I learned that, only a minute after the blast, fires would be already raging and "tens of thousands" of people dying, survivors "crawl[ing] from wrecked homes" to see an eight-mile-high mushroom cloud in the distance.

But—survivors! *See*, I pointed out to my little brother, even at that early age displaying the hopeful spirit that all Detroit-area natives learn by necessity to cultivate like a rare breed of flower. *One of us might live!*

* * *

Detroit used to be the greatest working-class city in the most prosperous country in the world. With the explosion of the auto industry, it had become the Silicon Valley of the Jazz Age, a capitalist dream town of unrivaled innovation and bountiful reward. My family came from Italy, our neighbor from Tennessee, my dad's friends were from Poland, Lebanon, Mexico. All had been drawn to Detroit, if not explicitly for the auto industry—my father sharpened knives and sold restaurant equipment—then because of what the auto industry had come to represent. The cars rolling off the assembly lines existed as tangible manifestations of the American Dream, the factories themselves a glimpse of the birth of modernity, in which mass production would beget mass employment and, in turn, mass consumption. Workers, eager to claim their share of the unprecedentedly high wages on offer, migrated to the city in droves, doubling Detroit's population in a single decade, from 465,000 to nearly a million, making the city, by 1920, the fourth largest in the nation. The art deco skyscrapers bursting from the downtown streets like rockets must have seemed like monuments to Fordism's manifest destiny. Everything pointed up.

Often, people incorrectly isolate the 1967 riot as the pivotal Detroit-gone-wrong moment, after which nothing ever went right. In fact, the auto industry had been in a serious economic slump for at least a decade prior, with tension in the black community festering for even longer and the axial shift of jobs and white residents from city proper to suburbs solidly under way. What the civic unrest, aside from hastening the process, did permanently change was the national story line about the city. If, once, Detroit had stood for the purest fulfillment of U.S. industry, it now represented America's most epic urban failure, the apotheosis of the new inner-city mayhem sweeping the nation like LSD and unflattering muttonchop sideburns. The fires of the rebellion launched a long-running narrative, one that persists today, of Detroit as a hopelessly failed state, a terrifying place of violent crime and general lawlessness. As John Lee Hooker, who had come north to work on the assembly line at Ford and later made his name as a bluesman in the juke joints of Detroit's Hastings Street, sang in "Motor City Is Burning":

My hometown burnin' down to the ground
Worser than Vietnam . . .

That, for as long as I can remember, might as well have been the unofficial slogan of the city. WELCOME TO DETROIT: WORSER THAN VIETNAM.

Things proceeded apace—that is to say, horribly—despite a brief lull of hope offered by the election, in 1974, of Coleman Young, the city's first black mayor. With the emergence of crack, drug violence bloodied the city, while Devil's Night, the night before Halloween, traditionally a time for relatively harmless pranks involving toilet-papered trees and soaped car windows, turned into an annual city-wide arson festival, peaking in 1984 with an estimated eight hundred fires. As a media event, Devil's Night proved irresistibly photogenic, the smoke hanging over the city seeming to taunt its distant twin in 1967. Rather than two lit ends of a time line, the fires came to feel like a single conflagration, one that had never been extinguished, the time line itself—the entirety of the seventies—merely a long, slow-burning fuse.

* * *

Detroit has long been a city observers find endlessly fascinating, often to the irritation of people who actually live in Detroit—the kind of place easily conscripted for overblown metaphorical theses or described as being a "symptom" of something bigger. Whenever I told people I'd grown up in metropolitan Detroit, they expressed a morbid curiosity, as if I'd revealed having been raised the next town over from Chernobyl or in the same apartment building as Jeffrey Dahmer. Other urban centers face very similar problems, but none have plummeted from the same heights as Detroit. The story of the city, of its meteoric rise and stunning fall, possesses the sort of narrative arc to which people seem hardwired to respond. It's an almost classically structured tale of humble origins transcended by entrepreneurial moxie and much diligent toil, all eventually brought low by tragic flaws (hubris, greed, long-simmering prejudices come home to roost).

Of course, on a basic level of storytelling, people also love tales of Detroit because there's just something inherently pleasing about having one's plot expectations so consistently fulfilled. When the chief of police takes to Facebook to warn Christmas shoppers in Detroit not to carry cash (because of the high probability of being mugged) or when, over the course of a single fiery afternoon, eighty homes in the middle of the city go up like trees in an old-growth forest, it does not disrupt the equilibrium of the world. In fact, such events reinforce existing ideas in a way that's perversely reassuring. These are the sorts of stories people want to read about when they read about Detroit—especially, perhaps, at times of economic instability, when a reminder of the existence of a place so much more profoundly screwed than your own offers a cruel comfort, one which, thanks to the moral aspect of the city's downfall, viz. the aforementioned hubris, greed, and prejudice, can be indulged more or less guilt-free, even with a dash of schadenfreude.

And yet Detroit's almost mythic allure isn't solely about misery. People have been drawn to The City Where Life Is Worth Living (an actual non-ironical historical nickname*) since the golden age of the automobile. To commemorate the 1927 rollout of the Model A, for example, the modernist photographer and painter Charles Sheeler was hired by an advertising firm to spend six weeks at Ford's gargantuan River Rouge plant, the largest factory in the world, with ninety-three buildings, sixteen million square feet of floor space, and 120 miles—miles!—of conveyor belt. Sheeler shot the plant the way an eighteenth-century painter might have depicted the interior of a cathedral, the elemental, almost sanctified vastness a seemingly intentional reminder of man's insignificance in the presence of God—or, in this case, Mr. Ford. "Our factories," Sheeler later wrote, "are our substitute for religious expression."† While touring America in 1935, Le Corbusier also stopped in Detroit, requesting immediately upon his

---

*See, for example, Newsreel LIX, of John Dos Passos's *The Big Money*: "the stranger first coming to Detroit if he be interested in the busy, economic side of modern life will find a marvelous industrial beehive . . . 'DETROIT THE CITY WHERE LIFE IS WORTH LIVING.'"

†The most famous shot in Sheeler's series, *Criss-Crossed Conveyors*, evokes neither grit nor noise but instead an almost tabernacular grace. The smokestacks in the background look like the pipes of a massive church organ, the titular conveyor belts forming the shape of what is unmistakably a giant cross. The photograph was originally published in a 1928 issue of *Vanity Fair*, where the caption read, "In a landscape where size, quantity and speed are the cardinal virtues, it is natural that the largest factory, turning out the most cars in the least time, should come to have the quality of America's Mecca."

arrival his own tour of the Rouge. In his book *Cathedrals*, he wrote of being "plunged in a kind of stupor" after leaving the plant. He was convinced Detroit's factories would be where his mass-produced "homes of the future" might one day be built.

On the opposite end of the reactive spectrum, Louis-Ferdinand Céline, then a young doctor working for the League of Nations, visited Detroit in 1927 to report on the health conditions of workers at Ford's factories. Appalled by what he witnessed, Céline recorded the degradations of the assembly line in his report and, subsequently, in his novel *Journey to the End of the Night*. The book's protagonist, Ferdinand, describes the factories where he seeks work as resembling "enormous dollhouses, inside which you could see men moving, but hardly moving, as if they were struggling against something impossible. . . . And then all around me and above me as far as the sky, the heavy, composite, muffled roar of torrents of machines, hard wheels obstinately turning, grinding, groaning, always on the point of breaking down but never breaking down." Later, while receiving a medical examination preliminary to being hired, Ferdinand informs the doctor that he, too, is an educated man. "Your studies won't do you a bit of good around here, son," the doctor says, shooting him a dirty look. "We don't need imaginative types in our factory. What we need is chimpanzees. . . . Let me give you a piece of advice. Never mention your intelligence again!"

In 1929, the New York monthly *Outlook* sent the poet and journalist Matthew Josephson to cover the auto show. A leftist intellectual (and a fierce critic of Henry Ford) who had just published a biography of Zola, Josephson writes of the city with scorn and condescension, but also with undeniable awe, in the same manner one might marvel at the aesthetics and scale of, say, an SS rally as filmed by Leni Riefenstahl. After noting Detroit's unlikely possession of one of the original castings of *The Thinker*, which still glowers distractedly from the steps of the Detroit Institute of Arts, Josephson proceeds to frolic in the irony of Rodin's masterpiece brooding at the heart of a city in which thought, to Josephson's mind, "has somehow been circumvented": "Something that was automatic, something that ran by an internal combustion engine had taken its place. In fact a new word was needed to express the trance, the fearful concentration with which all men awaited the approaching Automobile Show. . . . No one thought of the human body, or the body politic. All minds were bent whole-heartedly upon the new Fisher or Chrysler bodies."

And yet, unhappily, Josephson also recognizes the brute power of a metropolis that he says has "no past . . . no history." He calls Detroit "the most modern city in the world, the city of tomorrow." This is not meant as a compliment.

* * *

In January 2009, precisely eighty years after Josephson's hysterical dispatch, I returned to Detroit on an identical assignment, to cover the approaching Automobile Show—and, more broadly, the collapse of the domestic auto industry—for *Rolling Stone*. My family still lived in the suburbs, so even though I'd moved away in 1993, I had contin-ued to visit regularly. All the while, Detroit had remained Detroit, a grim national punch line. In the eight decades since Josephson's account of the city's vulgar ascendance, my hometown had gone from being a place with "no past . . . no history" to becoming one that barely possessed a present and certainly had no future. At least not the version of the city Josephson witnessed, that city having become *entirely* history by this late date, the very word *Detroit* threatening to turn into one of those place-names that no longer immediately signi-fies place but rather, like Pompeii, Hiroshima, or Dresden, the trau-matic end of one.

When Josephson reported his own story, in January 1929, the stock market crash was nine months away. Detroit's fortunes plum-meted during the Great Depression, and it required nothing less than the outbreak of World War II, when the car factories were retooled as tank and aircraft plants and Detroit became known as "the Arsenal of Democracy," for the city to recover. In the case of my visit to the auto show, on the other hand, the economic free fall had been occurring in real time since the preceding summer. I arrived on the week of Barack Obama's inauguration, an incautiously hopeful moment, despite the seismic tremors of financial uncertainty. In Detroit, though, all minds were bent wholeheartedly not upon the new Fisher or Chrysler bodies—Chrysler, in fact, debuted no new models at the 2009 auto show and would declare bankruptcy three months later, with GM to follow shortly thereafter—but upon questions of basic survival, as the city faced its worst crisis in decades.

For Detroit, this was saying something. Where to begin? The most recent mayor, Kwame Kilpatrick, had just begun serving a three-month jail sentence, having resigned in disgrace following a sex and corruption scandal. Meanwhile, the heads of the Big Three automakers, just weeks earlier, had appeared before Congress to publicly grovel for a financial lifeline—this after personally making the nine-hour drive from Detroit to Washington in hybrid cars, atonement for flying to the initial hearing on corporate jets. (All the humiliating stunt lacked was Burt Reynolds racing them in a souped-up Prius and they might have pulled in some extra cash with a reality TV pilot.) At just over 15 percent, Michigan would have the highest unemployment rate in the nation by the end of the year; in the city, where half of all children lived in poverty and one study identified nearly half of all adults as functionally illiterate, officials estimated the true unemployment figure at closer to 50 percent. The national housing-market collapse felt like old news in Detroit by January 2009, when the *Detroit Free Press* ran a story about a street on the city's northeast side on which sixty of sixty-six houses had been foreclosed on or abandoned.

The school system remained the worst in the country, its administrators astoundingly corrupt. Crime had also shot back up: Detroit had the highest murder rate in the country (40.7 homicides per 100,000 residents in 2008) and was ranked by *Forbes* as the most dangerous U.S. city overall (based in part on a stunning 1,220 violent crimes per 100,000 residents). Yet the police department's entire crime lab had been shut down the previous fall, after a state audit found egregious levels of systemic error. Though the Devil's Night fires that plagued the city in the eighties had tapered off,* Detroit still reported 90,000 fires in 2008, double the number of New York, a city eleven times as populous. A deep racial animus continued to pit

---

*Surprisingly, Detroit city officials managed to successfully rebrand the night before Halloween "Angel's Night" in 1995. Thousands of volunteers enlist each year to help patrol their neighborhoods during the last days of October severely curbing the outbreaks of arson.

Detroit's suburbs against the city (the most segregated major metropolitan area in the country)—this despite the fact that the suburban sprawl largely invented by Detroit automakers had begun evincing a structural failure of its own, with foreclosure rates in once-model suburbs like Warren actually higher than Detroit's.

Detroit's own population had plummeted from a high of two million to 713,000, with an estimated 90,000 buildings left abandoned. Indeed, huge swaths of the city's 140 square miles were poised on the cusp of returning to nature. Along with the empty skyscrapers and block-long factories fallen into ruin, entire residential streets, once densely populated, resembled fields in rural Arkansas after most of the houses had either burned to the ground or ended up demolished. A friend's mother said she now carried pepper spray on her daily walks—not for protection from potential muggers, but from the packs of wild dogs she'd been seeing in the neighborhood. A coyote had just been spotted near downtown.

* * *

One afternoon, to get a better sense of the state of the city beyond the confines of the auto show, I met up with John Carlisle, the proprietor of the marvelous *Detroitblog*, on which he filed dispatches from some of the least-visited corners of the city. By day, Carlisle edited a weekly suburban newspaper, but online, writing as Detroitblogger John, he'd become the Joseph Mitchell of the postindustrial Midwest, ferreting out stories about vigilante ex-cops, whites-only hillbilly bars, and an old blues singer doing a healthy side business selling raccoon meat. That afternoon, we drove alongside snow-covered plains where houses once stood, what locals had begun calling the "urban prairie," and crept around the perimeter of General Motors' immense Fisher Body Plant, closed since 1984, its six floors of broken windows—hundreds of them, *entire blocks* of them—giving the place an odd beauty, like a dried-out beehive. At the vacant lot where Motown's headquarters had been left abandoned for years, we observed a moment of silent contemplation, Carlisle recalling the time before the demolition when he'd snuck inside and stumbled across Marvin Gaye's old desk, with love notes to Gaye's wife still in one of the drawers.

Finally, back downtown, we parked in front of the Metropolitan Building, a fifteen-story, neo-Gothic office tower opened in 1924. It was a weekday afternoon, but the street was completely deserted. A block away, I could see Woodward Avenue, Detroit's main thoroughfare.

The Metropolitan, once the center of the jewelry trade in Detroit, housed a number of jewelry manufacturers and wholesalers, but it had been empty since 1977. Someone had painted a garish football mural on the ground floor, and a filthy brown teddy bear had been tied to a street sign. "Memorial," Carlisle said. "Someone was shot here." Walking quickly to one of the building's doors, Carlisle turned the knob and was surprised to find it unlocked. Then he noticed a woman behind the counter at a carry-out place across the street, eyeing us. "Here, pretend I'm taking your picture," he said, posing me next to the memorial bear. He snapped a few shots until the woman turned away. Then we slipped inside the building and Carlisle switched on his flashlight.

The room had been completely gutted. Shards of plaster and glass covered the floor, and an icy draft blew through all of the broken windows. Carlisle splashed the walls with beams of light. Other than a single, cryptic graffiti tag, scrawled in Day-Glo orange, even the defaceable surfaces were barren. We began climbing the stairs. It was dark, and the wires dangling from the ceiling looked eerie and weblike. On one of the doors, someone had written, "If You Want 2 Die—" I paused and tried to make out the rest of the sentence, but it was illegible. Carlisle stopped on the flight above me and hissed, "What's wrong? You hear someone?"

Eventually we made it to the top floor. A couple of rusty radiators had been dragged to the center of the room and abandoned. "Crackheads always try to take them for scrap, but then realize they're too heavy," Carlisle said. He led me out to the snow-covered roof. We blinked in the bright daylight, staring up at what we'd come to see: the building's beautiful stone facade, a carved knight's helmet topping a coat of arms and ornate fleur-de-lis garlanding each window. Carlisle snapped a few pictures. He had started photographing Detroit's ruins several years earlier. In his explorations, he had come across homeless encampments, drug addicts getting high, a couple having sex. In another building, eight cops showed up with their guns drawn. After realizing Carlisle had only a camera, they let him go. There was nothing for him to steal, anyway, even if he had been a thief.

"This city is like a living museum," Carlisle said. "A museum of neglect."

We moved over to the parapet of the roof, crenelated like the top of some fortress, and gazed out at the city skyline. "That building is empty," Carlisle said, pointing to the nearest skyscraper. He shifted his finger to the left. "So is that one." Then, sounding surprised—and the hitch in his voice reminded me that he was not a professional guide, that he didn't do this every day—he pointed to the next building over and said, "And that one, too."

In 1995, a Chilean photographer, Camilo José Vergara, had cheekily proposed allowing a cluster of buildings in downtown Detroit to molder and become "an American Acropolis." Dismissed by many locals as a smirking Ivory Tower provocateur, Vergara turns out to have been a prophet. I hadn't brought a camera, but I could have been a tourist in the off-season at a scenic overlook.

And yet, standing in calf-deep snow, my hands thrust deep in my coat pockets, staring out at this wintry scene of ruin, I had to admit I didn't really feel sadness, or anger, or much of anything. Depressingly, perhaps, it all just felt normal. For people of my generation and younger, growing up in the Detroit area meant growing up with a constant reminder of the best having ended a long time ago. We held no other concept of Detroit *but* as a shell of its former self. Our parents could mourn what it used to be and tell us stories about the wonderful downtown department stores and the heyday of Motown and muscle cars. But for us, those stories existed as pure fable. It was like being told about an uncle who died before you were born, what a terrific guy he'd been, if only you'd had the chance to meet him, see how handsome he looks in these old pictures . . .

Would my kids one day grow up thinking the same thoughts about America as a whole, about my ponderous tales of cold war victories and dot-com booms? It was easy to let your imagination drift in melodramatic courses. A malaise spreading through the rest of the country—a creeping sense of dread that, after spending the past eight years doing absolutely everything wrong, this time we really had reached the inevitable end of our particular empire—all of this had the effect of making Detroit, for the first time in my life, feel less like a crazy anomaly and more like a leading indicator. The mood of hopelessness had become palpable. I found myself fleetingly wondering if Detroit, in the end, might reclaim its old title after all—not the Motor City but the city of tomorrow.

John said we should go. I squinted out over the ledge one last time. The icy wind was almost harsh enough to make you cry, and Detroit, from up here, looked like it went on forever.

* * *

The story of Detroit has long functioned as a cautionary tale, as much a memento mori as one of those Roman catacombs lined with the skulls of dead monks. *What you are now, we once were; what we are now, you will become.* For this reason, observers have a tendency to approach Detroit as a forensic investigation, a sort of murder mystery. They examine the body, poke their gloved digits into the wounds, dust the crime scene for prints. Whom you ended up fingering in the drawing room could often say as much about your own biases as about the city itself. For instance, when people place all of the blame for the demise of Detroit on the riots, or white flight, or "political corruption," there's an implicit racial—sometimes racist—element to the critique, as Detroit, post-1967, would become a black city, still 85 percent African American today, run entirely by a black political elite, which lends the nostalgia for the "old" Detroit expressed by so many white suburbanites of a certain age an occasionally disquieting subtext.

Unsurprisingly, black Detroiters of a similar age can offer up a wholly different reading of these events, one in which the word *uprising* replaces *riot*, and in which the destructive fallout, while not celebrated, is contextually understood as a reaction to years of workplace discrimination, redlining, slum housing, and abuse at the hands of goon-squad cops. As for the city's subsequent decline, well, an observer sympathetic to this point of view might note that *of course* the oppressors would not simply flee, not without sacking the joint on the way out the door and doing everything possible once they'd gone (top-down disin-vestment, supporting lopsided suburb-favoring land use and tax struc-tures, dismantling public transportation, more redlining) to ensure the failure of, and effectively place sanctions upon, the hostile regime left behind.

Some blame the unions for their unchecked power and excessive demands, making Michigan an impossible place to do business; oth-ers, the Big Three automakers, for selling out the working class by moving factories abroad and to southern "right to work" states and for so badly bungling their own business model with chronic shortsight-edness and an inability to adapt to a world involving actual competi-tion with high-quality foreign product. Environmentalists might see the combustion engine as Culprit Zero; urbanophiles, the metastasiz-ing suburbs; leftist European academics, the rot of capitalism and the long-fated unraveling of our great Yankee folly.

But I wasn't really interested in any of that. Detroit-as-whodunit had been done, ad nauseam. Rather than relitigate the sins of the past, I hoped to discover something new about the city—specifically, what happens to a once-great place after it has been used up and dis-carded? Who sticks around and tries to make things work again? And what sorts of newcomers are drawn to the place for similar reasons? These questions seemed particularly pertinent now that Detroit was no longer such a freakish outlier. Cities in Florida and California, in the Rust Belt and the Sun Belt, in England and the Mediterranean and who knew where next, they'd all woken up to the same problems that have been pummeling Detroit for decades, including but not limited to structural bankruptcy, unsustainable city services and public obli-gations, chronic unemployment, vacant and increasingly worthless real estate, and the disappearance of a workable tax base. Left unchecked, Detroit levels of crime, political instability, and blight would certainly follow.

I wanted to think about how Detroiters struggled mightily to solve these problems—historically, yes, but more importantly right now.

* * *

I wasn't alone. In the waning months of the Bush administration, a curi-ous thing happened, as Michigan experienced a small but significant uptick in one very specific sector of its tourism economy: journalists started showing up. It turned out that explaining the origins of the financial crisis in any detail required elaborate definitions of complex and stupefyingly boring financial terms like *credit default swap* and *collateralized debt obligation*. But with the potential bankruptcy of General Motors, you had something tangible and wholly understandable to a layperson. We'd all at least *ridden* in an American car at some point, just as we all possessed opinions on various ways in which they sucked. Even better, Detroit provided the sort of breathtaking visual backdrop that shots of anxious-looking Wall Street floor traders or the exterior of Bernie Madoff's condo simply could not compete with. As the hurricane approaches landfall, journalistic convention dictates a live report from the field, wherein the correspondent must don a rain poncho and shout into a microphone while being buffeted by the elements, palm trees flailing wildly on the deserted beach in the background. A visit to the ruins of the old Packard plant or a "ghost street" of abandoned houses became the financial-collapse equivalent. It had taken the worst economic crisis since the Great Depression to do the unthinkable: Detroit had suddenly become trendy.

And so we all came. Reporters from *Fortune*, the *Guardian*, CNN, the *Economist*, *Vice*, from Tokyo and Paris, Sydney and Los Angeles. While attempting to get footage of the Packard plant, a Dutch film crew was carjacked, which itself became a news event, adding to the "Detroit so crazy!" story line in a satisfying, metanarrative kind of way. At a public school rally, I nearly bumped into Dan Rather. Was Dan Rather even *on television* anymore? Had he just turned up on his own dime, drawn by an old man's vampirish sixth sense to the most swollen vein in the circulatory system of the present news cycle?

Time also turned its gaze back to Detroit in 2009. This time around, the magazine had come not to engage in speculative nuclear annihilation but rather to launch Assignment Detroit, a project being billed as a bold new journalistic experiment—a team of reporters would cover the city over the course of a year, living in a company-purchased home in Indian Village, one of the last remaining swank neighborhoods in the city proper. Not coincidentally, one of the first stories produced by Assignment Detroit was about how residents of such besieged neighborhoods had taken to hiring private security details to patrol their blocks. The previous fall, around the time of the auto bailout hearings, a photo essay of ruined Detroit buildings on *Time*'s website titled "Detroit's Beautiful, Horrible Decline" had been a big hit, despite the unfortunate ordering of adjectives. The tagline of Assignment Detroit's new blog, "One year, one city, endless opportunities," also hinted, inadvertently, at the magazine's own opportunistic appropriation of Detroit's sudden chicness.

The new obsession with Detroit did not end with journalists, at least not according to the journalists themselves, who reported on how artists were also colonizing the city. Could this be a first wave of bohemian gentrification? Was Detroit the next Williamsburg? One young couple from Chicago had bought a home in Detroit for a hundred bucks. Brooklyn artists came and froze another house in a block of ice. Thanks to a nearly 50 percent tax incentive being offered by the state, Hollywood film crews also arrived, along with actors like George Clooney and Richard Gere. A glossy French fashion magazine even produced a special "Detroit issue" featuring shots of models in ruined industrial backdrops. The magazine cost twenty dollars in the United States—or, in local terms, one-fifth of the price of a home in Detroit.

Land speculators made the scene, too, as the new mayor, former Detroit Pistons basketball star Dave Bing, began to publicly acknowledge the need for the city to both shrink and radically reinvent itself, a pledge that urban-theorists, who had long regarded Detroit as the unsolvable math problem of their field, found tantalizing. And so they came, too, along with the Scandinavian academics, the neopastoralian agriculturalists, the deep-pocketed philanthropical organizations and the free-market ideologues and the fringe-left utopianists—they all came. For the most idealistic of these pioneers, which is how many of the newcomers self-identified, Detroit might very well be the city of tomorrow, but of a wholly different sort than described above. They'd come to see the place as a blank slate, so debased and forgotten it could be remade. The irony was almost too perfect: Detroit, having done more than any other city to promote the sprawl and sub-urbanization that had so despoiled the past century, could now become a model green city for the new century, with bike paths and urban farms and grass-roots sustainability nudging aside planned obsolescence.

So I joined the wagon train, alongside the hustlers and the do-gooders, the preachers and the criminals, the big dreamers looking to make names for themselves and the heavily armed zealots awaiting the end of the world. They—we!—came like pilgrims, to witness, to profit from, to somehow influence the story of the century. It might very well turn out to be the story of the *last* century, the death rattle of the twentieth-century definition of the American Dream. But there could also be another story emerging, the story of the first great postindustrial city of our new century. Who knows? Crazier things have happened in Detroit. It's a place so unspooled, one's wildest experiments, ideas that would never be seriously considered in a functioning city, might actually have a shot here. Nothing else had worked, and so everything was permitted. The ongoing catastrophes had, in a strange way, bequeathed the place an unexpected asset, something few other cities of its size possessed: a unique sense of possibility. On a psychological level, this played out as one of those instances when a hoary cliché (or, in this case, a Kris Kristofferson lyric) is basically true: having nothing left to lose really *did* open the mind to an otherwise tricky-to-come-by sense of freedom.

After I moved back to the city, people I met in dozens of different contexts described Detroit as "the Wild West." Meaning, it's basically lawless. Meaning, land is plentiful and cheap. Meaning, now, as the frontier quite literally returns to the city—trees growing out of tops of abandoned buildings! wild pheasants circling the empty lots!—so, too, has the metaphorical frontier, along with the notion of "frontier spirit." All possibly offensive notions to the people who'd never left, for reasons of choice or circumstance. But it's undeniable that Detroit feels like an extraordinary place, and at the same time, just as Greenland might be called ground zero of the

Service Street. The author's building is the third from left.

[Chris Ringler]

broader climate crisis, Detroit feels like ground zero for . . . what, exactly? The end of the American way of life? Or the beginning of something else?

Either way, that is why so many divergent interests are converging here right now. Who doesn't want to see the future?

I

GOIN' TO DETROIT, MICHIGAN

DETROIT IS 139 SQUARE miles and shaped, roughly, like an outboard motor. Looking at a map, you might also think of an anvil, but mostly because the northernmost border, the famous 8 Mile Road, traces such a perfectly planed line. My own return to the city began at the edge of downtown, in the Eastern Market neighborhood. Though best known for its weekly farmer's market, Eastern Market remained primarily a distribution hub for wholesale food: produce, imported dry goods, meat from several working slaughterhouses.

I'd made regular deliveries to Eastern Market for my dad as a teenager, and when I pulled my rental car onto Service Street, which ran behind the building housing my new apartment, I realized I'd navigated this very alley many times before, years earlier, in one of my father's knife-delivery vans, dropping off (as I recalled) newly sharpened meat grinder blades, which resembled little metal starfish and spun around in the grinders' gullets. Butcher & Packer, a supplier of restaurants and meat markets, was still in business, just down the block from my new place. A key component of the Butcher & Packer inventory had been an assortment of premixed spices for seasoning sausages. Twenty years later, I could immediately conjure the pungent, curried funk of the place.

The rest of the block, comprised of nondescript brick warehouses and commercial structures, had been converted into lofts. The buildings fronted Gratiot Avenue, a major Detroit boulevard. One of the street-level businesses was a place called the Unemployment Institute, which, according to signs in the windows, offered services like "pre-employment screening" and "online job searching." Large color photographs of people doing businesslike things had been incorporated into the signage—for example, a man touching his head pensively while staring down at a sheet of paper. The look on the man's face was inscrutable; either he was puzzling over a very difficult business-related problem or he'd just received terrible news. Conveniently, if the Unemployment Institute didn't have what you were looking for, the Lama Temple, right next door, sold lucky oils and candles and lottery tip sheets. A green candle painted on the window bore the word MONEY. Aside from Butcher & Packer, the Unemployment Institute and Lama Temple were the only two operational storefronts on the entire block, but this was not an especially poor occupancy rate for Detroit.

If you stood in front of the Lama Temple and gazed north, you would see the towers of the Brewster-Douglass projects, which housed residents displaced from Black Bottom,* a thriving black neighborhood destroyed in the 1950s by the I-75 freeway. Stevie Wonder, Marvin Gaye, several of the Supremes, Smokey Robinson, and Berry Gordy all grew up there. The projects were closed down years earlier, and now the towers kept watch over the freeway with a hollow menace, every last window of the fourteen-story high-rises—even their frames—having been removed by scrappers. A friend called them the "zombie towers": undead husks, stubbornly upright.

Approximately 30 percent of Detroit proper, though—nearly forty square miles—is now vacant land.† As I reacclimated myself to the city, I came to see the dominant tone, no matter where I ended up, as one of absence: the unsettling absence of people, and the missing buildings and homes, which left jarring gaps in the architectural landscape; the absence of regular commerce (fast food, liquor stores, funeral parlors, and the most minuscule pockets of gentrification

---

*The name was not as racist as it sounds: the area was originally named by the French for its dark, fertile topsoil.
†The entire city of San Francisco is approximately forty-seven square miles.

excepted) and the way, when night fell, long stretches of major city streets became pitch-black country roads, Detroit's lighting department remaining too broke to replace so many extinguished street lamps. And on those same streets—right here, in the Motor City— the absence of any normal semblance of vehicular traffic.

And then there were the ruins. When it comes to the sheer level of decay, Detroit is truly a singular place; among the city's ninety thousand abandoned structures, there were residential homes, mansions, storefronts, motels, factories (miles and miles of unplanned obsolescence, like the 3,500,000-square-foot Packard plant, spread across thirty-five acres of land and closed since 1958), Ford Auditorium (the former home of the Detroit Symphony Orchestra), banks, warehouses, Coney Island hot dog restaurants, YWCAs and YMCAs, the Reason Why Cocktail Bar, hospitals, churches, synagogues, porn theaters, schools, public libraries, a Chinese restaurant called Kung Food, a pair of geodesic domes, a club called Another Level, a children's zoo, a slaughterhouse, beauty parlors, my father's old knife shop, a car wash called Wash My Car, supermarkets, gas stations, an amusement-park ferry terminal, a bar called Stream in the Desert, the thirty-eight-story Book Building (1926), the nineteen-story David Whitney Building (1915), every building on Chene between Ferry and Hendrie (except for the Ideal Liquor Store), every building on Fort between Dragoon and Cavalry, and the All Star Barber Shop (its roof burned off, leaving a charred flattop).

Most of the blight in Detroit is just that, blight. Away from the skyscrapers and the unbelievably vast industrial structures, back down at eye level, the quotidian monotony of the blasted and empty storefronts quickly becomes numbing, even though the scale can be unmooring. Some buildings have been picked clean as skulls by thieves, others left gaping and ravaged in a way that made you feel as if you were violating someone's privacy by peering inside, somehow committing an act of voyeuristic sin, like a Peeping Tom catching a glimpse up a skirt. Apparently, by sneaking into the Metropolitan Building with John Carlisle for my original *Rolling Stone* piece, I'd committed a grievous journalistic faux pas—at least in the eyes of certain Detroiters, who were, understandably, quite touchy about the way the ruins have become favorite tour stops of visiting reporters. But what new-comer could ignore them?

Though most commuters in southeast Michigan never pass an opportunity to jump onto the freeway, even if they're only traveling as far as the next exit, I like to keep to the surface streets when I'm driving in Detroit, partly just to take in the scenery. One afternoon on Rosa Parks Boulevard, I spotted an enormous cloud of black smoke in the distance. It was startling, because I had been driving up Rosa Parks a few minutes earlier (trying to find the corner where the 1967 riot had started) before looping back to a film shoot I'd noticed on a side street. There had been no giant smoke cloud that first time around. I continued in the direction of the fire, which turned out to have started at a warehouse near the highway. A crowd had gathered for the action. I overheard a security guard ask her friend, "You ever see this many people out here? This is more than on payday!" Another woman called in a panicked voice, "They out of water. The firefighters are out of water!" But they weren't. A few moments later, jets streamed from one of the hoses.

The fire raged with fairly spectacular amplitude and intensity. Looking up, I thought I could see the moon behind the billowing clouds of black smoke. Then the clouds drifted away and I felt the heat of the summer afternoon beating down on me again and I realized I'd been staring at the sun, which the smoke clouds had almost completely blotted out.

I left shortly after that, worried by rumors circulating that the plant housed chemicals and we might be breathing toxic fumes. On the way home, I took a circuitous route and saw a plume of smoke on the horizon. I thought, "How the hell did I completely turn myself around?" But I hadn't. I was driving in the right direction and just looking at another fire.

* * *

If you're from Detroit, you're either from the east side or the west side, by which you would mean a "side" of Woodward Avenue, which splits the city down the middle. The east side neighborhoods, closest to the Detroit River and Lake St. Clair, were the first to be colonized and thus are older and generally less well-off than the landlocked, more tightly gridded western blocks. The proximity to water gives the east side a coastal lackadaisy, though the severe depopulation of many of the neighborhoods might also contribute to the ambience, the endless, grassy fields surrounding an occasional lonely homestead making for a decidedly countrified air. People from the west side say they never go to the east because it's too violent and dangerous (but people from the east side say the same thing about the west).

The east has the mayoral mansion, and the artist Tyree Guyton's internationally beloved Heidelberg Project, an entire residential block transformed into a sculptural installation, and Belle Isle, the city's bucolic island park, designed by Frederick Law Olmsted in 1883. The houses here tend toward the older, wood-frame bungalow. For a short few weeks during the summer, the streets closest to Lake St. Clair are overrun with millions of *Hexagenia limbata*, twig-bodied, long-winged insects known locally as "fish flies." Fish flies spawn and hatch miles from the shore, eventually shedding an outer layer of shell, which they employ as flotation devices for the landward journey—though, unfortunately, their two-day lifespan provides only enough shore time for the couples to mate before the males unceremoniously die and the females fly back out to the lake, deposit their fertilized eggs, and likewise expire. Despite the brevity of their time in the city, fish flies en masse mimic the effects of a top-drawer biblical plague. At the peak of fish fly season, the bugs fur every illuminated surface close to the water (lamppost, party store* entrance, front porch, parking lot), forming a thick carpet on lakeside streets that makes a crunching sound as cars roll by. It is possible that the absence of fish flies has made west siders softer.

Many of the major streets on the east side are named for French settlers: Dequindre, Gratiot, Cadieux. Other roads share names with one-term Republican presidents (Hoover, Hayes) and outmoded styles of beard (Van Dyke). There are also roads called Mound, Mack, Morang, Chalmers, Conant, and Caniff.

Street names on the west side, on the other hand, evoke the romantic idea of the American West, conjuring images of unspoiled

---

*Our term for liquor stores in metropolitan Detroit.

nature, wide open plains, and frontier optimism: Greenfield, South-field, Wyoming, Evergreen, Telegraph, Joy. Berry Gordy founded Motown Records on the west side, not far from where Aretha Franklin grew up and first sang at her father's church, New Bethel. The art deco sign at Baker's Keyboard Lounge, which claims to be the oldest con-tinuously operating jazz club in the world, still glows nightly on Liv-ernois. For black Detroiters, the west side traditionally stood for upward mobility. On the far western edge of 7 Mile, another church, the $35 million Greater Grace Temple, sits on nineteen acres of lush parkland. Greater Grace's holdings include a golf course, a senior hous-ing complex, low-income rental units, and a travel agency. The pastor, Charles Ellis III, has become known for his highly theatrical "illus-trated sermons"—for example, during the auto bailout hearings, his blessing, on the chancel, of three sport-utility vehicles (one loaned from each of the Big Three automakers).

My own Eastern Market neighborhood abutted the downtown center, where the fortresslike glass towers of the Renaissance Center, built in the seventies as a riot-proof lure for business and currently serving as the world headquarters of General Motors, gleam impreg-nably from the edge of the Detroit River. On a nearby traffic median, a public sculpture dedicated to boxer and city native Joe Louis hangs from a swinglike contraption. The sculpture is a twenty-four-foot, eight-thousand-pound black fist, pointing directly at Canada.

Outside of downtown Detroit, residential neighborhoods through-out the city have the feel of a place like Atlanta or Los Angeles—less urban density, more single-family homes with front lawns and garages. By the 1940s, according to historian Thomas Sugrue, just over 1 per-cent of the residential structures in Detroit were apartment buildings, while two-thirds of Detroiters lived in single-family homes. Workers had the means to spread out, and the room, and so they did. A series of parallel roads cross the city (and the surrounding suburbs) from east to west at one-mile intervals, although they are not labeled as such until 7 Mile. Beyond 8 Mile Road, the suburbs also cleave east and west. The east side includes the Waspy, old-money Grosse Pointe, though many of the neighboring communities are fading first-ring suburbs, blue-collar places like Warren, St. Clair Shores, Roseville, and Eastpointe, all largely working class and ethnic: Italian, Polish, Irish, German.

Most of the wealthier suburbs are on the west side, in Oakland County, still one of the richest counties per capita in the nation, with cities like Birmingham and West Bloomfield. Farther west, there's Dearborn, where the Ford family once farmed and where Henry, a pioneer not only in Taylorized mass production but in suburban homesteading, would move his corporate headquarters and primary residency, the Fairlane Estate. Closer to the river, the scenery shifts with disconcerting suddenness to an almost surreal Industrial Age tableau dominated by the Ford Rouge plant, smokestacks rising like the peaks of Mordor from its two thousand acres.

Back when business was booming, railroad lines connected the city's car factories, metalworks, chemical plants, and hundreds of tinier parts shops like the cells of a single, groaning organism, a "simply staggering" environment, in the words of historian Olivier Zunz, wherein "the density of factories was such that the city appeared to have a totally industrial landscape." Today, there's still a bleak light-industrial aesthetic to many of the commercial strips throughout the greater metropolitan area. A gray quietude hangs over many of the buildings, which, thanks to their windowless, painted-cinderblock functionality, offer few clues as to present-day habitation or disuse.

The blacks working at the Rouge didn't necessarily want to commute all the way from Detroit but they weren't welcome in Dearborn, so they began settling in the regrettably named suburb of Inkster (which in fact commemorates an early Scottish settler, Robert Inkster). For over three decades, Dearborn was ruled by Mayor Orville Hubbard, a morbidly obese open segregationist who once skirted a court-ordered travel ban by boarding a train disguised as a clown and, less charmingly, said things in public like, "If whites don't want to live with niggers, they sure as hell don't have to. Dammit, this is a free country."

Hubbard is long dead, but Oakland County is still ruled by L. Brooks Patterson, the paunchy Republican county executive who, in the early 1970s, made a name for himself by taking up the cause of suburban opponents of busing. Policies fostering regionalism, enacted in cities like Indianapolis, have been elusive in metropolitan Detroit. Instead, via unchecked suburban growth, counties like Oakland and Macomb have physically recoiled from the city, over the years continuing to spread north and west. On Oakland County's official website, Patterson himself has written, "I love sprawl. I need it. I promote it. Oakland County can't get enough of it."

Not coincidentally, there's also a distinct absence of any sort of regional public transportation. And so in the adopted city of Rosa Parks, the bus system remains essentially segregated, as the surrounding suburbs maintain their own regional bus line, wholly separate from that of the city, where the riders are almost entirely African American. Certain suburban bus lines will take riders from the suburbs downtown, but they go express as soon as they cross into the city proper and will not pick up new passengers.

Dearborn, meanwhile, has become home to the largest Arabic-speaking population in North America—primarily Iraqis, Lebanese, Syrians, Palestinians, and Yemeni. The best restaurants in metropolitan Detroit, for my money, are here, along stretches of Warren and Vernor that feel like neighborhoods in Damascus or Beirut, if either of those cities have mini-malls. As the state of Michigan continued hemorrhaging residents, one demographic experienced a minor growth surge, about five thousand new arrivals in the Detroit metro area in 2010 alone: Iraqi immigrants.

So that was something. Dire though things had become, Detroit, apparently, remained a more desirable place to live than postwar Baghdad.

* * *

Every morning, I walked over to the newspaper boxes in front of the deli in Eastern Market and picked up copies of the *Detroit News* and the *Detroit Free Press*. The city lacked many things, but it had managed to hang onto two major broadsheets, both servicing their audiences with headlines that felt like dispatches from the apocalypse. The summer I returned, for example, I learned about a dog plague: canine parvovirus, a disease that could be deadly, spreading throughout southeastern Michigan, primarily, the experts speculated, because owners could no longer afford to vaccinate their pets. Also, 750,000 people in Michigan were looking for work, the highest unemployment number in the state's history. And the home of the outgoing chief of police, James Barren, was burgled: the thieves made off with jewelry, a computer, a camcorder, and a television set, among other things. Asked for comment, Barren acknowledged, "They got me pretty good."

When location scouts for the movie *Little Murder* were checking out a block in the Woodbridge neighborhood, a pair of bandanna-wearing teenagers with sawed-off shotguns robbed them in broad daylight. The movie was set in New Orleans just after Katrina; apparently, minimal production design would be necessary to make certain neighborhoods in Detroit look as if they'd just been destroyed by a flood.

An off-duty police lieutenant was carjacked at a fast food drive-through window. A white suburban teenager was carjacked at a Quiznos in Eastpointe, not far from where I grew up. His body was discovered in an abandoned home in Detroit about a week later. Incoming police chief Warren Evans spoke with arresting frankness to the *Detroit Free Press* about the number of shootings in the city the previous year. "I don't know what 1,100 means to someone who figures they're part of an anonymous 800,000 population," Evans said. "But over 1,100 people being shot is getting kind of Third World to me."

In all, it was reported, thirty-five metro Detroit teenagers (and one twelve-year-old) awaited trial for murder in various detention centers. Among them: two boys charged with beating a homeless man to death, apparently for no reason, and the so-called Rib Rack Killer, accused of shooting and killing the night manager of a Rib Rack fast food restaurant during a botched robbery attempt. The accused killer and his two accomplices had also attempted to rob a man named Mr. Cash, known for selling Cartier sunglasses out of the trunk of his car. That robbery had been foiled by Mr. Cash, who was carrying his own gun.

"DETROIT COPS," we were informed, "LEAD NATION IN SUICIDE." "TEEN," they told us, "TOO PREGNANT FOR JAIL." "DETROIT FIREFIGHTERS HAVE THEIR OWN NAME FOR FORECLOSED HOMES," began another article. "FUEL."

* * *

None of these headlines had the legs or the national reach of Detroit's abysmal census showing. The decline should have been no suprise to anyone who'd taken even a cursory tour of the city's empty streets.

And yet, something about the hard numbers—Detroit had shed 25 percent of its population in the first decade of the twenty-first century, putting its population at a pre–Model T low of 713,777—brought a bracing empiricism to the problem and also, conveniently, fit an especially beloved subset of the Detroit-as-failed-state story line, the crazy statistic. Did you know Detroit experienced a *97 percent decline in residential property value* over the past eight years? Or that the Pontiac Silverdome sold for the price of a *Manhattan studio apartment*? Or that a family moved out of the state *every twelve minutes*?

The census story was trumpeted with a mixture of solemn condolence and barely concealed delight. The news raced around the Internet and made the front page of newspapers throughout the country. Local politicians also responded quickly—most, essentially, demanding a recount. The city council president insisted (on his Facebook page) that the count was "way low" and told a newspaper that one of the reasons had to do with the large number of Detroit residents who were serving prison time in other cities, which struck me as a poorly chosen line of argument.

Detroit's population explosion had begun nearly a century earlier. People came to the city because Detroit represented an idea about America they wanted to believe. Progress was inevitable; personal salvation could be achieved through hard work. Detroit, *New York Times* columnist Anne O'Hare McCormick wrote in 1934, "is twentieth century":

> It belongs to a period of democratized luxuries, with gas stations on every corner, chain stores, moving-picture palaces, glittering automats, broadcast symphonies. . . . In a way Detroit is the birthplace of this civilization. It is as truly a world capital as any city on earth, more fascinating to the outlander than New York, more influential than Washington, or even Hollywood. Paris dictates a season's silhouette, but Detroit manufactures a pattern of life. As a capital of revolution, it is far brisker and bolder than Moscow in transforming human habits and communizing the output of the machine.

With the onset of World War II, Detroit's assembly lines began running three shifts, turning out tanks, jeeps, and fighter planes and becoming the first modern manifestation of the naked profit at stake in what had yet to be termed the military-industrial complex. Postwar, metropolitan Detroit provided a model for the suburbanization taking place across the United States. Southfield was home to Northland Mall, the first shopping mall in the country, built in 1954 by the Austrian-born socialist architect Victor Gruen, who would later denounce his creations as the precursors to hideous suburban sprawl. Warren, home of the General Motors Tank Plant, was, at the time, one of the fastest-growing cities in the United States.

All of which put unique pressure on the city proper. Just as various factors converged perfectly to make Detroit the Motor City, so did harsh new realities conspire to steal the title away: the automakers' desire to escape the strong local unions, which benefited southern states; the lure of the low business taxes offered by the new suburbs, which could get by with less revenue, having far fewer expenses than an aging city like Detroit, with its larger, more impoverished population; pressure from the Pentagon for industry to move, with cold war leaders, afraid of nuclear strikes, convinced that the cluster of American military production in Detroit posed a threat; and the simple need for more land. It was much more difficult to expand a preexisting plant, let alone build a modern new facility, in a congested, older city, as opposed to the open fields of the suburbs. This problem led to a stronger push for "slum clearance" to make room for housing developments and factories, which, like today's downtown stadiums, were basically state-subsidized giveaways to corporations in exchange for their willingness to locate in the city. In the end, as businesses and working-class whites with means gained increasing mobility, all but the most elite of blacks had less and less.*

Racial tensions had already been growing in the overcrowded city. In the August 17, 1942, issue of *Life*, amid ads for Colgate ("No

---

*All of this is masterfully chronicled by Thomas Sugrue in *The Origins of the Urban Crisis*, his indispensable history of the decades leading up to 1967.

Male . . . For the Girl Who Has Bad Breath") and a cartoon in which Dagwood Bumstead makes himself a tongue-onion-mustard-sardine-horseradish sandwich, an article titled "Detroit Is Dynamite" described a city "seeth[ing] with racial, religious, political and economic unrest." "The news from Detroit is bad this summer," the piece began, ominously. "Few people across the country realize how bad it is. . . . Detroit can either blow up Hitler or it can blow up the U.S." Detroit's roiling citizenry, now numbering two million, "give their loyalty to their own group, creed or union. . . . In this melting pot flourish demagogues of every persuasion—Communists, Fascists, Ku-Kluxers, Coughlinites, pro-Nazi leaders of the National Workers League."

In fact, six months before the *Life* article, the opening of the Sojourner Truth housing projects in a predominantly white neighborhood had prompted armed resistance, and by the summer of 1943, a full-blown race riot erupted on Belle Isle, spreading throughout the city for thirty-six hours. Thirty-four people died, including an Italian doctor who drove into a black neighborhood on a house call (dragged from his car, beaten to death) and a fifty-eight-year-old black man waiting for a bus (shot by a gang of white youths). Twenty-five of the dead and the vast majority of the eighteen hundred people arrested were African American. Six thousand federal troops were eventually called in to quell the fighting, and the city remained occupied for the next six months; it was the worst case of civic unrest in the United States since the New York City draft riots of 1863.

Republican Albert Cobo was elected mayor in 1950 by playing on racial fears and running on, essentially, an anti–public housing platform. As mayor, Cobo ignored the advice of all public policy experts and clustered low-income minority public housing in isolated ghettos rather than attempt any sort of integration. Not that that would have necessarily worked. White flight was well under way by the 1950s, when real estate appraisers labeled any neighborhoods with blacks "hazardous." As late as 1970, according to the census numbers cited in B. J. Widick's *Detroit: City of Race and Class Violence*, Warren and Birmingham had five black residents each, Grosse Pointe two, Dearborn, Hazel Park, and Harper Woods one.

* * *

You rarely saw any black people in St. Clair Shores, the blue-collar suburb where I grew up, at least when I was a kid. There were a handful of black students at my all-boys Catholic high school (in nearby Harper Woods), but they commuted from Detroit proper. A nasty rumor circulated around that time regarding a supposed police-band code used by Grosse Pointe cops: "NOMAD," short for "nigger on Mack [Avenue] after dark."

St. Clair Shores had been the sticks when my mother and her family emigrated from Italy in the late forties. Back then, the roads were still dirt, and even though my grandparents were desperately poor, they managed to scrape together enough money to purchase a corner lot on which one could fit at least three normal-sized suburban homes. As kids, my cousins and I would run around my grandmother's yard, which felt to us like a park, chucking crab apples at one another and snapping the branches off the weeping willow tree for use as whips in obscure games involving slavery.

My father, Italo, arrived in Detroit in 1959, when he was twenty-six years old. He came from Pinzolo, a village in the Dolomites. While he was still a teenager, his parents pulled him out of school and sent him to Trieste to apprentice in a butcher's shop. One of his jobs involved massaging the blood of freshly slaughtered pigs (by hand) as it drained into a tub (preventing coagulative jellying apparently being a crucial preliminary step in the production of blood sausage). He'd always been good with machines and dreamed of becoming a mechanic, but at that time, with the postwar Italian economy reduced to rubble and my paternal familial economy long an austere one—my grandfather, Clemente, a bit of a drinker, had mostly worked a string of odd jobs, including plastering homes, tending cows, and delivering mail to neighboring mountain villages via horse-drawn cart—his parents had impressed upon him the unshakable necessity of making his way across the Atlantic to seek fortune, or at least a steady job, in America.

For years, one of the primary exports of Val Rendena, the mountain valley where my dad grew up, had been knife sharpeners. According to local lore, the heavily forested valley was originally famed for its lumberjacks, but then at some point one of them hit upon the marketability of a key secondary skill of their trade: keeping one's axe sharp. And so, during the long winter off-season, they began hauling their whetstones to balmier climes, where they would find work as itinerant knife grinders.* The first knife sharpeners to make their way to the Detroit area had been Binellis from Pinzolo—although, in an unsettling twist, they came from the maternal side of my dad's family. My father unconvincingly insists this line of Binellis bears no relation to the paternal Binelli line my grandmother married into, but the total population of Pinzolo and its two largest neighbors is something like two thousand people, which makes his protestations suspect. To sound less Italian, one of the first Binellis to arrive in Detroit dropped the "i" from his surname and thus became a "Binell." (In a fairly sizable oversight, however, he neglected to change his first name, Mario.) My grandmother's younger brothers, Caesar and Angelo, followed, along with my dad's best friend, Fausto, and soon my father himself joined them. At first they operated out of the back of a van, eventually securing a brick warehouse building on Davison Street, on the east side of the city. They called their business Detroit Cutlery.

My mother, Anita, was born in Madonna di Campiglio, a mountain resort town overlooking Pinzolo. Her family emigrated to Detroit in 1947, when she was only two years old. Her parents had managed various hotels in Campiglio, but the war had a predictably deleterious effect on local tourism, necessitating the move. As it happened, her mother, Josephine, had been born in Manhattan, where my great-grandfather had also worked as a knife sharpener. They lived in a tenement building on First Avenue near 125th Street, now Spanish Harlem but at the time the largest of the city's several Little Italys. Through a series of misfortunes, my grandmother found herself back in Val Rendena with a new stepmother but without her father, who stayed behind in New York to sharpen knives and send over money.

My grandmother Josephine began working in one of the hotels in Madonna di Campiglio, which was where she met my grandfather,

---

*The quirky local dialect developed, in part, as a means of secret communication between clannish traveling *moletas* (grinders), who incorporated Italianized versions of stray foreign words into their private language.

Pio. Also the son of an Italian knife sharpener, he had grown up in Wiesbaden, the German spa town, fought for the Germans in the First World War, and studied in art school in Frankfurt, before making his way back to Italy. After marrying my grandmother, he considered moving the family to New York, where one of his best friends from the *Kunstgewerbeschule*, Ludwig Wolpert, a master silversmith who has been described as "one of the greatest Judaica artists of the twentieth century," invited Pio to join him at the Jewish Museum as an art instructor. But New York proved an impossible sell to my grandmother, whose memories of tenement slums were not exceptionally happy ones, and so instead they moved to Detroit, where her own father and brother, drawn by the beachhead of other Italians from Val Rendena, had settled and opened a knife shop. Nonno Pio, close to fifty by the time he left Italy, tried finding work that interested him (cooking at the Grosse Pointe Yacht Club, teaching art classes at a local high school, sculpting headstones for a cemetery), but nothing ever bore fruit, and so he borrowed some money and bought a knife route from one of the Binells. He called his business, which he ran out of a shed next to the family's cramped, slant-floored wooden home, the Sharpen Shop. Uncle Dave (my grandmother's younger brother) also had a knife shop, Dave's Cutlery, which he ran out of his garage, across the street from my grandparents' place. Meanwhile, my father's uncle, Caesar, had broken away from Detroit Cutlery and formed a rival knife shop, Statewide Cutlery (which was eventually sold to another cousin and became John's Cutlery, John sprucing up the company logo with the tagline "Never a Dull Moment"), and then there were the Ferraris, cousins on my mother's side, who had the Ferrari Brothers Cutlery, and the good old Binells. Basically, we were related to everyone who sharpened knives in a professional capacity in Detroit.

My parents met at a picnic at Uncle Dave's. After they married, they settled a few blocks away from my grandparents in St. Clair Shores, although my father continued to work in Detroit. Every so often, after moving back, I'd drive by his old shop, a warehouse building on Davison, between McNichols (6 Mile) and Mound. It was a rougher part of town than I remembered: lots of warehouse buildings that had seen better days, a prison, strip clubs, Coney Islands. There used to be a fast food joint called Marcus Burgers, "Home of the Loose Burger," which my brother and I rechristened "Home of the Loose Bowels" and which seemed to have either closed or moved. We both helped out at the shop during our summer breaks and on Saturdays during the school year. I hated working inside, though, so as soon as I became old enough to drive, I began making deliveries all over the city, including to Service Street, my future block.

The shop had a fenced-in parking lot topped with barbed wire. There was a crack house just down the block. A clicker opened a section of fence remotely, the fence wobbling noisily as a motorized conveyor pulled it back along a groove. Fortified against the hostile forces in the neighborhood with heavy metal doors requiring buzzing in, the shop felt decidedly unwelcoming and contributed, like many other unadorned buildings, to Detroit's bleak and battered physiognomy. That whole stretch of Davison was not different from the many industrial zones criss-crossing the city like fattened arteries. You couldn't call it blight exactly, since many of the facilities, at least at the time I was working for my dad, remained going concerns.

Since then, of course, many of the shops had closed.

* * *

I remembered Service Street as an unremarkable back alley. But once I started living there, pulling onto the redbrick cobblestone always felt like entering a secret world. Doors to several of the buildings had been painted vivid colors—one was bright orange, with various-sized and -colored polka dots receding into the background—and a pair of old kitchen sinks had been converted into window boxes. There were landscaped flower beds, wind chimes hanging from a post, a fire pit at the rear of a dirt parking lot.

My downstairs neighbor, Las, a personal chef, could often be heard shouting, "Shiva! Be still, girl!" Shiva was a pit bull given to loud barking. Las himself struck me as an incongruous pit bull owner: gentle-voiced, with a round baby face, except for the traces of gray stubble, and such a mellow demeanor you might take him for a transplant from Laguna Beach, though he'd been born and raised in the city.

When we first met, I told Las my story about making deliveries to Butcher & Packer as a kid. Having driven to the apartment straight from the airport, I was, perhaps, a bit overeager to impress him, the first black Detroiter I'd had the opportunity to tell about my book project, with my own Detroit bona fides. Las nodded and said, "Right on," but didn't seem terribly wowed. He said the Butcher & Packer guys would occasionally give them old pallets to burn in the fire pit. Then he asked where I lived in New York, and told me that he had worked, for several years, at a Soho interior design studio not far from my apartment. Having established street cred in our respective neighborhoods, we gazed out the window for a moment, and then Las asked if I had any other questions about the block.

Las was just one of an appealing mix of residents, among them a jazz drummer, a clothing designer, the founder of the Detroit chapter of the Black Panthers, several DJs and artists (including a creator of art neckties), and, during occasional visits from Amsterdam, John Sinclair, the poet and former manager of the MC5 famously busted in 1969 for possession of two joints and sentenced to ten years in prison.* It also turned out that Detroit techno, a seminal early genre of electronic dance music, had basically been invented on Service Street. This had been back in the eighties, by the so-called Belleville Three— high school classmates Derrick May, Juan Atkins, and Kevin Saunderson, who had all had recording studios on the block. In no small measure, the long-standing European romanticization of Detroit can be traced back to the borderline-deranged partisanship of the Continental techno enthusiast. I would still occasionally see May, whose record label office remained on Service Street, driving down the alley in his blue convertible BMW, when he wasn't DJing at some club in Tokyo or Rotterdam, which is how he still spent most weekends. If he wanted to play in Detroit, Derrick told me, he would have to throw his own party.

My favorite new neighbors were Steve and Dorota Coy, young

---

*By 1971, Sinclair was still doing time, so his supporters organized a "Ten for Two" rally in Ann Arbor, featuring John Lennon and Yoko Ono, Stevie Wonder, and Allen Ginsberg. It was here that Lennon debuted his song "John Sinclair," featuring the unforgettable lyric:

Gotta, gotta, gotta, gotta,
gotta, gotta, gotta, gotta,
gotta, gotta, gotta, gotta,
gotta, gotta, gotta set him free.

artists who had met and married in Hawaii and then, in what might be an unprecedented move in the history of human migration, decided to relocate to Detroit. The first night we hung out, Steve told me, "This is the last frontier in this country. What else is left? There's Hawaii. There's Alaska. And there's Detroit." It made a strange kind of sense, although we were both very drunk. Dorota (born in Poland) and Steve tagged abandoned buildings with stencils promoting their nonexistent corporation, the Hygienic Dress League. Often, they depicted themselves in their artwork, wearing gas masks and carrying machine guns or mysterious briefcases. In real life, they never went anywhere without their tiny dog, Bob, often carted around by Steve in a shoulder bag. They were subletting an entire floor of an old furniture warehouse, about three thousand square feet of raw studio space, for $250 a month.

Another neighbor, Holice Wood, a stocky guy with a ponytail, had a variety of moneymaking gigs, or "hustles," as he liked to say. Detroit was the sort of a place where even the people who held down a real job also had a hustle going, Holice told me, adding pointedly, "And now most people have *lost* their real jobs." Holice's own hustles included, but were not limited to, promoting blues concerts, starting his own T-shirt company, and plotting the opening of a marijuana dispensary. Despite the ponytail, Holice evinced none of the mellow grooviness such a hairstyle choice generally implied. He spoke with a loud, sandpapery voice and had a habit of fixing you, right in the middle of conversation, with a highly scrutinizing, cold-blooded stare, giving the impression that he might at any moment begin shouting for no reason or else challenge you to a fist fight. He lived in a windowless cinderblock bunker on the very corner of the alley, adjacent to a garage that I'd always taken for a chop shop (since the mechanics seemed to work only in the middle of the night) but that apparently was being rented by a muscle-car enthusiast with a regular day job. I never had a conversation with Holice that did not, at some point, involve his taking a massive, lung-puckering toke of a joint, which gave even a veteran smoker like Holice a croaking voice for a few moments afterward. That, too, did nothing to reduce his intensity.

Many of Holice's stories involved fights or near fights. One night, he said, he'd spotted a guy breaking into a pickup truck in the parking lot. Without thinking, Holice had grabbed the only weapon at hand, which happened to be a broom handle, and dashed over to the truck, where he discovered the would-be thief was a six-foot-two crackhead. Holice himself had been "high as a three-peckered goat" (his phrasing). He swung and missed. The thief lunged with a sharpened screwdriver and also missed. Holice jabbed him in the face with the end of the weaponized broom handle. The thief howled and ran off.

The first time we met, Holice told me, "When I moved here five years ago, I couldn't walk my dog without carrying my gun with me." Leaning forward, he warned, "This is not a block where you can be timid!" I tried to remain nonchalant, as if crazy-seeming strangers invaded my personal space so often I'd become inured to anything less than a sucker punch. At first, I thought he might have meant timid journalistically—like, I shouldn't be shy about approaching people for interviews. He went on, "If you hear any noise or commotion, you need to come down and see what's going on and help out, because that's the only way we keep this street the way it is." He took a step even closer. "This is where we *live*," he pronounced carefully. "If you see someone pissing on that wall over there or trying to break into a car, you need to *chase them down*."

I nodded. Of course I would chase thieves. It was Detroit.

Detroit burning, 1805. [Painting, Robert Thom]

2

THE TOWN OF DETROIT EXISTS NO LONGER

NOT ALL OF THE news coming out of Detroit was horrible. Some workers at Detroit Edison's Conners Creek power plant reported a number of downed trees displaying curious chewing marks, possibly bites. The report landed on the desk of a safety specialist whose duties included "wildlife coordination" on the plant's vast grounds. He expressed skepticism of the bite claims but agreed to set up a motion-detecting camera.

The ensuing photographic evidence prompted breathless headlines: "The Beavers Are Back!" It seemed to be true: though hunted to near extinction during the rabid European fur trade that occasioned the founding of the city, the beaver, not spotted in the area for at least seventy-five years, had returned, against all odds, to the Detroit River. Or at the very least this one particular beaver, looking, in the grainy black-and-white surveillance photograph, like an appropriately rough fellow, standing pear-shaped on his hind legs, his chin and stubby front paws raised in the direction of a hanging branch, burglar's eyes aglow; even his tail, flat on the ground behind him but lying at an awkward angle, seemed fake, as if the rogue sawyer were actually an obese rat with a crude prosthesis trying to outsmart pest control. I'm just saying that if cities had the power to conjure animal familiars, Detroit would have conjured this beaver.

For the first European interlopers, the primary attraction of eighteenth-century Detroit's straight-up wilderness was undoubtedly the beaver trade. The city had been founded as a French trading post and garrison, strategically located at the narrowest point of the strait, *le détroit*, connecting Lakes Erie and Huron, providing easy access for fur trappers combing the Canadian hinterland for beaver fur and other goods to export back to the Old World as well as martial advantage for the soldiers meant to keep rival English would-be colonizers at bay. The first French settlers had arrived from Montreal in the summer of 1701, an exploration party of a hundred men in twenty-five canoes led by a forty-three-year-old hustler and rather inept military tactician named Antoine de la Mothe Cadillac. The previous year, Cadillac had managed to convince the French government of the need for establishing a new outpost on the river, of which he would, naturally, assume command. In a letter to his patron, Count Pontchartrain, Cadillac insisted that establishing a fort at *le détroit* would not only make the French crown's commercial interests "entirely safe" but "cause the certain ruin of the English colonies."

Hats made from beaver fur were sturdy yet easily shaped and naturally waterproof (in the least pleasant sense of the adverb: beavers rub themselves with an oil secreted by glands near their anus) and had been all the rage in European society since the fifteenth century. According to the historian Nick Bunker, felted North American beaver fur hats made their Parisian debut in 1577. With the Continental beaver population depleted to essential extinction, the discovery of the beaver-rich rivers of the New World resulted in a hot new import, "sensuous, durable, but chic, visibly expensive but open to subtle reinvention," writes Bunker, ". . . a Jacobean version of the tweed suits designed by Miss Chanel." Both men and women wore the new style of hat, festooned with gold and silver and silk and available in a variety of shapes and shades. By the 1620s, the price of a single pelt had reached nearly forty shillings, enough (again, Bunker) "to rent nine acres of English farmland for a year."

A furious North American beaver harvest predictably arose, pitting rugged French Canadian *coureurs de bois* against colonial English trappers from the Eastern Seaboard, with both nations also jockeying for superior trading status with the Indian population. When Cadillac first began pitching Fort Detroit to France, he borrowed the descriptions of an earlier explorer, Robert LaSalle. Of course, *le détroit* would have strategic importance when it came to the fur trade. But with the establishment of a Cadillac-headed fort and settlement, the crown would also be gaining command of a river (per LaSalle) "as richly set with islands as is a queen's necklace with jewels," the "beautifully verdant" shores serving to "complete the picture of a veritable paradise" where deer "roam in graceful herds" and even the bear were "by no means fierce and exceedingly good to eat," and be sure not to overlook (Cadillac pulling out all the Gallic stops) the wild vines, "heavy with grapes," which produced wine "that, considering its newness, was not at all bad." Cadillac was proposing more than just a fur post; he envisioned the beginnings of a colony, a real beachhead in what was, by any other measure, untamed land.

When Cadillac came ashore, his party included a motley assortment of soldiers, traders, artisans, and *coureurs de bois*, along with two priests (a Jesuit and a Franciscan Recollect), three horses (two of which quickly died, though the third, Colon, was still alive and doing plow work in 1711, providing Cadillac with a lucrative monopoly), and eighteen swords (Cadillac loved fencing). The original settlement, Fort Pontchartrain du Détroit was one arpent (roughly one acre) square, with fifteen-foot-high oak picket walls sunk into three-foot trenches. Among the deal-sweetening incentives offered Detroit's earliest pioneers were land grants, in the form of so-called ribbon farms, the first European homesteads in the area, which ran up from the riverbank like the keys of a xylophone, each individual plot long and narrow enough to give every settler a bit of water frontage.* A handful of streets in Detroit, running north from the river, mark the locations of some of these original farms, taking their names from the French landholders: Chene, Dequindre, Dubois, St. Aubin,† Beaubien, Riopelle, Beaufait, Orleans.

---

*There was a muddy, often impassable road running along the base of the river, but the settlers simply slipped a canoe into the water and paddled up- or downstream if they wanted to visit the fort or a neighbor. Most of the farms were basically orchards: apple, cherry, and pear trees.

†Edwin St. Aubin, a direct descendant of one of Cadillac's original one hundred men, lived in the suburbs and, appropriately enough, sold real estate. We met for lunch one afternoon at an Italian restaurant in a strip mall past 17 Mile Road. A group of old Italian men were playing cards in a side room decorated with a mural of Rome; a poster on the wall advertised a Christmas concert with Dean Martin, Frank Sinatra, and (inexplicably) Roy Orbison impersonators.

St. Aubin was in his fifties, with a thinning bush of white hair, along with a mustache and

Shortly after the British defeated the French (and their Indian allies) in 1760 and took over the fort now called Detroit, the Indian chief Pontiac convinced his fellow Ottawa tribe members, along with historically feuding neighboring tribes, to join him in simultaneous attacks on multiple English posts. Thus Detroit staked its initial claim to a reputation for danger, violence, and general mayhem. The population was still under five hundred at that time, despite efforts by the French to lure more Canadians into the reputedly paradisiacal wild.

The siege of Detroit ended up lasting for five months and became the stuff of national legend. In the wonderful *Conspiracy of Pontiac* (1851), historian Francis Parkman relays the ill omens blanketing the land in the months preceding the attack: the "thick clouds of inky blackness" that had spread over Detroit, darkening the river and choking the surrounding forest in a "double gloom"; raindrops so pitched and sulfurous "that the people, it is said, collected them and used them for writing." When the attack began, the Indians filled their mouths with bullets in order to be able to quickly reload their guns, popping up and then vanishing behind trees, ridges, barns, and fences. The English returned fire, blasting cannons filled with red-hot spikes. The naked bodies ("gashed with knives and scorched with fire") of Lieutenant Cuyler's detachment from Niagara were occasionally seen floating down the Detroit River by the men in the fort, who took note, in Parkman's words, of the "fish [coming] up to nibble at the clotted blood that clung to their ghastly faces." An ensign cap-

---

goatee that added to his catlike appearance. He drank three glasses of wine with lunch, the effusiveness of his storytelling increasing with each round. St. Aubin said he had grown up not knowing about his rich ancestry, but then one afternoon he had somehow ended up in the basement of the Detroit Public Library flipping through historical documents, where he discovered his grandfather's name in direct lineage from the original St. Aubin. Since then, he and his brother had immersed themselves in early Detroit history.

"You know," St. Aubin told me, "there's a whole France-mafia parallel?" He glanced around the room. "I've got to be careful what I say in here. But there was a group back then called the Red Poppy Society. St. Aubin was a member. They were basically enforcers, like mafia guys. If you didn't donate to the church, they'd shake you down. They'd break your fucking legs." An old man with floridly dyed hair and a cane walked by. St. Aubin mumbled, "Bookie." Then he went on, "There's a book called *Frontier Metropolis* that mentions selling land for two cents an acre. Which is about what it's selling for now in Detroit." He ate a forkful of salad, then said, "It's funny how Detroit was originally encased in a fort to protect the city. Now you don't need a fort. You can't pay people to go down there."

tured at Ohio's Fort Sandusky, meanwhile, was brought before Pontiac and pelted by a crowd with sticks and stones, "forcing him to dance and sing, though by no means in a cheerful strain."

The siege dragged on. One Indian was killed and scalped by the British just outside the fort. He happened to be the nephew of a Chippewa chief, and so in retaliation the Indians hacked a British prisoner to death with tomahawks, eating his heart and feeding the rest of his body to dogs. Two other English officers were attacked and killed above Lake St. Clair: Sir Robert Davers was boiled and eaten and, according to an anonymous soldier's letter, someone "had seen an Indian have the Skin of Captain Robertson's Arm for a Tobacco-Pouch!" The most English blood was spilled on July 31, nearly three months after the initial attack, during a disastrous 2:00 a.m. maneuver in which three hundred soldiers silently crept from the fort and marched directly into an ambush near what is now the entrance to the Belle Isle bridge but which was known for years as Bloody Run. Fifty-nine of the British were killed before the contingent retreated to the fort. One of the soldiers at Bloody Run, Major Robert Rogers, later wrote a play called *Ponteach, or The Savages of America: A Tragedy*, which, though described in the introduction to a 1914 edition as "almost pitifully devoid of intrinsic merits," retains the distinction of being the second play written by an American (the first being Thomas Godfrey's *The Prince of Parthia*, a romantic tragedy), and one with nuanced views of the Indians and the English, the latter, in particular, sharply satirized as bartering with scales "so well conceived / That one small slip will turn three pounds to one." While stationed at Detroit, Rogers had gotten to know Pontiac, "the proud chieftain" who, Rogers claimed, offered him "a major part of his kingdom" in exchange for passage to England and introductions into British society.

* * *

After an eventual negotiated peace with Pontiac, nothing much interesting happened in Detroit for the next thirty or so years. The British fort was three weeks' travel through hostile Indian country from the nearest American settlement and so remained a wild frontier, more or less wholly isolated during the course of the Revolutionary War. In 1789, George Washington considered attacking Detroit, but then he didn't. Nevertheless, Henry Hamilton, the lieutenant governor in charge of the fort, paid Indians to attack American settlers in nearby states like Ohio and Pennsylvania, at the going rate of five dollars per scalp. This practice earned Hamilton the nickname "the Hair Buyer."*

A Detroit census from 1789 lists John Drake, captain of a ship called the *Beaver*; James Allen, "mere hand"; Joseph Malbeuf, deaf man; John Durette, captain of the *Weasel*; Madam Sterling, who made shirts; along with about three hundred other residents, including farmers, furriers, merchants, carpenters, blacksmiths, tavern keepers, shinglers, bakers, and Indian traders. The 1794 census included "Joseph, with the frozen feet." The great Detroit historian Clarence Burton titles this section of his epic five-volume *The City of Detroit, Michigan, 1701–1922* "Public Morals at Low Ebb," chronicling Indian-fighting soldiers drunk on moonshine whiskey, local courts filled with "many cases of rioting," and Detroit taverns as "rum holes of the worst kind." A British engineer, visiting the fort in 1800, described peering down an alley and being "pounced upon by an immense animal," which turned out to be someone's pet panther. "He is very young," the cat's owner reassured the visitor, "and has no harm in him."

It's possibly comforting to note that semihysterical dispatches regarding Detroit's terrifying nature—riots! wild animals roaming the streets!—have been filed since the eighteenth century. With the arrival of the Americans a few years later, another trope of the city's official story line would be established: burning the place to the ground.

Aside from Pontiac's Rebellion, the most well-trod historical marker of Detroit's frontier century is the Great Fire of 1805. Just as the Michigan Territory of the United States was officially established with Detroit as its capital, the fort was almost entirely destroyed by a

---

*Around this same time, Hamilton's justice of the peace handed down a death sentence to a Detroit couple for stealing six dollars from the cashbox of a trading firm and starting a small fire. No one could be convinced to perform the execution; finally, the woman (a slave who had been having an affair with her accomplice) agreed to hang her partner in exchange for a pardon. A public outrage followed, and the Hair Buyer, who it turned out had had no authority to mete out capital punishment, was charged with murder and ended up fleeing Detroit and being captured by Americans. Hamilton's replacement, Colonel Arent De Peyster, published his own verse, which was not very good, despite such promising titles as "To a Beautiful Young Lady, Who Had on One of Those Abominable Straw Caps or Bonnets in the Form of a Bee-Hive" and "The Ghost of Old Cocosh (a Pig). Shot by the Guard in the King's Naval Yard at Detroit."

freak conflagration. The temptation to ascribe Detroit's misfortunes to conspiracy is apparently an old one, and a theory quickly developed—arson!—supposedly committed by lumber barons up in Black River, now Port Huron, who wanted to sell the city more wood. In fact, the fire was started by an employee of John Harvey, a baker, who knocked some ashes from his clay pipe, igniting a pile of hay. Detroit was made up of old wood buildings built very close together on narrow streets, and by the middle of the afternoon, the entire village was ablaze. There was only one fire truck. Citizens tried to put out the fire with river water and "swabs at the ends of long poles." Eventually they evacuated the fort in canoes and watched the settlement burn. The Reverend John Dilhet noted that it was a windless day, which "allowed the flames and smoke to ascend to a prodigious height, giving the city the appearance of an immense funeral pyre. It was the most majestic, and at the same time the most frightful spectacle I have ever witnessed."

The starkness of the devastation resonates morbidly. "The town of Detroit exists no longer," begins a dispatch in the August 7, 1805, edition of the *Intelligencer*, in which the writer posits that "history does not furnish so complete a ruin, happening by accident, and in so short a space of time. All is amazement and confusion." Father Gabriel Richard, the Frenchman who had ended up parish priest of St. Anne's Church after jumping from a window in Paris to escape from a mob of Jacobin soldiers during the Reign of Terror, took the occasion to write the Latin motto (*Speramus meliora; resurget cineribus*) that would end up on Detroit's flag and prove so depressingly durable, forever apropos, so that quoting the good Father's "We hope for better days; it shall rise from the ashes" would become the hoariest of applause lines at civic functions as long as the buildings of Detroit kept burning down. But the hope always felt of the hollow, Catholic variety to me, and I suppose I prefer an alternate fiction, a story, likely apocryphal, related by the historian Robert E. Conot,* in which a baker (not John Harvey, employee of the fire starter, but another baker, Jacques Girardin), combing through the ruins of his shop, discovers his oven still

---

*Author of *American Odyssey*, a masterful, idiosyncratic history of Detroit, unconscionably out of print.

intact, and when he cracks the oven door he twitches his nose at a familiar aroma and realizes the dough he left inside has been baked "to perfection." Even though Conot provides no further detail, and it's all a bit too close to the ending of *Bright Lights, Big City*, still, here, I like to imagine Girardin reaching tenderly inside and tearing off a piece of baguette, still warm, and as he bites into the crust the sunlight glints on the river, which would have been visible from wherever he was standing, because everything else was gone.

* * *

A few weeks after the fire, President Jefferson's newly appointed territorial governor, Judge Augustus Woodward, arrived on the scene. The timing was coincidental but propitious: Woodward might be described as the city's first disaster capitalist. "He made himself a committee of one to rebuild Detroit," wrote the popular *Free Press* columnist Malcolm Bingay in 1946. The reconstruction of the city was also the first government-led attempt at urban planning in Detroit. A man of science, Woodward "proclaimed . . . that he had devised his plan through his vast knowledge of the celestial system." Enacting it, however, the judge took heed of more earthly concerns, securing generous amounts of land for himself, along with the presidency of the city's first bank and near-totalitarian control of the court system. Conot describes one trial in which Woodward acted as judge, prosecutor, complainant, and (presumably star) witness. On the plus side, he cofounded the University of Michigan (my alma mater) and was, by most accounts, a bookish oddball who drank too much and dreamed with a grandiosity all the more endearing in its shortfalls.

His scholarly writings, such as *Considerations on the Substance of the Sun* (1801)—spoiler alert: "the substance of the sun is electron"— exude in all their learned wrongness a charmingly loopy innocence. But Woodward was not well liked by the still largely French populace and so became the first in a long line of suspect and ultimately despised outsiders charged, by the state or federal government, with the unenviable task of "fixing" some aspect of Detroit. During the War of 1812, when a white tablecloth was mustered into service as a flag of surrender by the guardians of Detroit, who gave up to the British without firing a shot, Woodward continued to run the territory for the enemy, and then again for the Americans when the war ended. In 1824, after Congress passed a law limiting the term of judges to four years (Bingay: "All this to get rid of Judge Woodward without actually firing him. He was still a friend of Thomas Jefferson"), celebratory bonfires lit up the city for an entire night.

What he left behind was indeed a city, however, and as the wilderness surrounding it became less impenetrable, thanks to the steamboat and the railroads and the Erie Canal—the opening of which yanked trade routes away from old colonial cities like Boston and Philadelphia to favor New York and, by extension, the Great Lakes—Detroit began a century-long boom in both population and commerce.* Suddenly, you didn't have to be a backwoods fur trapper or Indian fighter to get to the Michigan Territory. You might be a land speculator, or an entrepreneur, or simply someone looking for work. You might be an immigrant: Irish, German, Scandinavian. By 1870, Detroit's population had reached eighty thousand and, Conot notes, four-fifths of the children attending school had foreign-born parents.

The state's great wealth of natural resources fueled the city's growth, as factories exploded along the easily accessible Detroit River. Northern Michigan had a seemingly limitless supply of lumber, and so Detroit became the shipbuilding capital of the United States, as well as a hub of production of wooden railroad cars. The Michigan Car Company, the largest of the local manufacturers, gave a sixteen-year-old just off the farm his first job, paying $1.10 an hour. Henry Ford lasted only for a few days before he went to work at a nearby machine shop, which proved more to his liking. The discovery, midcentury, in the state's Upper Peninsula, of one of the richest copper mines in the world, along with numerous iron and lead deposits, resulted in an eruption of foundries and concomitant industrial concerns: Detroit became the number-one stove manufacturer in the country and a top

---

*Though, writing a decade later, Gustave de Beaumont, Tocqueville's coauthor, cautioned against the mistaken belief "that Detroit is very civilized," noting the occasion, only a year before his visit, in which a pack of hounds bayed a bear out of the forest, sending it down the entire length of one of the main streets of the city, most likely Jefferson or Woodward—"to the entertainment of the Americans," the French traveler added with apparent fondness, "whose gravity probably did not betray them even on this occasion."

producer of steam engines and lead-based paint and varnish.* The Berry Brothers were apparently the Fords of the varnish world, with an operation so gargantuan it boasted its own Western Union telegraph office.

Detroit factories also produced shoes, soap, pharmaceuticals (Parke-Davis was founded in Detroit in 1866), and matches. The first hints of the problems of housing and demography Detroit would face in the twentieth century surfaced during this apprenticeship boomtown period. Workers crowded slums; there was such a housing shortage that churches and stables were hastily converted into tenements. One of the worst of the ghettos lined the riverfront and was derisively called "the Potomac," according to Conot, who describes streets teeming with beggars and prostitutes, barnyard animals and opium dealers.†

Black workers were also drawn to the city, which, in the years leading up to the Civil War, had become a major terminus of the Underground Railroad, with the safety of Windsor, Ontario, just across the river. In 1833, an escaped Louisville slave named Thornton Blackburn and his wife were tracked down in Detroit by their former master and jailed there. Mrs. Blackburn swapped clothes with a visiting friend while awaiting trial, snuck out of the building and made her way to Windsor. Her husband was whisked away by a black crowd while being transported from the jail to the courthouse and also wound up in Canada, where he joined his wife, moved to Toronto, and, according to Burton, "acquired considerable property." (After which, even more excellently, he snuck back into the United States in disguise and managed to rescue his mother from the selfsame Louisville slave-owner.) During Blackburn's liberation, a black man was shot and a police officer suffered a fractured skull and had his teeth knocked out. This melee was dubbed Detroit's "first Negro insurrection," and the military was called in, as it was 134 years later with the second, much better-known insurrection. Any black citizens spotted on the street were arrested and thrown into jails that quickly became, as Burton

---

*"The manufacture of varnish in itself is an absorbing story," writes Clarence Burton, unconvincingly.
†Conot also notes how Thomas Edison, who grew up in rural Port Huron, Michigan, but worked as a newsboy on Detroit-bound trains, often "expressed his frustrations in the explicit language he had learned along the docks of Detroit. 'Shit! Glass busted by Boehm!' he wrote in his notebook."

describes, "crowded to the door. . . . Bugles were sounded, and the firebells added to the alarm. The announcement was made at every corner that 'the niggers have risen and the sheriff is killed.'" Eventually, one Mrs. Madison J. Lightfoot received a $25 fine for acting as ringleader of the rescue operation, a charge she never denied. Burton insists the true mastermind was "a one-handed barber named Cook."

The passage of the Fugitive Slave Law of 1850 was inspired, in part, by the case of David Dunn, a politically connected St. Louis burgher who tracked one of his escaped slaves to Michigan, dragged the young man (Robert Cromwell), to a local courthouse and was promptly arrested himself for attempted kidnapping, ultimately spending six months in a Detroit jail while awaiting trial. In 1859, the abolitionist John Brown arrived in Detroit with fourteen freed slaves from Missouri. That evening, in a candlelit home on Congress Street, he met with Frederick Douglass, who was in town to deliver a lecture, to plan the raid on Harpers Ferry. Douglass objected, as did the local Underground Railroad agent George DeBaptist, who favored a less conciliatory approach, suggesting that Brown instead stage simultaneous attacks on a number of white churches throughout the South, blowing them up with gunpowder. (Brown rejected this idea.)

Like that of many other Northern cities of the time, Detroit's progressive facade proved flimsy as a (white) sheet, barely covering the city's own rank history of race hatred. Four years after the Brown plot, a light-skinned African American saloon owner named William Faulkner (really) was accused of molesting a nine-year-old white girl, Mary Brown, and her nine-year-old black friend, Ellen Hoover, after they stopped by his establishment one afternoon to warm their feet. Both girls later recanted their story, with Brown admitting she'd made up the charge in order to avoid being punished for her tardiness. Unfortunately, their admission came six years after Faulkner was tried, convicted, and sentenced to life in prison. (He was subsequently released.) During Faulkner's trial, a white mob gathered outside the courtroom. An article in the *Detroit Advertiser and Tribune*, headlined "Case of the Negro Faulkner," described how the mob, thousands strong, surged as the convicted barkeeper was escorted by police out to Gratiot Avenue, in the direction of the jail.

The riotous gang rampaged up and down Beaubien Street,

targeting black residents. "The mob," according to the *Advertiser and Tribune,*

> was composed, to a large extent, of young fellows brought up in the "street school"—rowdies and vagabonds, ignorant, unreasoning, and crazy with whiskey and prejudice. Their spirit and their shouts were full of bitter and violent hatred for the negro. "Kill the nigger!" "D——n the nigger!" "Butcher all niggers!" "Stone that nigger house!" "Tear down that nigger dive!" "Every d——n nigger ought to be hung!" We will do the mob the justice to suppose that but a few of them could read, and that they despised, above all things, the free school and the church.

After the hooligans threated to cut his hoses, the fire marshal allowed the black homes to burn, though fires that had spread to neighboring white-owned homes and businesses were extinguished in the name of the common good. In all, thirty-five buildings were burned to the ground. Other outrages were detailed in the oral history *A Thrilling Narrative from the Lips of the Sufferers of the Late Detroit Riot, March 6, 1863, with the Hair Breadth Escapes of Men, Women, and Children, and Destruction of Colored Men's Property, Not Less Than $15,000.**

Interesting side note: Faulkner was apparently light-skinned enough to be described, by the anonymous compiler of the *Thrilling Narrative,* as "to all intents a white man." "If [Faulkner] thought he had one drop of colored blood in his veins, if he could, he would let it out," an elderly Detroiter is quoted as saying, his claim bolstered by the inclusion of a poem titled "The Riot," written by one "B. Clark, Sen., A Colored Man," containing such stanzas as:

---

*After his home was burned by the mob, Thomas Holton spent the night hiding in the woods with his wife and child, later telling the compilers of the *Thrilling Narrative,* "With frosted feet and all our property destroyed, did the morning sun rise upon us, as destitute as when we came into the world, with the exception of what we had on, and without a friend to offer us protection, so far as we could learn. Oh, Detroit! Detroit, how hast thou fallen! No power in noonday to defend the helpless women and children from outlaws, till they have fully glutted their hellish appetites on the weak and defenseless. Humanity, where is thy blush!"

Now be it remember'd that Faulkner at right,
Although call'd a "nigger," had always been white,
Had voted, and always declared in his shop,
He never would sell colored people a drop.

He's what is call'd white, though I must confess,
So mixed are the folks now, we oft have to guess,
Their hair is so curl'd and their skins are so brown,
If they're white in the country, they're niggers in town.

Still, did we mention—business was booming! Conot notes that by the eighties Detroit, a city "whose egalitarian character had struck Alexis de Tocqueville in 1830, . . . now contained a significant number of the nation's four thousand millionaires." Detroit's first skyscraper, the ten-story Hammond Building, was erected in 1889 with much hoopla (state holiday, bands, an aerialist pushing a wheelbarrow across a tightrope). And four years later, Ford, by this point chief engineer at the main branch of the Edison Company, fired up a crude homemade engine in the kitchen of his family's new home. It was Christmas Eve. The room immediately filled with smoke and fumes, displeasing Ford's wife, Clara, who had been pouring gas into the motor (which had no carburetor) by hand.

And yet, for all that, the engine had worked. Henry Ford removed it from the kitchen sink, and his wife went back to preparing Christmas dinner.

An urban garden in Upper Chene, tended by a storefront preacher.
The roofless building was once a furniture warehouse.
[Corine Vermeulen]

3

DIY CITY
Or, Okra as Metaphor

It has also been my good fortune to have lived long enough to witness the death blow dealt to the illusion that unceasing technological innovations and economic growth can guarantee happiness. . . . Instead of putting our organizational energies into begging Ford and General Motors to stay in Detroit, we need to go beyond traditional capitalism. . . . Instead of buying all our food from the store, we need to be planting community and school gardens and creating farmers markets.

GRACE LEE BOGGS, *The Next American Revolution*

Brothers and sisters, I wanna tell you something. I hear a lot of talk by a lot of honkies sitting on a lot of money telling me they're high society. But I'll let you know something. If you ask me, *this is the high society.*

MC5, "MOTOR CITY IS BURNING" (live intro)

SPEND ANY TIME IN DETROIT and you'll quickly see that the city's ongoing and multi-sectored collapse has made room for a kind of street-level anarchy. Red lights: optional. Buildings: porous. All manner of vice could easily be had. More positively, self-reliant Detroiters exploited, with admirable vigor, the twin strengths of their particular failed state:

space and lawlessness. Artists, musicians, and other bohemian types tended to hog all the ink when it came to manifestations of the do-it-yourself spirit, but painting foreclosed homes "Tiggerific Orange" as a conceptual art prank or throwing a rave in an abandoned auto factory were not the only creative reclamations of negative space. Detroit had become a DIY city unlike any other, the kind of place where regular civilians took it upon themselves to tauten the civic slack.

Des Cooper, a local journalist and demographer, moved to Detroit from the D.C. suburbs in the early eighties and she came to see the DIY nature of her adopted hometown as one of its "huge, huge strengths." The amount of work people do for themselves simply to live in the city, she told me, was truly stunning when you stopped to think about it. "Because the problems are so huge and the people have so few resources, it doesn't always look that way," she went on. "There's a perception that people here are kind of lazy and not really trying. But then you think of somebody who doesn't have a car and has to take two buses to get to work and worry about child care—and *then* they come home and do neighborhood patrol and go to block club meetings. Nobody in West Bloomfield has to do neighborhood patrol!"

She had a point: once you began to pay attention, the sorts of activities to which Cooper referred were apparent everywhere, and despite all evidence (historical, economic, you name it) to the contrary, the transformational potential of Detroit could start to appear boundless.

In 2010 alone, the blog *Rethink Detroit* pointed out, the *New York Times* ran ten articles on Detroit's DIY revitalization, spotlighting the plucky entrepreneurial resolve of the owner of a downtown creperie, a group of guys who opened an art house theater in a shuttered public school, and the Detroit Zymology Guild, "a weekly canning session held in the back of an art gallery." There were vigilante demolition teams, such as the Motor City Blight Busters, who, like a weird, Detroit-specific version of the Guardian Angels, tore down unsalvageable abandoned homes, and guerilla landscapers like the Lawn Mower Brigade, which (yes) went around trimming the grass in vacant lots.

One winter afternoon, I joined the members of Detroit Dog Rescue, an unlicensed, technically illicit dogcatching operation as they drove around in a van looking for strays. Estimates had placed the number of roaming dogs in the city in the tens of thousands. Detroit's animal control lacked resources to deal with the magnitude of the problem and had enacted a policy of automatic euthanization for any unclaimed pit bull breeds after four days. We visited one empty bungalow taken over entirely by pack of wild dogs. Through the gaping hole where the ground floor picture window would've been, the leader of the pack, a pregnant black Lab, growled at us from behind a shredded couch. Two more dogs, a malamute and another black Lab, watched from a second-floor landing. We left a mound of dry food and moved on.

The Detroit 300 were citizen crime fighters who'd been credited by the police with helping to capture several suspects, including a serial rapist and the murderer of a thirteen-year-old girl. One night, the group marched on a block where a woman had been killed over sixty dollars during a home invasion. Raphael Johnson, one of the Detroit 300's founders, was himself a convicted murderer, having shot an older man when he was seventeen, during a petty squabble at a house party. After serving his prison sentence, Johnson had come close to winning a seat on Detroit's city council. Detroit police chief Ralph Godbee told me he embraced the group. "Some detractors think this is vigilantism, but I think that's a very narrow view," he said. The Detroit 300 could penetrate neighborhoods, the chief explained, where police officers would not have been welcome.

The struggle by Detroiters to reinvent their city has been under way for decades and does not necessarily await a Marshall Plan or some other consultant-driven solution from above. When I'd go for bike rides in the urban prairie sprawling just a few blocks from my apartment, amid the empty fields and bedsheet-curtained crack houses, striking repurposings of the open space had already taken place. There was the lovely house where the owners had ornately fenced several neighboring lots, decorating the lush yard with Italianate statuary. A few blocks away, four old men had chained a table and some chairs to a tree in a field, where they would sit and play cards on sunny afternoons. Farther up the street, another guy lived in a mobile home permanently parked in an empty corner lot. He'd draped a giant

American flag over the side of the RV, either as sincere patriotism or an extraordinarily committed act of satirical commentary.

Along with the influx of homesteading artists, by far the most breathlessly covered aspect of this neo-frontier autonomy has been the urban farming movement. Very rarely are journalists treated to a story so metaphorically apposite—hope *literally* growing from the fallow soil of the postindustrial necropolis. By the count of a 2009 study, 875 farms and community gardens had sprung up throughout the city, one of the largest such networks in the United States; organizations like Earthworks and the Greening of Detroit had been promoting urban agriculture for years, with all that Detroiters lacked—for one thing, a single major grocery chain in the entire city*—resulting in the sort of unspoiled ecosystem in which farming not only could thrive but made perfect sense. In recent years, the ballad of the urban farmer dovetailed as if scripted with the budding locavore movement, and the narrative of an underserviced minority population in the poorest big city in the United States seizing control of their nutritional destiny by embracing a preindustrial, communitarian way of feeding themselves proved irresistible.

With the amount of press devoted to Detroit gardeners like Mark Covington, the personal beneficiary of coverage by *Time*, MSNBC, the *Guardian*, the Associated Press, and the official White House blog, you'd think he'd invented celery. But Covington also happened to be an incredibly engaging character. A thirty-seven-year-old heavy-equipment operator, he'd begun cleaning up and then tilling the garbage-strewn fields in his blighted east side neighborhood out of boredom, after losing his job in 2008. He'd started out with four beds, eventually "adopting" the lots through a city program that gave citizens permits to beautify unused city-owned properties, as long as no permanent structures were erected.

When I stopped by for a tour, Covington was wearing a blue

---

*This was actually true, until a $4.2 million subsidy convinced Whole Foods to open a mini-store in the relatively thriving Midtown neighborhood. Still, outside of a few select neighborhoods, the term *food desert* was not by any means a stretch. For those without a car in a city lacking adequate public transportation, many grocery options consisted of grim liquor stores fortified like banks. A 2007 study found that 92 percent of food stamp outlets in the city were, indeed, liquor stores, gas stations, or pharmacies.

T-shirt that read "I'm an East Sider" and a Denby High School football cap. He had close-cropped hair and one of those thin mustaches that circle around the bottom of your mouth to become a chinstrap-looking beard. Covington said he'd lost fifty-five pounds over the course of the barely two years he'd been gardening, solely due to healthier eating. I pictured him fifty-five pounds heavier—he remained a massive presence—and nodded, impressed. The neighborhood was a battered quilt of houses and vacant fields, except for Covington's community garden, which stretched across a park-sized patch of land comprised of a half-dozen former home lots, including, at the time, twenty-three beds of tomatoes, Brussels sprouts, bell peppers, okra, turnips, bok choy, Napa cabbage, carrots, bush beans ("my family alone picked fifteen pounds this year," Covington told me), Swiss chard, collard greens, vivid orange clusters of marigolds (which "bring beneficial bugs, red and black aphids, that eat cabbage beetles"), and jalapeño peppers. The different vegetables were labeled with hand-painted signs. Raspberries grew out of an old tire. Pallets corralled a compost heap of grass clippings.

Covington seemed at once bemused by and grateful for the amount of attention his efforts had received; along with the media coverage, he'd been invited to speak at a number of conferences. His last day job had been working for an environmental services company, cleaning oil, bodily fluids, and other waste products from refinery tanks, machinery, and Amtrak trains. Vomit, he said, "was the *nicer* stuff." He said he hoped to expand the garden to include goats and chickens and maybe one day opening a little farmers market in the abandoned party store on the corner. The last owner of the party store had been selling drugs out of the back. "You couldn't buy Pepsi or bread, though," Covington said. Now prostitutes used the space to turn tricks.* On a telephone post outside the shop, a little yellow sign read "Top Cash Paid Gold Diamonds." A dead possum, about the size of a large cat, lay in the middle of the street.

Continuing the tour, Covington pointed out a couple of hoop houses (homemade greenhouses constructed out of PVC piping and plastic sheets) and some raised "lasagna beds" (organic gardening plots

---

*Covington did eventually gut and remodel the party store, transforming it into a community space.

layered with sheets of compost), which resembled fresh graves. One of his friends, a barber, had been setting aside bags of hair, good for keeping away rabbits, and in an ambiguous spirit of city-suburb cooperation, a riding club in Grosse Pointe had been donating horse manure. I asked if people in the neighborhood had been excited by the garden. He smiled faintly and said, "Noooooo. Workdays are Monday and Thursday, and we can't get anybody out here. We had three people say they wanted to plant things, but it ended up just being me, my mother, and my wife." He was holding a shovel, and when we stopped walking, he leaned forward on the handle, chin thrust out, in that classic pose they must teach you at farmers' school. "I guess our trade-off for not getting a lot of help is they don't tear it up, either. I'll take that over the help. We have our guards, too. I'll get a call at two in the morning: 'Hey, Mark—some guy out here taking dirt!' We've only had one real incident. Someone took a few small rose bushes in the spring. A lot of people just don't understand the concept of a community garden. They'll come at eleven at night, think they have to sneak in. I planted pumpkins and people started picking them in August. Who picks a pumpkin in August? It's kind of hard to kill off a pumpkin plant. They did it. My plan was for kids to pick them."

As we spoke, a guy drove by and honked at us. Covington lifted one of his giant hands and said, "Hey, Mario," even though there was no way the guy would be able to hear him. There hadn't been any other signs of life, apart from a teenager in a hoodie who'd marched sullenly through the garden, cutting over to Gratiot. "That kid?" Covington had said. "They break into people's houses. Can't call the police. They won't do nothing. It's been like this for so long, it seems normal." Covington said if someone's car was stolen, you didn't call the cops; you drove around in a friend's car looking for it. People came into the neighborhood at night and illegally dumped trash in the empty lots and behind the liquor store. He'd found a bunch of mail from St. Clair Shores.

"With urban agriculture, there'd be less dope houses," Covington said. Thinking for a moment, he went on, "Maybe there would be more meth labs, because it would be more rural. But less crime. What you gonna do, steal chickens? You pull up one of my collard plants, okay, I'll plant another one. It's not a TV."

* * *

There was something unassailably wonderful about the urban farming movement, especially in Detroit, with its extra little raspberry directed at Henry Ford, whose absolute detestation of farmwork had driven him from then-rural Dearborn to the city and played no small role in motivating his wholesale reinvention of the American way of life.* A study at Michigan State University determined that the city of Detroit alone owned nearly five thousand acres of vacant land, spread over forty-four thousand parcels, which, if cultivated, could provide over 75 percent of fresh vegetables and 40 percent of nontropical fresh fruits for all Detroit residents. The researchers described this as a conservative estimate; certain dreamers, such as the nonagenarian activist Grace Lee Boggs and the investigative journalist Mark Dowie, have argued that Detroit, with the proper infrastructural investments, had enough unused land to become the first entirely self-sustainable city in the world, food-security-wise—in other words, the only city on the planet producing all of its food within its own borders.

This experiment was already being tested on the ground, by community gardeners like Covington; by farmers like Rich Wieske, whose Green Toe Gardens produced three thousand pounds of honey from more than sixty inner-city beehives, and Greg Willerer, whose Brother Nature Produce stretched across an acre of property in North Corktown, producing two hundred pounds of salad greens a week, along with produce for the twenty-seven families who took part in his farming co-operative; at places like the Catherine Ferguson Academy, a high school for pregnant teenagers where all the students were required to work on the campus farm.

Still, among the visions of Detroit's future, urban agriculture was not exactly the most practical. As genuinely inspirational as stories like Covington's might be, most Detroiters showed limited interest in turning to subsistence farming. But the notion of a pastoral, premodern

---

*Ford biographer Steven Watts points to Ford's specific hatred of horses, his charge on the family farm, where, as a teenager, he was once dragged home by a colt after falling off the animal and catching a leg in its stirrups. Watts implies this might have been a possible vindictive factor in Ford's perfection of the horseless carriage, offering as evidence Ford himself, in one of his notebooks, gloating uncharitably, "The horse is DONE."

salvation for Detroit had an appeal that far exceeded its plausibility, fitting, as it did, the world's Mad Max fantasies of the city as a place where the vestiges of humanity might build makeshift lives for themselves out of the wreckage of modern society.

A rival model for greening the city was also emerging. Perceived as corporatist (and therefore likely villainous) by activists of a more community-based bent, Hantz Farms was the brainchild of John Hantz, who had made millions in the financial services industry; Hantz had announced his intention to save Detroit, or at least perform some serious landscaping, by creating the world's largest urban farm in the city limits. Hantz's spokesperson was Matt Allen, who had been a press secretary during the Kwame Kilpatrick administration. In the midst of defending the mayor's misbehavior, Allen had managed to out-disgrace his boss and get himself ousted from his own job first, after police officers showed up at his home to break up a violent domestic dispute involving Allen's drunkenly grabbing his wife by the neck and smashing her head through a bathroom window.

In person, Allen seemed like a mild-mannered guy. He was reedy and sharp-featured, with thin-framed glasses and a manner of speaking at once highly excitable and curiously wholesome. Several times he mentioned going to church, and he would occasionally refer to himself in the third person, saying things like, "There have been experts working on urban farming issues for years. Matt Allen has only been doing this for eighteen months." Of his boss, he told me, "John's the berries!" As Allen drove me around one of the proposed sites of Hantz's farm—a depopulated neighborhood near my apartment—he explained how Hantz's initially vague idea about "doing something with all of this land," perhaps merely cultivating miniature forest, had expanded into a wild plan to make Detroit "a model for sustainability." Ex-convicts and recovering addicts would be hired to work the farm; where the soil had been found too contaminated for vegetables, Hantz proposed planting Christmas or fruit trees, eventually promoting farm-tourism with attractions such as equestrian trails, pumpkin patches, and a cider mill.

Allen stopped his car at a crossroads so desolate we might have been in Romeo, the rural Michigan community where Hantz had grown up. "Most of these neighborhoods, you can't even call them neighborhoods anymore—they're 'areas,'" Allen said. "Okay, count these houses with me. One, two, three, four. Five over here. Six, seven over there. That's ten blocks, seven structures. Two of them definitely vacant. Look! Over there. That's literally a tar-roofed shack." A couple of men stared at us from their front porch. "We've just gone fourteen blocks and we could not count fifteen structures. I can't make this up."

One of the stickier issues when it came to large-scale use of vacant land in Detroit was the near unfeasibility, short of a savage eminent-domain fight, of assembling the scattered lots into anything sizable and contiguous. Smaller cooperative farming operations, long established in the city, also feared the scope of Hantz's project, describing it as a land grab, one that would only produce low-paying manual jobs. Malik Yakini of the Detroit Black Community Food Security Network raised the specter of a "corporate takeover" of what's historically been a grassroots movement, adding, "At this point the key players with [Hantz] seem to be all white men in a city that's at least 82 percent black." (When I brought up Hantz Farms to Des Cooper, she was even more dismissive, asking, "You mean the plantation?") The very size of Hantz's operation also prompted concerns about pollution and water usage.

Allen pointed out that Hantz had lived in the city of Detroit for over twenty years and also possessed a far from superficial knowledge of the world of agriculture, his father having sold farming equipment in Romeo. They hoped to launch Hantz Farms with a twenty-five-acre starter site, ultimately expanding the operation into larger pod farms. "In our wildest dreams, we could see five thousand acres," Allen said. "And even that would only be one-tenth of the available land in the city! If we fail, unlike an empty skyscraper or a half-built stadium, you get the land back, in better shape than we got it. People say, 'He's gonna make a lot of money.' That's a faulty premise."

I expected Allen to point out the great inefficiency of land speculation via mass-scale urban farming for a fabulously wealthy individual like Hantz. Instead, he went on, "The premise of a land grab assumes the housing market has even *bottomed out*."

In the end, however, the critics' fears proved unfounded. The project, in spite of all the hype, remained stalled for years, until the Bing administration finally allowed Hantz to plant a starter orchard on (but not actively farm) five acres of land.

* * *

The frontier's endless horizon has always proved attractive to those with the facility for conjuring utopian mirages. The logical conclusion to such thinking is something I like to call the Dystopian Happy Ending. You've seen this one before: after humankind finds itself close to eradicated by, well, take your pick (lab-produced plague, doomsday weapon, supercomputer, band of highly intelligent apes), the hardy survivors manage to come together and restart civilization, only this time (the hopeful implication goes) we learn from our ruinous missteps and finally get it right. In this vein, the waning of the auto industry might create short-term pain for out-of-work employees, but why mourn the end of Detroit's hideously polluting industrial history, the deadening repetition of the assembly line, the inherently exploitative tethering of the proletariat to a giant, soulless corporation like General Motors or Ford? In the same way that the microsocieties formed at Zuccotti Park and other Occupy encampments in 2011 provided, for the simpatico, an exhilarating glimpse of freedom, postindustrial Detroit could be an unintentional experiment in stateless living, allowing for devolution of power to the grass roots.

The sharp cultural critic Rebecca Solnit famously embraced this view in a *Harper's* essay titled "Detroit Arcadia." While acknowledging that it is "unfair, or at least deeply ironic, that black people in Detroit are being forced to undertake an experiment in utopian post-urbanism that appears to be uncomfortably similar to the sharecropping past their parents and grandparents sought to escape," Solnit ends the essay in mawkish celebration of the city as an antidote to privileged liberals with their "free-range chickens and Priuses." The future, she writes, "isn't going to be invented by people who are happily surrendering selective bits and pieces of environmentally unsound privilege. It's going to be made by those who had all that taken away from them or never had it in the first place." To Solnit, the "most extreme and long-term hope" offered by Detroit is that "we can reclaim what we paved over and poisoned, that nature will not punish us, that it will welcome us home."

Solnit presumably wrote these sentences back home in San Francisco. But there are Detroiters who share her viewpoint, or versions of it, from the young white anarchists living collectively in a pair of rambling Victorian mansions on Trumbull Street (dubbed the Trumbullplex) to the black residents of the east side neighborhood known as the Hope District who planted fruit trees in vacant lots, constructed prayer circles, and sold local goods at an open-air market called Little Egypt. A sign in the Hope District proclaims, "1967 is Detroit's 1776."

The local hub of such neighborhood-level leftist utopianism has long been the Boggs Center for Social Progress, headed by the aforementioned Grace Lee Boggs. After graduating from Yale with a philosophy degree, Boggs, who is Chinese American, became involved in the civil rights movement. In 1953 she married James Boggs, a Detroit autoworker and labor activist whose books included *The American Revolution: Pages from a Negro Worker's Notebook*, and for the next forty years, until James Boggs's death in 1993, the couple agitated together for radical social change. Though enfeebled by age—tiny, and mostly confined to a wheelchair, with a boyish mop of white hair and an air of wizened impishness—Grace Lee Boggs has rallied to the moment. She contends that the ongoing crisis of Detroit has created room for the "kind of community that was not possible during the years where there were lots of jobs and the industry was expanding," and that Detroit's collapse is an opportunity to foster "a whole new way of looking at life in the future."

One morning, I met up with a group from the Boggs Center who were taking a driving tour of Detroit meant to showcase the sorts of granular DIY projects applauded by Grace Boggs in her vision of the new Detroit. The tour had been laid on for Mark Rudd of the Weather Underground, in town to promote a book, and was conducted by Rich Feldman, an avuncular, genially distracted Brooklynite who'd moved to the area in the late 1960s to attend the University of Michigan and then stuck around to work as a community and labor activist.

I met the group in front of the ruins of the old Packard automotive plant. Feldman suggested that I leave my car on a nearby residential street, so I followed him down a leafy block, parking in front of a rundown home. There were no signs of any people. Abandoning my rental car struck me as a potentially irresponsible act, but Feldman seemed to think it would be fine, so I reluctantly climbed into his ride, in my mind cursing the trusting, pigheadedly naive neo-Marxists, or whatever they were, and in fact remaining vaguely preoccupied for the duration of the tour with the certitude that my vehicle was being van-dalized or stolen.

In the car, Feldman and Mark Rudd sat up front. I squeezed into the back with a local college professor and Feldman's son Micah, who had a cognitive learning disability but was attending college and had become a disability-rights activist. Rudd was a hulking, excitable pres-ence, corpulent and white-bearded, with a generous, toothy grin. He wore a corduroy shirt jacket over white pants, and at one point, men-tioning how he'd been his wife's "project," he gestured to his outfit as evidence that she'd reformed him. I wondered what sorts of clothes he used to wear before his wife came along.

Feldman, a scattered but entertaining tour guide, wore a padded blue union vest and spoke with a slight Brooklyn inflection. I knew that he'd begun working at the Ford Rouge plant after graduation as a political act, in hopes of spreading a radical doctrine to the working class. "Back then, my friends were going to work for car factories the same way people went to work for the Obama campaign in 2008," Feldman had told me earlier. "I was there because I thought we could make a revolution. I still call someone to change a lightbulb! I came in romanticizing what workers would be like. But the old-timers from the South all hated me. The plant was where people got their pay-check. I started off painting underbodies, myself. The trucks would come out of an oven. They didn't dip them in rustproofing, because that would have been a capital investment. I painted the underbody with scrap paint, whatever was left over. I'd be standing near a hot oven all day, with paint from the spray gun dripping in my eyes. I'd come out a different color every night. Eventually they moved me to the trim shop. I'd try to get a job that didn't involve small parts, because I'd drop them."

We drove by General Motors' Detroit/Hamtramck assembly plant, one of the few auto factories still operating within Detroit's city limits, though Feldman wasn't there to celebrate that fact: he meant to point out the contentious history of the place, how eminent domain had been used to destroy a thriving immigrant neighborhood called Poletown. Then we stopped by a twenty-four-lot farm operated by a Capuchin monastery. They also raised bees and made their own honey. After that, we made our way to perhaps the most visible and enduring symbol of Detroit's DIY positivity, the Heidelberg Project, the artist Tyree Guyton's beloved outdoor art installation, which had spread over several residential blocks surrounding the house on Heidelberg Street where he'd grown up.

Guyton had studied at Detroit's Center for Creative Studies after serving in the army during Vietnam, but his endlessly morphing project had always reminded me of the mad folk art environments I'd seen in the South by untrained artists like Howard Finster. In the eighties, as Guyton watched his neighborhood violently rended by poverty and the drug trade, he began painting bright polka dots on vacant houses on the block. He also decorated the sidewalks with totemic faces and erected plywood sculptures of taxi cabs in empty lots and covered an entire two-story home with stuffed animals* and built all manner of other sculptural pieces using old tires, part of a bus, bicycles, rusty oil drums, telephones, decapitated doll's heads, shopping carts, a men's room door, broken televisions, football helmets, Camel cigarette signs, vacuum cleaners, and discarded ballet shoes, among other things. The city government loathed the Heidelberg Project for many years. (Two different mayors, Young and Archer, ordered sections of the artwork demolished.) But since then, everyone has pretty much left Guyton alone. I had tried to set up an interview with him but his wife informed me that he would need to be financially compensated for his time, as so many requests from journalists and documentary film crews had been submitted.

In many ways, the Heidelberg Project is the ultimate manifestation

---

*Stuffed animals, it turns out, become incredibly unsettling when exposed to the elements for several years.

of a Boggsian vision of Detroit's future—a working-class African American artist, through a stubborn, solitary act of imagination, crafting a better world out of his blighted surroundings. Heidelberg Street, once left for dead, has become a regular stop for tourists from all over the world, and you never hear about anyone being robbed or hassled or about Guyton's artwork being stolen or vandalized, the city's own efforts at destruction notwithstanding.

Just as we parked, Guyton himself, who no longer lived on the block, happened to be pulling up in his Ford pickup truck. Feldman knew Guyton, and they greeted each other warmly. Guyton was drinking a fruit smoothie he'd made at home, sipping it through a straw from a plastic cup. He had a short, military-style haircut, almost entirely shaved in back, and wore jeans and Timberland boots and a blue University of Detroit Titans sweatshirt.

He'd come by to check on a flag he'd draped around one of the Heidelberg houses. The flag was so oversized, you only saw its stripes if you looked at the house head-on. The stars had ended up hanging somewhere on the roof or in the backyard. It was a windy morning, and the flag billowed dramatically.

Mark Rudd said, "You're the Detroit Christo!"

Guyton said, "People have called me lots of names."

We paused in front of the polka-dot-covered house. Guyton told us he'd grown up there. He said he could remember sitting on this very porch as a kid and listening to his grandfather tell stories about the lynchings he'd witnessed during his own boyhood in the South. Guyton had asked his grandfather, "But what, exactly, did you see?" And his grandfather had said, "I saw their soles blowing in the wind." These stories inspired Guyton to decorate the great oak tree in front of the house with dangling pairs of shoes, hundreds of them. Guyton said when people who'd visited the Heidelberg Project died—one lady was murdered in a crime and another guy, an aspiring artist, hung himself, and afterwards this aspiring artist's father hung himself as well—sometimes the families would bring a pair of the dead person's shoes to Guyton and ask him to add the shoes to the tree.

Guyton had just returned from a show in Berlin. He talked about wanting to unite all peoples, and how, when he first started the project, his neighbors despised it. Some of them didn't appreciate the fact that it was bringing white visitors to the block. Guyton spoke with a very precise, slightly nasal diction. He said some tourists from China had recently stopped by. He said that when he was in the army he'd been ordered to get rid of a bunch of the marijuana the government had been growing as part of an experiment about the effect of pot on soldiers during times of stress. He said he'd sampled some first. He said he was not surprised by anything the government might do.

Then he said, "I know you guys are in a hurry, but let me ask you," and he gestured toward the sky. "Do you believe in a Divine Creator who made everything?" Earlier, he'd made reference to a Creator's having put him here for a purpose, but no one had said anything. The topic of religion had not come up during our car ride. We all shifted around uncomfortably. I muttered something unsatisfying about being a nonpracticing Catholic. The college professor said he believed in more of a "source," something that we could all tap into, but not so much a divine being. Mark Rudd said that he believed in something but didn't like to talk about it and didn't really know how and that talking about God at all was a form of blasphemy, and for good reason, because once you started naming God, you got into religious wars. Feldman said he was into the cultural traditions of Judaism but not the idea of a divine being looking over us. Micah said he *was* God, at least that's what his sister always said, because he was always smiling and that struck her as godlike.

Guyton said he'd been pondering why he did what he did, and how he got to this point in his life. Waving his arms skyward again, he said he believed in a purpose for all of us. The sky did look strikingly beautiful this morning. It felt miserly, somehow, to argue with our host.

When we got back to my car, everything was fine. I'd worried all morning for nothing. A few blocks earlier, a pheasant had dashed in front of our path. We seemed to all cry out at once, delighted. One so inclined might have interpreted the moment as auguring something good.

* * *

On Sunday afternoons during the summer, if you drive up St. Aubin, passing a few grim-looking light industrial buildings (one called Elevator Technology), several fields threatening to overtake dilapidated wooden houses, and a boxing gym for kids run by a former gangbanger, you will eventually notice cars tightly lining either side of the street, a highly unusual sight for this part of town. If you happen to have a window cracked, you will also hear amplified blues chords echoing over the prairie. Finally, you will arrive at the corner of St. Aubin and Frederick, where, in a field taking up nearly the entire block, a man named Pete Barrow has erected a crude stage and begun hosting weekly blues concerts.

Actually, the stage is just a bunch of pallets nailed together and covered in carpet. A sizable crowd gathers by late afternoon, with spectators forming a U around the field's perimeter, leaving a large, open expanse of grass between themselves and the stage. The standing room, kibitzing portion of the crowd mingles behind the seated folk and spills all the way down Frederick—it being pretty much all field around here, so no private homeowners to bother. A couple of early arrivers set up tents to protect themselves from the sun and Pete Barrow has constructed a wooden outhouse. Other people bring lawn chairs, coolers, and little grills to cook out on. You can also buy tamales from the tamale guy working out of the back of a van or peanuts from the peanut man, who moves around the crowd in the manner of a ballpark vendor, except instead of a neck-slung hot dog or beverage container he carries a brown duffel bag stuffed with hand-baggied portions of peanuts, the bag itself—the duffel, not the individual baggies, which would've likely been prohibitively labor intensive for his pricing structure—helpfully marked PEANUT MAN.

Barrow, a retired autoworker, never sits in with the band. "Well, I sing once in a while," he says, "but there ain't nothing to it." You see him working the crowd between sets, exhorting people to "chuck it in the bucket," "it" meaning cash money, "the bucket" meaning the bucket he hauls around to collect the optional cover charge. "I need money to cut this lawn, people!" Barrow also shouts, when he's not telling people to chuck it in the bucket. What he doesn't say, not until the very end of a long conversation, and then only as a casual aside, is that he happens to be related to one of the neighborhood's most famous sons. His first cousin was Joe Louis Barrow, who grew up in Black Bottom, worked after school at Eastern Market, and learned to box at a recreation center near the Brewster-Douglass projects.

The corner of Frederick and St. Aubin could be an historical reenactment of the very rural Southern past left behind by the ancestors of so many African American Detroiters, and however temptingly easy and perhaps even inevitable the romanticization of such a scene might be, it's nonetheless not unreasonable to worry about how the best and the brightest diligently taking their pencils to the map of Detroit with the intention of "rightsizing" the place might fail to budget for this sort of thing, unthinkingly squeezing out the cherished alchemic components necessary to make a truly great city: the messiness, the clamor, the unplanned jostlings and anarchic eccentricity. Raising any sort of gentrification fears at this earliest stage of Detroit's would-be comeback feels like an academic luxury. And yet, when phrases like "the most potentially ambitious urban planning initiative in modern history" are being bandied about (to describe Bing administration's rightsizing efforts), it's hard not to grimace at the thought of the plasticized, deadening nature of planned communities.

Many would consider nearby Lafayette Park, the Mies van der Rohe development that partly replaced the razed Black Bottom neighborhood, one of the more successful residential areas in Detroit: middle class, diverse, safe. Even the chilly architecture, by this date, has aged into an appealing *Alphaville* sort of retro chic. And yet, I'd venture to guess you could spend as much time in Lafayette Park as you fancied and you would never see a house band jamming on a stage made of pallets while a singer in his seventies named Kenny Miller, dressed casually in a tan windbreaker, gray denim pants, and white Fila sneakers, his only nod to show business being his gold-rimmed brown-tinted glasses, performed "Paying the Cost to Be the Boss." Nor would you be able to wander among a standing-room crowd and spot a guy dressed in the official-looking vest of a casino employer dealing out a poker game. You wouldn't have seen thirty people move into the center of the field to join an elaborate step dance to a song called "Wobble" and you wouldn't have noticed the number of men arriving on motorcycle and seemingly affiliated with one of the city's many black biker clubs, their leather jackets, per custom, signifying which club precisely, e.g., the Black Dragons, the Outcasts, the Black Gentlemen, the Sons of Zodiac, and (a personal favorite) the Elegant Disciples. You wouldn't have the opportunity to shake the hands of one of the Outcasts or to be the recipient of the salutation "They call me Satan. But my name is Joe." You wouldn't hear Satan's thoughts on the Bing rightsizing plan ("I think it's a bunch of bullshit. Let people do what they want to do, live where they want to live"), nor would you learn that Satan, who just turned sixty and has massive arms and long silver hair and a light, almost South Asian complexion, used to work as an underwater welder on oil derricks in the Gulf, doing commercial deep diving—he was certified at two hundred feet—and that he'd also been a cop, briefly, in Louisville, though he didn't like it, and now he mostly builds and fixes Harleys, having lost one of his legs after being hit by a drunk driver in 2001 while riding his motorcycle and left for dead. You also wouldn't get to ask a stupid question like *So how did losing your leg affect your riding?* nor would you receive a response combining a good-natured slap of the prosthetic with a cry of *It didn't make it easier!*

A female blues singer whose name I didn't catch had told the crowd to "put some cotton in the children's ears" before launching into a song called "I'm a Dirty Old Woman with a Dirty Mind." You wouldn't have heard that, Lafayette Park, nor would you have caught that cherry red '66 GTO driving down Forest or have had the following exchange with the guy standing next to you in the leather vest and dark glasses:

GUY IN LEATHER VEST: Man, I used to have that *exact* car!
ME: What happened?
GUY IN LEATHER VEST: They stole it! Don't mean no disrespect, but *white boys* stole it.
MY FRIEND BILL: Some of us are dicks.

ME: Ever find it?
GUY IN LEATHER VEST: In Detroit? *Shit.*

Later, Harmonica Shaw took the stage with a sort of gunslinger's belt strapped around his middle, only the belt had different harmonicas. It would have been a shame to miss that.

Neighborhood watch leader James "Jack Rabbit" Jackson,
a retired Detroit police officer living on the city's east side.
[John Carlisle]

4

NOT FOR US
THE TAME ENJOYMENT

IF YOU WERE TO make the five-minute walk east from Mark Covington's Georgia Street Community Garden to Gratiot Avenue, then
turn north and stroll a single block, you would reach the Slumberland Child Development Center. In a city of haunted ruins, it takes
special élan to stand out as an unusually haunted ruin. For the Slumberland Child Development Center, the crude mural featuring
Mickey Mouse and the Tasmanian Devil provides that extra boost,
especially if you live in the neighborhood and happen to know the
recent history of the place—how, in 2009 and again in 2010, the
former day care center was used to hide the cadavers of murder victims. Including the two Slumberland corpses, the bodies of eight
women were discovered in the immediate vicinity over the same
time period. Two years on, there had been no arrests in connection
with the killings. In one of the local articles on the case, a resident
wondered if the neighborhood was becoming a "mecca for dumping
bodies."

Though his community garden earns most of the attention,
Covington also serves as vice president of a group called the City
Airport Renaissance Association. As the body count piled up, the
members of CARA, dedicated to stabilizing what remained of their
neighborhood—called "City Airport" because of its proximity to the

barely used Coleman A. Young Municipal Airport,* which for years has handled only cargo and the occasional private commercial traffic— began knocking on doors and distributing flyers warning residents of the killings.

If you ask a Detroiter about saving the city, it's unlikely that she will mention tech start-ups or urban farming. The first thing most Detroiters want to talk about is crime.

* * *

I was robbed at gunpoint when I was twenty, just a short walk from Service Street. A group of us had decided to drive from Ann Arbor, where I was an undergraduate at the University of Michigan, to Greektown, one of the few parts of downtown Detroit that can pass for a shlocky tourist zone in a regular, fully operational city. I rode with Jill, a friend of a friend I'd just met that night. We parked and entered the stairwell of the parking structure. Hiding on the other side of the door was a man with a gun. He hissed for us to look away from his face and hand over our money, in that order. I remember giving him my wallet and, bizarrely, clenching my stomach, as if preparing to take a punch. That was where he'd pointed the gun. Then, to my horror, Jill began arguing about having to give up her purse, which, she insisted, was a gift from her grandmother; it had "sentimental value."

"What you got in here, bitch?" the mugger wanted to know, suspicious, as he rifled through her bag. I did my best to telepathically signal that I'd just met this young woman and had no sentimental attachment to her. Eventually, he thrust the purse back into her hands. I couldn't tell if he was disgusted by her audacity or filled with a strange respect. Then he let us go.

Moments after we staggered out of the stairwell, Jill burst into tears, and I felt obligated to put my arm around her and comfort her, even though she'd endangered our lives for her stupid purse.

* * *

---

*Detroit's main Metropolitan Airport is actually twenty-five minutes west of the city, in suburban Romulus.

As urban pathologies go, crime as an issue can feel prosaic. The problem is fairly similar—specific stats aside—from one inner-city neighborhood to the next, even if the first happens to be in New Orleans and the second in East Brooklyn. What makes Detroit's crime situation particularly interesting is not the crime itself but the civilian response.

Along with groups like CARA and organized anticrime patrols like the Detroit 300, private citizens, in do-it-yourself Detroit fashion, attempted to fill the void left by the hobbled police department, which possessed one of the worst 911 response times in the country. (Thirty-four minutes in 2009—and that was for priority calls, as in, "A burglar is climbing through my bedroom window right now!" Nonpriority callers could expect waits closer to an hour.) Not coincidentally, metro Detroit accounted for 43 percent of all concealed weapons permits issued in the entire state of Michigan.

It could get sort of crazy. A few days after the new city council was elected in the fall of 2009, it was reported that five of its nine members had CCW (carry a concealed weapon) permits and regularly carried firearms. Around the same time, a robber made the mistake of breaking into the Westside Bible Church—where he was promptly shot by the pastor. A resourceful AP reporter had followed up on the gunslinging minister story by conducting a quick poll of Detroit churches and managed to turn up a number of other armed men of the cloth, including Holy Hope Heritage's Rev. William Revely, who admitted to occasionally preaching while wearing his .357 (and who kept in practice by target shooting at a gun range with a fellow pastor), and Greater Grace Temple's Bishop Charles Ellis III, who insisted he didn't wear his concealed weapon during services, but then again, he didn't have to, as the church had its own armed, eighteen-member Ministry of Defense present at all major functions. Speaking to the AP, Revely remained unapologetic: "I've always felt that the only way to handle a bear in a bear meeting is to have something you can handle a bear with."

The police could be just as nonchalant about gun ownership. One time, John Carlisle—"Detroitblogger John"—took me to Club Thunderbolt, a strip club run by a guy named Jay out of his dead parents' house, in one of the worst neighborhoods in the city. Jay had been shot in the face when he was eleven. (Now in his forties, he looked as if he'd recently suffered a stroke.) He showed me around the house, the butt of a pistol sticking out of the back of his pants, eventually leading me upstairs to his "War Room," which contained a stack of cardboard boxes. "Brand new AK-47 here, and 10,000 rounds of ammo," he said, patting one of the boxes. Then he leaned into the open doorway of his bedroom and emerged holding a double-barreled shotgun. "I've always got this ready to go," he said. "I sleep with numerous weapons." I could see a pair of nunchucks and a crossbow hanging above his bed, and there was a Kevlar vest hanging closer to the door. "You really don't want to fuck with me," Jay continued. "Shit, with the police here? I could dig a hole in the backyard and nobody would know. I saw a cop car seven days ago. And I saw a sheriff at the gas station yesterday. That's *it*, in this neighborhood, in a week."

Jay told me that he'd been sitting in bed one night, watching Jay Leno, and he'd heard a burglar creeping up the stairs. He grabbed his shotgun and chased the man outside, firing at him through the door.

"I shot high, because I didn't want to kill somebody," Jay said.

A cop showed up five-and-a-half hours after Jay called 911. When the officer arrived, he told Jay, "Next time, aim lower."

* * *

To obtain a CCW permit in Michigan, one must first complete a gun safety and proficiency class with someone like Rick Ector, the proprietor of Rick's Firearm Academy, who was quoted in the AP story. Ector said he'd taught pastors and "people from all walks of life." As he explained it, "Detroit is not a very safe place."

On Ector's website, he'd splashed across the top of the page: "If You Live, Work, or Play in Detroit, You Need a CCW/ CPL!" Below this imperative, visitors could scroll through such statements as:

Detroit is the most violent city in the USA.

Each and every single day within the Detroit city limits one (1) person will be murdered, two (2) people will be forcibly raped, nineteen (19) people will be robbed, and thirty-six (36) people will be victims of an aggravated assault.* (Be advised that these numbers only reflect crimes that were reported; criminals, as a rule, do not report crimes committed against them.)

I was surprised to discover, via the website, that Ector was African American. In a case of reverse stereotyping, I'd always considered this specific type of right-to-bear-arms proselytizing as distinctly Caucasian behavior. Curious, I gave Ector a call, and he invited me to take a class. The next one would take place on a Sunday, in the bland conference room of a suburban hotel located on a freeway service drive, beginning at 8:00 a.m. sharp.

There were nine other students, six of them women, everyone black but for a towheaded, Polish-accented man who looked about six foot five. Pastel watercolors (floral bouquet, covered bridge) adorned the thin walls. Ector stood at the front of the room, forty-two years old, fit, conservatively dressed (blue slacks, tucked dress shirt), with short hair and a five o'clock shadow. By day, he worked as a systems analyst for a company whose major client was one of the Big Three auto companies.

Ector's pedagogical style seemed the product of a Dale Carnegie–inspired handbook on effective public speaking. He projected his crisply enunciated words toward the back of the room and made deliberate eye contact with each of his students, occasionally underlining a point with a sudden and intense grin. Unlike Carnegie, Ector was wearing a pair of bulky handguns, visibly holstered on either hip, which made his telegraphed confidence appear sinister and slightly unhinged. (There is something unnerving about a motivational speaker whose motivational purpose is to convince you to carry a weapon and understand precisely when it is legal under state law to use that weapon to kill.) Ector told the class the reason to carry two weapons was so you'd have a backup in case one of the guns misfired.

Among the other students, there was one young couple, a paunchy retirement-aged man wearing a UAW cap, and a compact, fussily made-up woman in a camouflage Detroit Tigers cap. The woman had brought along her own handgun in a black carrying case. Seated directly

---

*These numbers are fairly close to accurate—at least the murder part. (In 2009, there were 361 murders in Detroit and 17,553 violent crimes.)

beside me, a pretty, broad-faced woman with a regal posture took copious notes on a yellow legal pad. Even the students who didn't take notes listened raptly as Ector worked his central thesis: the crucial necessity of constant vigilance and hyperawareness of one's surroundings, sleep being the only exemption. If you're a heavy sleeper, Ector recommended buying a dog.

Ector laid out a number of "be aware" scenarios where a crime might occur. Some seemed universally applicable (a car following you home), others specific to Detroit (a car stopping next to yours at a red light after dark). Whenever Ector wanted to emphasize a point, he narrowed one end of his mouth and cocked it sharply, at the same time puffing his cheek and making a clicking noise with his tongue.

The class covered practical gun-related concerns—the pluses and minuses of various-calibered handguns,* the inefficiency of certain pistols, how the difference between store-bought and home-swaged bullets was akin to the difference between an off-the-rack and a custom suit (perhaps as a nod to the number of women in the room, Ector noted he typically pressed his bullets while watching *Oprah*), and how hollow-point bullets tended to "solve the penetration problem."

"At what point does someone stop being a threat to you?" Ector asked the class.

A woman in a faded teal sweatshirt raised her hand. The effort seemed to exhaust her. "When they can't move?" she asked.

"You shoot until he stops!" Ector shouted, his eyes flashing as if lit up by gunpowder. Lowering his voice, he continued, "You may have to shoot a person more than once. You may have to shoot a person *a lot* of times. It's getting colder, so people wear a lot of clothes. A person might be high on drugs."

His voice turning grave, Ector told us it was better not to carry a gun at all than to have one and not be prepared to pull the trigger.

"Do you have it in you to defend yourself?" he asked. "Or would you pull out your gun and wave it around and hope they magically disappear?" The "they" referred to a would-be assailant. He paused, arranging his face into a disgusted look, before continuing, "This is

---

*According to Ector, gun instructors joke that if you shoot a guy with a .22 caliber, he'll probably find out about it.

ripped from the headlines: what if your assailant is twelve years old?" A few months earlier, a twelve-year-old boy had, indeed, been arrested in Detroit for murder, after shooting a young woman during an attempted carjacking.

"What if," Ector went on, "a twelve-year-old with a shotgun in his pants rolls up on a bicycle? Would you have it in you to shoot him?"

A low chorus of yeses rose from the seats, though one of the women, demurring, began, "Well, it depends on how big—"

"He could be a runt!" Ector interrupted. "If you are not prepared to shoot a twelve-year-old, you should not carry a handgun!" Shifting to a faux-whiny voice, he said, "'Ooh, Rick's *hard-core*. He's talking about shooting *children*.'"

The woman in the teal sweatshirt said, "If he's big enough to point a gun in your face, he's big enough to take a bullet."

A plurality of my classmates nodded approvingly.

Eventually, Ector introduced the attorney who would lecture us on the specific instances in which we could legally defend ourselves. You weren't allowed to shoot someone for trying to steal your car. But if that same person made the mistake of breaking into your home, you, the home owner, could assume that person meant you bodily harm and so you had permission to shoot to kill, thanks to a law passed in 2006 eliminating a gun owner's so-called duty to retreat. The catch was, the home invader had to be inside your home, not simply, say, standing on the front lawn throwing a brick through your front window.

A copiously freckled woman wanted to know if you should drag the dead body of someone you'd shot into the house before the cops arrived.

The lawyer said, "That would be a bad idea." He spoke through his nose.

"A police officer told me I should do that!" the woman exclaimed, sounding annoyed. Her question had not exactly been hypothetical, as a few of us learned during a break, when she explained how a group of her nephew's friends tried to break into her home one afternoon. They'd expected her to be at work when she'd been home sick—a severe miscalculation. "When I heard people running up my back door, I put my baby girl in the bathroom and came out blazing," she said, the pitch of her voice rising with recalled excitement. "They got to running, I got to shooting and chasing!" She'd followed the would-be burglars into the street, firing after them, but nobody ended up hit. Still, the body-dragging question had possible utility for the future.

When the lawyer finished this section of his talk, he said, "Okay, so that's how you get to shoot someone."

He went on to discuss "overkill," which basically meant shooting someone an excessive number of times, after they no longer posed a threat.

"Unfortunately, you can shoot yourself out of the right to kill," the lawyer said. "If he's on the ground twitching and bleeding, you can't stand over him and shoot him."

A smattering of *awww*s rose from the class.

"You just ticked off a few people, man," Ector said from the back of the room.

My note-taking neighbor, who, later, when we graded one another's written tests, would receive a perfect score, raised her hand. She spoke in a crisp tone befitting her posture. "Let's say I'm sitting in my living room with all the lights off and Pookie and Ray Ray come in the dark," she said. "Is that an ambush, if I'm waiting with my gun? Am I allowed to put a cap in their ass? Because I'm about to move back to the hood and I'm gonna have two guns with me. It's a neighborhood where things happen."

The lawyer indicated that a shooting in this instance would likely be justified.

My neighbor muttered, "I know those Negroes gonna try me. I got a vacant house they keep messing with."

Ector resumed his portion of the lecture, this time to discuss marksmanship. "This is where you want to shoot the bad guy," Ector explained, pressing an 8½ × 11 sheet of paper to the center of the lawyer's chest. The lawyer stood still, making no indication of any discomfort in his role. "No aiming for the arm or the leg because"—Ector shifted to his mewling, effeminate voice—"*you don't want to hurt them. You're not a sharpshooter!* That's why we have this area—" He tapped the lawyer's chest, rustling the paper. "So you can put them down."

Near the end of class, Ector issued a final warning: "Just because you have a CPP"—a concealed pistol permit—"does not mean you can carry that throwaway. Get rid of it."

The freckle-faced woman who'd chased her nephew's friends down the street raised her hand and asked, "All of them?"

* * *

During one of the breaks, Ector stepped outside for a cigarette and I joined him for a chat. He said he'd been uninterested in guns until seven years prior, when he'd been robbed in his own driveway. He lived in Rosedale Park, a neighborhood on the northwest side that holds a reputation as one of Detroit's more stable. One night in October, he'd arrived home after dark and, exiting his car, found two teenagers waiting in the shadows, one packing a gun. The kids ordered him to sit down in his driveway and empty his pockets. Ector had so little cash, they attempted to force him to drive to an ATM, but he managed to convince them he had wildly overdrawn his account after a long night at a bar.

"They weren't that big," Ector told me. He did his thoughtful cheek-puffing thing. You could still detect the sting in his voice. "Average kids. I think I could've took 'em. But I'll never know. Because they had a gun and I didn't."

Ector had kept a twelve-gauge shotgun in his home for protection, but he'd never used a handgun before. The next day, he went to his local police precinct and asked about acquiring a permit. "They tried to discourage me," Ector said. "'The solution is not everyone getting a gun. That only adds to the problem.' It incensed me a little bit. I thought, 'You were not there when I got robbed.'"

That same day, driving along 8 Mile, Ector spotted an ad for a CCW class on the side of another car. It wasn't that much of a coincidence: such ads are common sights all over the city. Still, Ector took it as a sign and called the school and learned that the next class (Basic Pistol) was scheduled for the following day. He took it. Six months later, he'd become a certified instructor.

Today, Ector evangelizes for gun rights with the zeal of a recent convert. Sometimes, just to test himself, he'll attempt to get through an entire day without allowing a single stranger to get within ten feet of him. (He allots himself one point if he spots the stranger approaching and penalizes himself ten points if someone "sneaks up" behind him.) Citing more Detroit crime statistics, Ector went on, "You know, there's no civil liability if the police don't respond in a timely manner.

You're officially on your own. The chief of police called Detroit the Wild, Wild West. Detroit gets picked on a lot, sometimes unfairly. But a lot of the criticism is justified. It's really bad in the city now. If the city is this bad, I'd think, as a public service, they'd come out and say, 'Go buy a gun for your protection until we get it together.'"

Ector also pointed out that some of Michigan's earliest restrictions on gun possession came in direct response to the Ossian Sweet case. In September 1925, Sweet, an African American doctor, moved into a white neighborhood on Detroit's east side with his wife and infant daughter. The booming automobile industry had resulted in severe housing shortages in the city's black ghettos, forcing Sweet—upwardly mobile and ambitious but no rabble-rousing activist—to risk crossing Detroit's clearly demarcated lines of segregation. Shortly after the family's move, a mob of angry whites gathered in the street and began to pelt the home with rocks and bricks, eventually storming the front door. In the ensuing melee, shots were fired by either Sweet or one of his dinner guests and two white men were wounded, one fatally. Sweet, his wife, and seven other men present were arrested and put on trial for murder. The defendants' eventual acquittal, after a pair of sensational trials in which they were represented by Clarence Darrow, is considered a milestone of the modern civil rights movement and has been chronicled in gripping detail by Kevin Boyle in his 2005 book, *Arc of Justice*.

"He was a very successful doctor who wanted to move to a nice diverse neighborhood where he wasn't wanted," was how Ector put it. "That law was designed strictly for the purpose of denying people of color from getting firearms." Ector admitted that the NRA had an "image problem" when it came to race. "People hear NRA and they think militias, rednecks," he said. "But there are other black people in the NRA. Not many walk around with a black NRA cap, like me." He smiled ironically, then recommended a book called *Black Man with a Gun*.* "Actually?" Ector told me, "I don't think the NRA goes far enough."

* * *

*By Rev. Kenn Blanchard, a former cop and Marine who insists gun control is racist.

On an unseasonably balmy fall afternoon, a couple of weeks after the gun class, I took a walk downtown to check out the site of the original French settlement of Detroit, Fort Pontchartrain. A twenty-five-story hotel called the Portchartrain had been built on the footprint of the fort in the midsixties. The hotel had been one of Detroit's most luxurious upon its completion, but in 2009, Mutual Bank had initiated foreclosure proceedings on the property, which had been steadily losing what little Detroit hotel business remained to the newer casino hotels, and now "the Pontch," the affectionate local diminutive for the place for as long as I can remember, stood empty.

Since it was such a lovely day, I decided to stretch out on a grassy embankment overlooking the river and read. A pair of homeless men sat on a bench on the promenade; a Middle Eastern tourist was taking his wife's photograph. To the east, Belle Isle smoldered in seasonal auburns. The absence of people made it easy to stare at the river, pixilating brilliantly in the sunlight on this cloudless autumn afternoon, and imagine Cadillac's convoy emerging from the distance, the stoic oarsmen fighting back grins at the sight of land, Cadillac himself assuming a Washingtonian prow stance on the lead vessel.

At some point, a couple appeared on the river walk. When the male portion of the couple spotted me, he waved and called out, "Hey! What are you reading?" Before I could answer, he began jogging up the hill in my direction.

The man was African American, probably in his forties, average height, slender build, wearing jeans and a black Marine Corps sweatshirt. He looked like he'd had experience sleeping outdoors, and I pegged his curiosity as an unsubtle opening bid for loose change. Upon reaching the top of the hill, though, he surprised me, saying, "I'm only asking because I love to read." From his back pockets, he pulled out a pair of battered paperbacks: *The World According to Garp* and something called *Algorithms*. "Man, I love John Irving," he said. "I see one of his books, I've got to read it." After giving me a demonstrative, brotherhood-of-readers handshake that incorporated a slapping of fives, he introduced himself as Tony and picked up my book, a doorstopping history of Detroit. Flipping open to a random page, he began to read aloud, assuming a mock-declamatory tone: "The electric industry would set off a new boom in the copper mines, and make Michigan's Calumet and

Hecla the most lucrative mine in the world. But it was lumbermen who were coming almost to rival the wealth of their railroad acquaintances. It was, in fact, the unparalleled expansion of the railroads that created the demand for lumber."

Tony frowned, seeming unimpressed, and closed the book. He told me he used to read all the time in jail, despite the fact that one particular drill-sergeant-acting corrections officer (Tony said "C.O.") always wanted to be messing with him. But Tony had been in the Marines, so he knew how to handle *real* drill sergeants, who, granted, also generally tended to be assholes, but you couldn't ever back down, that was the key. Tony spoke fast, and his voice had an edgy, intense quality, though his eyes remained cold and disengaged.

I started to tell Tony how my brother worked at a place called Children's Village, a juvenile detention center for kids under eighteen who had been accused of crimes and were awaiting trial. Tony interrupted me and said he knew the Village, that he'd been through O.C., meaning Oakland County's lockup, and then proceeded, under the assumption (incorrect) that I had a deep familiarity with the local criminal justice system, to rattle off references to numerous judges and jails and probationary terms, making use of increasingly cryptic jargon and undecipherable acronyms. I nodded as if I knew what he was talking about. In what sounded like a non sequitur, Tony mentioned how he wasn't prejudiced and told a story about a recent bus ride on which he'd overheard three white boys calling each other nigger, and how this had offended some of the black bus passengers but how Tony had told his wife, "They from the ghetto. They hustling just like us." Then he gave me what seemed like a pointed look and added, "Now, not *everyone* can say it." I agreed that that was the case.

Then Tony told me about how he'd been shot eleven times and stabbed three times. He began to display his various wounds, something I've noticed people with multiple wounds like to do—suddenly, shirts and pant legs start getting yanked up and it's like being around tattoo enthusiasts showing off their ink. "This is my .38 watch," Tony said, pointing with some pride to a jagged circular bullet wound on his right wrist. Rolling up his left sleeve, he flashed another entry wound farther up his arm. "Here they had to cut me to relieve the pressure," he explained. Tugging the sleeve up even higher, almost to his shoulder, revealed a long knife scar. Then he pulled down the neck of his sweatshirt to uncover his most cherished engraving, a gnarly slug of discolored skin curled up to the edge of his jugular. "Someone tried to cut my throat," he said, obviously pleased with himself at having survived such an attack.

All of the wound talk prompted Tony to return to the theme of how it was not a good idea to fuck with him. As he spoke, he began to lift his sweatshirt. For a moment, I thought he was going to show me a gun. But instead, tucked into his pants, he had a butcher's knife, alongside the scuffed, silver blade of an even larger hatchet. (The hatchet had been pantsed handle-side down.) "See, I'm not allowed to carry a gun, because of my record, but I do carpentry work sometimes, so I can carry my tools," Tony said, deadpan.

I didn't get the sense that Tony was preparing to attack me with the axe, or even that he meant any sort of implicit threat. He quickly readjusted his sweatshirt and went on with whatever he'd been saying. I nodded, acting unmoved. Eventually, Tony asked if I had eighty-three cents he could borrow.

"Sorry, man, I don't have any money," I said.

"Really?" Tony said. Affecting a look of concern, he pulled a crumpled dollar bill out of his pocket and held it out to me.

"No, I'm good," I said, smiling.

"You sure?" Tony asked. "I hate to see people with an empty pocket." Then he shrugged and stuffed the bill back into his own pocket and invited me to come join him and his wife over by the river, where they would be having a couple of brewskies—he actually said "brewskies"—if I happened to get thirsty.

After Tony walked away, I wrote "Tony/Antoine (de la Mothe Cadillac)" in my notebook and underlined it, twice. Then I realized there was no one else around. The two other homeless men had disappeared, as had the Middle Eastern tourists. I hadn't been frightened when Tony flashed his blades, but now I wondered if I should leave. But then I glanced down the hill and saw Tony sitting on a bench near the river. He took a sip of beer and said something to his companion. They stared out at the gently rippling current, not giving me a second look, just enjoying the beautiful day like anyone would.

A home on Detroit's "urban prairie." [Geoff George]

5

HOW TO SHRINK A MAJOR AMERICAN CITY

THERE WAS NO GETTING around it: Detroit had too much space. Having experienced a decades-long, ongoing population bleed, the city had begun to feel like an overstretched empire in its decadent phase, sprawling far beyond its means. But after years of obstinate resistance and denial, a new consensus was finally emerging, at least in policy circles, about what to do with those forty square miles of vacant land. Detroit would have to shrink, in some sense of the word, in order to survive. The main obstacle had long been a psychological one: there seemed to be a bone-deep American reluctance to even flirt with the idea of thwarting manifest destiny, let alone embrace the notion of getting smaller. "I teach land use and planning and there's nothing in there about downsizing," was how John Mogk, who has spent decades studying urban policy as it applies to Detroit, put it when I dropped by his office at Wayne State University's law school. "Most of the scholarship relates to development and growth—the assumption is that a population is expanding, so how best do you control it. There's very little of value at all written about what do you do about decline."

It was in the air, though—notions of American fallibility, our fading sole-superpower status, China's rise, India's rise, unsustainable long-term deficits, all of that. The difference in Detroit was that the contraction would be *literal*. Mayor Dave Bing had run for office peddling a vision of benevolent retrenchment: condensing the city's government agencies and its job rolls to bring them more in line with its population. Then in February 2010, as Detroit began grappling with the bleak findings of the census, Bing announced more details of what would euphemistically come to be known as "rightsizing"—a geographic shrinking, not of the city's borders, but of its population footprint, wherein citizens living on isolated urban prairies would be incentivized to move to denser, more easily serviced neighborhoods. "If we don't do it," Bing told the *Detroit News*, "you know this whole city is going to go down."

There was talk of a multimillion-dollar federally funded light rail plan to anchor development along Woodward Avenue, of vacant land being bundled and cultivated as public parks or other green spaces, of assessing and ranking individual neighborhoods according to factors such as strength of housing stock, population density, and economic activity. Since the city remained too broke to fund an effort this complex on its own, the nonprofit Kresge Foundation had agreed to pay the salary of Harvard urban planner Toni Griffin, who would oversee what was being called, surely as a means of conjuring images of New Deal largesse—President Obama was still talking up generous stimulus spending and infrastructure building at this point—the Detroit Works Project.

What do you do with a discarded city? Political leaders had been struggling with the issue of sustained blight for decades. Whereas in a normal town, a mayor loves nothing better than to unveil plans for an ambitious civic building project (and, by extension, an enduring monument to mayoral vision and leadership), in Detroit, where all rules about how cities work have been upended, elected officials since the 1960s have sweet-talked constituents by promising to tear down more derelict structures than their predecessors. Most recently, Dave Bing made the leveling of ten thousand vacant homes within four years "a centerpiece of his administration," in the words of the *Detroit News*. In early April 2010, the slated demolition of the first of these homes, on the 1100 block of Lewerenz Street in southwest Detroit, was promoted by Bing's people and covered by the local press as a major media event. In Detroit, this is what passes for a ribbon-cutting ceremony; I was surprised Bing himself didn't show up in a hard hat, hoisting a sledgehammer, ready to deliver the inaugural blow to the load-bearing wall.*

This was not part of Detroit Works but simply standard mayoral practice, a more or less baseline promise you had to make to get elected. In fact, when the demolitions started, all details pertaining to what, exactly, the Detroit Works Project might encompass were still pure speculation. To assuage the fears of skeptical citizens, the Bing administration promised that the initiative would begin with a "listening" phase of at least forty-five town-hall-style community meetings, taking place over the course of eighteen months. While garnering community input, or at least paying lip service to the idea of doing so, made sense from the standpoint of desirable optics, the lack of urgency implied by such a leisurely approach made the mayor seem wildly out of touch. At the meetings, Bing and his representatives insisted, again and again, that Detroit Works was no Trojan horse hiding another, secret plan to sell large chunks of the city to moneyed suburban interests, a real fear of many Detroiters. And in fact, forget secret plans, *there's no plan, period* became the constant public refrain—*really, trust us on this one, guys, we got nothing.*

Still, the very prospect of such a comprehensive reckoning with land use, depopulation, sprawl, and the future of the American city felt like an important moment, one with potential application for

---

*John Adamo Jr. owns and operates the biggest demolition contractor in the city, the Adamo Demolition Company. If one family's immigrant story stands as an allegory for Detroit's past century, it is the Adamos'. John Adamo Jr.'s grandfather, a builder, emigrated to Detroit from Alcamo, a town in Sicily, in the early 1920s, just as the auto industry was exploding. A newly flush class of workers wanted to expand their homes, many of which had "Michigan basements"— a crawl space beneath the cinder blocks on which the houses rested. Here, Adamo's grandfather discovered his niche. "He'd get under the houses," Adamo told me, "jack them up a couple of feet, and put guys under there with shovels and picks to dig a full basement."

By the time Adamo's father took over the business in the 1960s, however, expansion had stalled. "At some point," Adamo said, "he thought, 'Man, if I had a wrecking license, I could take down a few of these houses.'" Within a few years, the demolition company had grown large enough to be incorporated, while the long-withering construction side of the business was slowly phased out. After the riots, Adamo said, the number of city demolition contracts went through the roof. "Timing is everything, I guess," he noted drily.

Detroit demolition guys, Adamo added, were always thinking about how to take down buildings. He and his demo friends, in fact, had a running joke going: if they'd never been to your house before, the first thing they'd do would be to look around and ballpark how many loads of debris the building would yield. *Oh, yeah*, one of them might say. *You've got yourself a ten-load house.*

the aging metropolises, large and small, which in aggregate made the present-day state of our union so atypically morbid. If anything like the rumors were true, Bing's plan could end up being one of the boldest reimaginings of urban space in modern U.S. history.

* * *

People liked to compare the amount of vacant land in Detroit to equivalent-sized spaces. All of Paris could fit into Detroit's forty square miles of nothing, or two Manhattans, or a slightly shaved Boston. Such formulations, though, inevitably led one to imagine a contiguous landmass, severable as a rotten limb, or possibly something to be cordoned off and beautified, like a Central Park—which, of course, was not the case. Vacant parcels were spread throughout the city, closer in spirit to tumors riddling a body.

When enough of those parcels happened to cluster together, you had urban prairies: entire neighborhoods nearly wiped from the map, the inevitable result of a place built for two million servicing less than half that number. An exemplary swath of prairie had crept within walking distance of Service Street; some call the neighborhood I'm talking about South Poletown—Polish factory workers populated the area several decades ago—but I started thinking of it as Upper Chene, after Chene Street, which runs straight up from the Detroit River. On the two-mile stretch of Chene itself, once a thriving commercial strip, you could count the viable, operating businesses on two hands. Several of the now unrecognizable storefronts, having burned and partially collapsed years earlier, looked like funeral pyres left untouched as a monument to the dead. On the residential streets, entire blocks had gone to field. The remaining houses ranged, schizophrenically, from obvious drug spots to beautifully kept-up brick ranches, from old wooden bungalows to foreclosed properties scrapped to the joists by copper thieves.

Once I shucked my trepidation at venturing into such lonely and forbidding territory, I began taking long bike rides around Upper Chene. On summer afternoons, the insect noise could be deafening, and though the people sitting out on their porches would stare, I soon learned that country rules applied here, too—if you smiled and gave a little wave or a head nod, you'd generally get the same back, saving, of course, the dope boys, whose hard-gazed dedication to radiating inscrutability and menace convinced me to drop the smiling part. Mostly, though, the menace was due to the absence of people, and thus far more rural than urban, putting me in mind of Seventies exploitation movies like *The Hills Have Eyes* or *Texas Chainsaw Massacre*, in which naive cityfolk venture down the wrong dirt road and find themselves on the business end of a meathook.

The scrappers were everywhere. One Sunday morning in broad daylight, on a desolate stretch of Grandy, I rode past a guy pulling pipes twice the length of his body and loading them out of the basement of a foreclosed home into a white minivan. A few blocks later, a couple of entrepreneurs came driving in the opposite direction in a pickup truck, its bed overflowing with twisted pieces of metal, including what looked to be a number of shelving units.

In another field, at Chene and Canfield, Tyree Guyton, the artist from Heidelberg Street, had arranged a bunch of discarded shoes in the shape of a river; shortly after he'd laid out his installation, I'd noticed some kids from the neighborhood wading right through the middle of it like anglers. When I asked what was up, they said, "Free shoes!" A little girl warned me that it was hard to find your size, or even a matching pair. A few blocks away, just past the Church of the Living God No. 37, a white pit bull began barking furiously at me from the yard of a home that I'd thought abandoned. When I got closer I noticed a young man in a crisp Tigers cap staring coldly at me from one of the front windows.

I bicycled down a block of Dubois with just a single house left standing, almost dead center of one side of the street. The whole of the other side had turned feral, forested by a tangle of unmowed grass and gnarled trees. Despite its isolation, the two-story wood frame house had been neatly maintained, with a handsome gray paint job and a lush garden of rose bushes and fruit trees surrounded by a picket fence. A round-faced man in a bright red T-shirt and Bermuda shorts sat on the top steps of the porch. I stopped and said hello. His name was Marty. When I got closer, I noticed he had a cane next to him on the porch. The writing on Marty's flip-flops proclaimed him Big Slugger #1 Dad.

Marty used to work in the auto industry and also at Thorn Apple Valley, a sausage plant near Eastern Market that closed in 1998. I'd made frequent deliveries to Thorn Apple Valley as a teenager; my dad sold them sausage casings. Marty and I bonded over this odd coincidence, though we figured out we'd probably never met back then. "I did things with pigs—*live* pigs," he told me, widening his eyes theatrically to signify, *You really don't want to know.* He told me anyway: while he'd never butchered, he'd had the karmically unpleasant job of herding the soon-to-be-slaughtered pigs into the abattoir, using a whip. He'd gotten into the habit of naming his favorite pigs and keeping them in the back with him as long as possible, though eventually they all had to go.

I asked Marty if he'd be willing to move if the neighborhood got rightsized. He shook his head. "This is our house for generations. We pay our taxes. That's not happening." Someone opened the gate at the side of the house. "Who's back there?" Marty asked. It turned out to be his aunt, who also lived in the family home. She tended the flowers and this afternoon was pulling a red wagon laden with gardening supplies. "I do it as much as I can," she said. Marty said the house had been in his family for fifty years. "*Sixty-four* years," his aunt said. "My mother bought this house when I was three months old."

"You got to analyze this," Marty said. "These are some rough times we living in. Most of our jobs went overseas. I ain't never seen an economy like this, ever." He'd lived on the block his entire life, watching the neighborhood disappear around him: the barbershops, bars, ice cream parlors, all gone. "This neighborhood used to be straight," he said. He squinted at the thicket of trees across the street. "You get used to it, though. One thing, it's quiet here. Don't be all that crazy stuff around here. I like the serenity of my environment. To me? All this is a big plasma screen. You just have to be strong and keep God with you. What does the Bible say? 'You're in this world but not—' No, wait." I said I thought it was "of this world but not in it," and he nodded, *right, right.* Though later, I realized I'd screwed up the quote. Of course we were all in it.

* * *

Detroiters are rightfully wary of top-down urban renewal plans. The city's wild budgetary and population woes date back to the peak of the auto industry, when workers from Europe and the rural South flooded the city, hoping to reap the benefits of Fordism. In 1919, James Couzens, the longtime financial manager of Ford, was elected mayor. Couzens had built the company's extensive dealership network and was the primary architect of the five-dollar workday, which had sparked the mass migration of labor to Detroit in the first place and created a problem for Couzens unimaginable to Dave Bing: a city with far *too many* people. In the ten years prior to Couzens's election, Detroit's population had more than doubled, leaving thousands of citizens, according to Robert E. Conot, "packed into leaky and unheated barns and shacks without plumbing" or into slapdash tent cities.

The desire to escape this Boschian tableau was a sensible one. Workers in Detroit also happened to be making enough money to buy the very cars they were building, which promoted mobility, as did the new, rapidly expanding highway system being built in large part because of the lobbying efforts of their employers.

With, of course, the notable exception of one demographic group. Detroit's African American population, which doubled between 1940 and 1950, was generally restricted, through redlining tactics, to living in packed slum housing in neighborhoods like the roughly sixty-square-block Black Bottom. These neighborhoods had the city's oldest housing stock—Sugrue again: "tiny, densely packed frame homes jerry-built by poor European immigrants in the mid and late nineteenth century"— and thanks to discriminatory banking practices that severely restricted loans to minorities, black residents had difficulty raising money to prevent the slums from further degrading. Pressure to build new housing projects met with deep neighborhood resistance.

But the builders of Detroit, having radically changed nearly every aspect of the lives of Americans—where we could live, how much we could earn, how far we could travel—believed there was a solution. As far back as 1939, General Motors, in its massively popular Futurama exhibition at the New York World's Fair, had begun predicting what a techno-utopianist's "city of the future" might look like. Not surprisingly, GM's vision included fourteen-lane expressways and elevated civilian walkways to double the available width for car traffic below.* The film accompanying the exhibit, *To New Horizons*, set in

---

*By the time of Futurama II, the sequel launched for the 1964 New York fair, the future included fantastic "road-building machines" that could cut through the jungle laying concrete and steel highways at the rate of a foot a minute.

the "wonder-world of 1960," imagined "an American city replanned around a highly developed modern traffic system," where "along both banks of the river, beautifully landscaped parks replaced the outworn areas of an older day" and "on all express-city thoroughfares, the rights of way have been so routed as to displace outmoded business sections and undesirable slum areas whenever possible." As the camera panned over a diorama of the future city, the narrator portentously intoned, *Man continually strives to replace the old with the new!*

Directly behind and to the west of my loft is the neighborhood that used to be Black Bottom. Beginning in 1946, Mayor Edward Jeffries condemned 129 acres of Black Bottom in the name of progress, uprooting nearly two thousand black families. As presaged by Futurama—almost to the year!—a freeway was eventually routed through the former neighborhood, "displac[ing]" the bulk of this specific "outdated slum area," including Hastings Street, the vibrant center of working-class African American life in Detroit (famously name-checked by John Lee Hooker in "Boogie Chillen"). The rest of Black Bottom became Lafayette Park, a cluster of identical podlike "homes of the future" designed in the International Style by Bauhaus master Mies van der Rohe. The stark, glass-fronted town houses and high-rise apartment buildings received mixed reviews as architecture; but in any event, they weren't built for poor people. As is often the case with the promises bundled into large-scale civic development schemes, construction of its lower-income housing was slated for the back end of the timetable and ultimately wound up dropped altogether.

* * *

I happened upon another failed urban renewal plan by accident, through a young Dutch photographer named Corine Vermeulen. In 2001, Corine had moved to the city to attend Cranbrook, the famous art and design school whose past instructors had included Charles Eames and Eliel and Eero Saarinen. Her work avoided predictable images of grit and decay, instead focusing on what kept the city alive: inner-city beekeepers, lowrider car enthusiasts, storefront mosques, pastoral scenes of the urban prairie. "I feel like Detroit is the most important city in the U.S., maybe in the world," she told me one night, utterly serious. "It's the birthplace of modernity and the graveyard of modernity. My American experience is Detroit. Detroit is America for me."

At a certain point, she brought up Andrei Tarkovsky's *Stalker*, her favorite film, explaining how much of the movie is set in a mysterious postindustrial netherworld called "the Zone"—a desolate, forbidden place that also offers supernatural promises of transcendence, at least according to the titular Stalker, who has agreed to guide the film's other two main characters, called only the Writer and the Professor, into the Zone in order to fulfill their deepest desires. Yanking a book by the anarchist writer Hakim Bey out of her bag, Corine began to tell me how Bey's theories of anarchic "temporary autonomous zones" connected with *Stalker* and, ultimately, Detroit, where anything could happen.*

"Detroit is a temporary autonomous zone," she said.

"Like the Zone in *Stalker*?" I asked.

"No, not all of Detroit. But it has Zones. The dichotomy between the parts of this city that are very magical and the parts that are miserable can be pretty overwhelming. But it's precisely these extremes that create the urgency to override the existing reality with something completely different. Detroit in the present moment is a very good vehicle for the imagination." She gave me a curious look. Her face had a mischievous, elfin quality. "Do you want me to take you to the Zone?" she asked.

I said, "I would go to the Zone."

The following Sunday, Corine picked me up in her ancient, boxy Volvo, a lush Detroit techno track, awash in synthesizer, playing on her stereo.† We drove past the ruins of the Packard plant, heading deeper into the east side. It wasn't an especially cold day, but the sidewalks and front yards were mostly devoid of life. We passed a house with no windows or doors; a poster on the front of the house warned "This Building Is Being Watched." You'd see these posters on forsaken structures throughout the city, their words splashed above a menacing

---

*Corine had never heard of Geoff Dyer, but in his collection *Yoga for People Who Can't Be Bothered to Do It*, he makes the same connection, sprinkling his account of a trip to the first Detroit Electronic Music Festival with references to *Stalker* and the Zone.

†Being European, Corine had been drawn to Cranbrook in the first place partly out of her fanatical appreciation of techno.

pair of human eyes, presumably meant to scare off scrappers or arsonists, but having the odd effect of making entire rows of ravaged homes resemble scarred, angry faces glowering at passersby, as if the potential home invader were Being Watched by the buildings themselves.

We eventually came to the edge of a cleared space. This was unlike the other fields we had been driving through, in that there weren't stray houses dotting the renatured yards—here, for a dozen or more blocks, absolutely *everything* was gone. Corine turned down the only street not barred with cement barricades. Strewn with detritus, at points nearly impassable, the block made me think of Humvee footage from the early days of the invasion of Baghdad. We maneuvered around shredded tires, jagged stacks of roofing tile, torn panels of Sheetrock, neat little mounds of broken glass, busted pallets, tangles of tree branches, unspooled cassette tapes, VHS tapes still in the box, a broken television, an empty purse, a pair of blue jeans. You could no longer see the sidewalks, the grass had grown so tall. There were one or two stop signs left, and a light post so stripped to the frame a person from a part of the world without light posts would have been hard pressed to discern its purpose. A cat padded out from between two piles of garbage and stared at us calmly before bounding back into the weeds. The one building still standing was an old school, Jane Cooper Elementary. Workers had begun to demolish it, but the job had been halted for months, so only part of the back wall had been torn off. There were no earthmovers or bulldozers in sight.

The street ended at a fence. Beyond it, we could make out the distant white walls of a factory, still in business. Corine parked the car between a pair of giant earth mounds—the taller of the two rose at least twenty-five feet—and we got out. Nodding, Corine said, "We need to go up there," and started moving toward the taller of the mounds. Soon I was following her along a sort of goatherd's path roughed out by previous visitors, which, after dipping into a little valley, eventually climbed a much steeper grade, forcing us to clutch handfuls of grass to prevent ourselves from toppling backwards.

When we reached the top, though, we had a panoramic view of the Zone. Corine said the mound we were standing on had been formed when the city had bought and plowed over the old neighborhood in hopes of transforming the area into a suburban-style industrial park. But the factory had been the only tenant to move in, and the rest of the cleared lots had been overtaken by grass the color of hay. There were also wildflowers, and those spiny nettle weeds that cling to your socks like Velcro, and scattered bushes and midget trees whose leaves had already gone amber. From up here, it was difficult to believe we were minutes from the downtown of a major American city. The homes in the distance, just outside the Zone, looked like farmhouses.

I later learned that the total size of the Zone was 189 acres. Its official name, the I-94 Industrial Project, hinted at the big plans once held for the place, a federally designated tax-free "Renaissance zone." Looking to convert the already largely barren neighborhood into a more development-friendly area, the city had spent $19 million buying up some two hundred properties and plowing them under. Over the course of ten years, beginning in 1999, only one new tenant (Exel Logistics, the white factory) had moved in. Now, with soaring vacancy rates in the city, there was no demand for industrial space, and work on the Zone had come to a halt.

An article in *Crain's Detroit Business* estimated that 130 private parcels remained scattered across the site, making it impossible for the city to market larger parcels of land to developers, barring eminent domain. Beyond that, a prominent local realtor noted in the article, industrial vacancy rates had risen so precipitously that even if developers were given the land *for free*, it wouldn't make economic sense to embark upon any new construction. Conrad Mallet Jr. of Detroit's Economic Development Corporation, the body that initially spearheaded the project, told *Crain's*, "Let's call a 4-H club and say, 'Plant some corn.' There is no one coming to an I-94 industrial park."

As Corine and I climbed back down to her car, the clouds hung low, shifting their weight at a sluggard's pace and doing funny things with the light. It was getting ready to storm. We drove over to Jane Cooper Elementary to look around and just then the sky opened up, so we ran inside to take cover. The part of the school that had not been demolished was still largely intact. The hallways, emptied, felt like tunnels, and despite the middle-school-yellow paint job, now faded and dusty with plaster, I thought of the noirishly lit chase scene in the sewers at the end of *The Third Man*. A fluttering noise came from one of the classrooms. Corine poked her head inside. There was a math book lying open on the floor, and when the wind gusted into the room—the back wall of the classroom was completely missing—it made the pages flap like the wings of a bird.

Other signs of the school's past life hung on, all through the building. We saw shattered trophy cases, and piles of textbooks still neatly stacked on shelves, and another book on the floor, titled *Critical Thinking That Empowers Us to Choose Nonviolent Life Skills*, and a flooded gym, the climbing rope still hanging from the ceiling, only now over water, which captured ghostly reflections of the denuded basketball hoops, "like a meditation pool," Corine said, tossing in a pebble.

By the time we made it back outside, not only had the rain passed completely but the sun had reemerged, astonishingly bright after the storm. We had exited from the back end of the school, where the demolition had begun. What had once been the rear of Cooper Elementary was now piled into an enormous heap of brick and rubble. From here, we could stare back into the school's rooms as if it were a doll's house opened in cross section. Suddenly it felt quite warm in the sunlight. In the rubble, I saw a giant bucket of Elmer's Sno-Drift Paste, empty. "Man, in spring?" Corine said. "It's crazy what starts blooming." She had thought of making a sound recording of the birds and insects. "Even today," she said, "just listen." Corine cocked her head and we took in the shrill, chirrupy hum all around us.

* * *

While all that vacant land failed to make Detroit attractive to developers, it did further the city's reputation as the nation's premier urban laboratory. Politicians from *other* cities began weighing in: Dan Kildee, a county treasurer from Flint, with a push for "land banks" that would amass, bundle, and ultimately redevelop delinquent properties; New York mayor Michael Bloomberg, with the suggestion that Detroit swell its population ranks with immigrants. A local nonprofit had a similar idea to Bloomberg's, only with college-educated young people, launching a plan called "15x15" meant to lure 15,000 new residents under the age of 35 to Detroit by 2015. The American Institute of Architects proposed clusters of dense "urban villages" surrounded by green space. In a more radical vein, Lansing public policy consultant Craig Ruff called for "repurposing" the city as "the world's greatest bio-urban hub," with bicycle paths instead of highways, green space where factories once loomed, and locally grown food and handcrafted goods replacing anything you could buy at Walmart. Other farm-related proposals involved a winery on Belle Isle. The prize for most symbolically problematic solution must be awarded to Jai-Lee Dearing, a City Council candidate I'd gone to high school with (though we hadn't known each other at the time) who suggested bundling a bunch of the plots and selling them to black-owned cemeteries.

All these ideas should have fueled the ambitious Detroit Works Project. But unaccountably, by the fall of 2010, the Bing administration's slow rollout of the plan was proving an unmitigated fiasco. The initial public meetings drew spillover crowds, which the administration admitted to being unprepared for, and the city officials present adamantly refused to provide any specifics of the plan, the mayor's PR team having apparently decided to adopt a Denny's suggestion box strategy—they would pretend to listen. Video stations where Detroiters could record their thoughts on the future of the city were set up throughout the venues, though the suspension of disbelief required to think Bing and company might actually weigh the opinions of a retired autoworker with a high school education alongside those of a team of urban planners from Harvard struck many as ludicrous, if not vaguely insulting.

At the first of the rightsizing meetings, held at a Baptist megachurch on the city's far west side, Bing himself showed up late, creeping into one of the confusing "break-out sessions" where citizens were supposed to be giving their feedback. "I didn't come here to speak," Bing said, sidling up to the podium. "I came to listen. We have some ideas, but I don't want to force them on the community. I've got to go to other rooms, but I want to make sure *you* speak out."

Beside Bing, the moderators had arranged several easels holding variously shaded maps of the city that were far too small to read and a stack of oversized cue cards listing a series of condescending questions concerning what the future Detroit might look like. These included:

> What will we be driving?
> Where and how will we be shopping?
> Will we live in bigger or smaller houses?
> What will schools look like?
> How and where will we be spending our free time?

Another cue card read: "Detroit's neighborhoods are clean, safe, and walkable." One of the hapless moderators quickly clarified, "This is what the city *should* look like by 2030."

A woman shouted, "Who's checking that there's gonna *be* a city in twenty years?"

After the first meeting's lambasting in the local media, certain tweaks were made. At the follow-up, held at the Serbian National Hall, Bing made a formal address to the crowd. Though falling short of pounding the podium with his fist, he attempted to work up a folksier, man-of-the-people rapport with the audience, ending with a practiced Bush 41-style applause line: "Not gonna happen on my watch!" As Bing spoke, his face was projected on a giant screen behind him; over his left shoulder, the right hand of the sign-language interpreter occasionally loomed into the frame, looking like a disembodied ghost hand readying to give the mayor a judo chop or vicious throttling if he said the wrong thing. Eventually, someone tightened up the camera shot to cut it out.

The speech was so boring I began to pay special attention to Bing's body language, which was how I noticed, every so often, the mayor's habit of drawing one of his long fingers gently across his forehead, just above his eyebrow, as if he were smoothing a stray hair. I realized this must be Bing's "tell," though I couldn't single out, based on this speech alone, which portion was the bluff.

It later emerged that relations between Mayor Bing and Rip Rapson, the head of the Kresge Foundation, which had been funding much of the initiative, including Toni Griffin's entire salary, had soured. Griffin, an outsider who'd tried to import a team of consultants, had never been trusted by many in the city. Nor had Rapson, a white guy from suburban Troy, Michigan, who talked about a "suite of coordinated investments" that could foster a green economy, who referred to vacant land as "a canvas of economic imagination" and envisioned what he called "neighborhoods of choice." The Bing administration became nervous, both about the power Rapson hoped to exercise and on the simple level of public relations, and so despite the Kresge Foundation's largesse, the city tried to freeze out Griffin and declined to include Kresge officials in the announcement of the federally funded light rail project. Rapson, in turn, began to threaten cutting funding.

After months of delay, Bing finally announced the lame opening phase of the plan, in which neighborhoods eventually would be ranked one of three ways—steady, transitional, or distressed—and be allocated services accordingly, the idea being to shore up the first two types of areas and persuade residents to move out of the last ones. The administration also announced an initial three-neighborhood "demonstration area" in which such service changes would be implemented. Stable neighborhoods would receive the bulk of $9.5 million of federal money designated for home rehab and development, along with increased code enforcement—trash pickup, mowing of vacant lots, the lighting of streetlamps—while the focus in distressed areas would be on demolition of vacant homes.

Still, it all felt vague. A private effort by deep-pocketed Marathon Petroleum to move five hundred families out of the southwest Detroit neighborhood where the company wanted to expand its oil refinery came with a price tag of $40,000 per household; Robin Boyle, a Detroit urban studies professor, did the math and figured moving only 5 percent of existing Detroit households, at the same cost as Marathon, would result in a bill of $600 million.

And what about the rest of the city?

* * *

Of course, "rightsizing" did not necessarily have to mean "shrinking." As the debate over Detroit Works festered, I remembered a conversation I'd had with a lifelong Detroiter who'd held a prominent position in the administration of former mayor Dennis Archer. We were hanging out in a bar downtown, and possibly several drinks into the evening, when our talk turned to Bing's initiative.

"Man, to me?" the political operative scoffed. "That's hustling backwards. It betrays who we are." When I wondered what the alternative might be, he said, "We should be doing the *opposite* of rightsizing. How did Philly grow? Grabbed up the suburbs. How did LA grow? Grabbed up the suburbs. Think about it: Detroit is fucking older than the country. This place was founded with frontier spirit. And now we're here in 2010, a bunch of wusses."

In fact, my friend's riff was a favorite thought experiment of a certain subset of Detroit-area urbanophiles. Sometimes they reference David Rusk, the former Albuquerque mayor whose book *Cities Without Suburbs* makes the case for the economic vibrancy of "elastic" cities (like Houston, Austin, Seattle, and Nashville) whose central hubs have the capability to annex or otherwise regionalize their surrounding suburbs into a unified metropolitan area.

In Detroit, the chances of something like this ever happening were slim—okay, nonexistent—but daydreaming about the real benefits of such a move could be a tantalizing exercise. The takeaway from the census stories revolved around Detroit plummeting to nineteenth place on the U.S. city-size list, behind Austin, Jacksonville, and Columbus. (Columbus!) But the Detroit metropolitan area, which I'll define for these purposes as Wayne, Oakland, and Macomb counties, still retained a population of nearly 4 million. If our territorial-expansion fantasia could be magically enacted with even two-thirds of this figure, Greater Detroitopolis would easily vault past Chicago, with its measly 2.5 million residents, to be the third-largest city in the United States, behind New York and Los Angeles. This would translate into more state and national clout (and allocated funds, many of which are based on population) and eliminate the need for much of the wasteful duplicate spending inherent in maintaining multiple separate municipalities, especially at a time when many of these suburban communities, just as broke as Detroit, have been announcing their own cutbacks of nonessential services. (Along with services that strike many as fairly essential: in February 2011, the west side suburb of Allen Park announced plans to eliminate its entire fire department.) When Indianapolis enacted a similar "Unigov" city-suburbs merger in the late sixties (under Republican mayor Dick Lugar), the region enjoyed economic growth (and the benefits of economy of scale), AAA municipal bond ratings, and a broader, more stable tax base.

Rusk also convincingly argues that elastic cities are less segregated and have fewer of the problems associated with concentrated areas of poverty. And though sprawl wouldn't necessarily be reined in, the region could finally adopt a sensible transportation policy. (The planned light rail project will nonsensically stop at 8 Mile Road, the suburban border.)

Beyond all of that, consider the branding implications. Unlike the New Detroit of *RoboCop* infamy, this New Detroit would no longer find itself sitting near the top of those annual "World's Most Dangerous Cities" lists, thanks to the juking a trebled population would do to the existing crime stats; similar dilution would occur with statistics involving vacant property, unemployment, and packs of wild dogs. Detroit would become, on paper, a city like any other, with scary neighborhoods and safe ones, and much harder to caricature.

There are a number of reasons why this will never, ever happen. For one thing, Michigan has laws making such annexation extremely difficult. And even if the laws could be changed, long-nurtured, largely racial city-suburb resentments would never allow for such bedfellowing. White suburban residents would reel from the possibility of merging with a city so long demonized as a terrifying war zone; the black leadership in Detroit, meanwhile, would surely be loath to see its own political power subsumed within a majority-white supercity. Even the idea of a regional sales tax, which could help provide money for costly undertakings like Detroit Works, remains a nonstarter in the Detroit area. "Why should I pay for the city's mistakes?" noxious Oakland County Executive L. Brooks Patterson asked the website *Remapping Debate*. "Tax base sharing is anathema to me."

Edwin St. Aubin, the real estate agent related to one of the city's founding families, confessed that he could not envision a mass suburban repatriation anytime soon. "These people would rather live in a shack in a field than go anywhere near downtown," he said. "They've completely insulated themselves from that economy." Lowering his voice, he said, "You talk to some of these old developers? They'd want to line up bulldozers—" We were sitting in a restaurant, and here, he put his hands together, his fingers touching and his palms facing his chest, and slowly moved them across the white tablecloth. "And get rid of everything. Start over."

In the eighties, St. Aubin had been married to a German woman. They spent one New Year's in the former West Berlin, and he recalled sitting on a rooftop watching a spectacular fireworks display and then glancing east and seeing nothing but darkness. At the time it made him feel like he was staring into Detroit from the suburbs. "That's exactly what it's like here," he said, "only there's no wall."

* * *

As for Detroit Works, by April 2012, the planning team had announced . . . more meetings. "At least" sixteen more, to be followed by the launch of "a Strategic Framework Plan for Detroit's future." Detroit Works officials declined interview requests, though the team did post a number of "policy audits" on its website, completed during the earliest stages of the project, and reflecting "the observations and analysis of the technical team at that time." Buried in the text, a list of neighborhood typologies laid out by one of the working groups hinted at the possibilities inherent in a fully realized vision of Detroit Works. The high-density City Hub, with high- and mid-rise buildings, would receive priority for regional rail and bus service, while in the Urban Homestead Sector:

> a family lives in a large, older home surrounded by a natural land-scape, growing vegetables to sell at a farmers' market. In return for giving up services such as street lights, the homeowner would get lower taxes (in exchange for experimenting with alternative energy and, where possible, using well water).

In low-maintenance Naturescapes, devoid of homes, pipe-encased creeks would be re-exposed and wildlife would flourish; in Green Venture Zones, on the other hand, vacant land and industrial build-ings would be converted to fish hatcheries, hydroponic and aquacul-ture centers, nurseries, small market farms, and other enterprises; Green Thoroughfares would transform lesser-used highways and boulevards into "green gateways," presumably akin to New York's successful reclamation of the High Line elevated train line.

All grand visions. But with the city's financial status in such turmoil that a state takeover was being threatened, the only thing Detroit Works could promise was an end-of-summer deadline for presenting its Strategic Framework to residents and "whomever may be in charge of the city at that point."

Tiffini Baldwin, 18, and her daughter Nicole, 3. Baldwin
graduated from Catherine Ferguson Academy, a Detroit
public school for teenage mothers, and is now studying
physical therapy at a local college.

[Corine Vermeulen]

6

DETROIT IS DYNAMITE

NOT LONG AFTER THE dreadful census news broke and Detroit became the poster city of the undone American economy, an old 1965 promotional film began to circulate widely on the Internet. The unwittingly deadpan host was Jerry Cavanagh, the mayor of Detroit at the time, introducing the city to the world in a now deranged-seeming bid to host the 1968 Olympics. Sitting stiffly behind a desk in a wood-paneled office, Cavanagh, slightly paunchy, with a conservative haircut, dark suit, and fingers forming a diamond in a way surely promoted by pop middle-management books as a means of conveying alpha male gravitas, seems to embody a holdover authority-figure archetype from the days just prior to the counterculture's triumphant rise. His cause certainly isn't helped by the script he's been given or by the style and content of the film, belonging as it does to that era-specific genre of documentary that includes the cold war instructional movie and nature specials hosted by Walt Disney. From the title—*Detroit: City on the Move*—on down, every line appears to have been written for maximum future ironic effect.

"Yes, we are enjoying our finest hour," Cavanagh says, before informing the viewer that Detroit is "frequently called the most cosmopolitan city of the Midwest," that the city "stands at the threshold of a bright, new future," while civic planners are "creating a new concept of urban efficiency" (here, the voice-over accompanies images of white men in suits sitting around a long desk in front of a wall-sized map of the city, its neighborhoods painted different colors) and her people "work shoulder to shoulder regardless of national origin, color, or creed" (here the illustrative images, weirdly, include a Native American pow-wow and German Americans dressed in lederhosen doing some kind of circle dance). "The inner city," Cavanagh concludes, "is becoming an exciting place to live."

It's a funny video. But there's also something obnoxious, almost cruelly triumphalist, about taking glee in the naive optimism of the long dead, just because we were born late enough to know how the story ends. Plus, in the case of Cavanagh, to listen to his clipped narration and write him off as a stereotypical Establishment square equally misses the mark, as the mayor was, in fact, widely considered one of the most glamorous and charming political figures of his day, only thirty-three when elected, a brilliant young talent of endless promise and presidential-short-list caliber. President Kennedy saw a kindred spirit in Cavanagh, and the press, in turn, cast him—another youthful Irish Catholic Democrat with a Rat Packer's swagger, a pretty wife, and an ambitious, forward-looking agenda—as a loyal vassal of Camelot, *Life* describing him as "the Golden Boy among U.S. mayors . . . a vigorous, young politician . . . who seemed to personify the surging prosperity of Detroit. . . . Civic officials from across the country were flocking to Detroit to see how Jerry Cavanagh did it."

The seeds of Detroit's current problems had already taken hold by the time Cavanagh assumed office, and he understood the seriousness of the challenge he faced. At the same time, a number of key indicators had been pointing to signs of positive development in Detroit: property values on the rise, the auto companies doing solid business, and even the population, after several years of steady decline, apparently stabilizing. Unlike a number of other big-city mayors, Cavanagh also had a serious plan in place for dealing with the possibility of a riot and remained exceedingly popular with the black constituents whose votes had swept him into office. In 1963, Cavanagh linked arms with Martin Luther King Jr., during King's Unity March down Woodward Avenue, which ended at Cobo Hall, where King delivered a longer preview of the "I Have a Dream" speech that would be made famous at the March on Washington two months later. Cavanagh had sent his liberal police commissioner, George Edwards, to greet King at the airport with the message, "You'll see no dogs and firehoses here," and the teeming crowd of marchers swelled behind King and Cavanagh with such rapturous goodwill that Cavanagh later told the *Detroit News* he'd only been able to say four words to King: "Hang on, hang on!"

Cavanagh possessed a bottomless faith in technocratic Good Society solutions to the problems besetting the modern American city. He created after-school and job-training programs, multimillion-dollar "neighborhood centers" to serve specific communities, and computerized data banks to aggregate progress points (and warning signs) on a microneighborhood level. In another odd parallel to the Detroit of today, the city was regarded as the perfect laboratory. When the Johnson administration began developing a real urban policy, Cavanagh lobbied hard for federal dollars, pushing for Detroit to become a so-called model city—like a model home, a showcase for the myriad possibilities of state-drafted urban renewal. In speeches, Cavanagh began referring to Detroit as "Demonstration City U.S.A."

* * *

To many conservatives, Detroit's failures have since made the place a Demonstration City of a different sort—a major bullet point in the postsixties, Reaganite précis on the shortcomings of liberal urban policy. But the truth is, Mayor Cavanagh's good-government reforms never had a chance to be properly tested or even fully enacted. The Cavanagh administration's federal funding proposal, probably always a pipe dream, came to nearly $1 billion over a ten-year period. President Johnson balked at this number, countering with $2.5 billion over six years, to be shared not by a select group of "model cities" but by somewhere between fifty and sixty urban centers throughout the country. Along with a lack of resources, Cavanagh faced problems of his own making, including a slowness to fully integrate the police department, a distracting and ill-fated run for one of Michigan's U.S. Senate seats, rumors of drinking and marital stress, and a public, impolitic break with LBJ over the Vietnam War.

"Here's what the word was on Detroit in the movement circles: that ain't nothing gonna happen in Detroit, because people in Detroit are working and they're making too much money and life is too good," General Baker, a black activist arrested on the first night of the 1967 riots, told me. "So nothing's going to break in Detroit. We were different than every other city. Most of the movement cities, most of the people in the movement around the country, were pimping the poverty program money. We weren't doing that shit. We were *working*. We had our own goddamn money, and we was militantly independent, wasn't nobody telling us what the fuck we gonna do. So it was a different kind of movement that grew up in Detroit, a real practical, down to earth, pragmatic movement, you see, not a lot of ideological bullshit. This city has a history. My mom and dad and them used to tell me, even when they left the South—they were sharecroppers in Georgia, moved up here in '41—they said, 'If you want to work, go to Detroit. If you want to play and pimp and all that shit, you go to Chicago.' So Detroit drew a different kind of people. It had a *history* of drawing a different kind of people. People were coming to work. And that's what helped set them up for the rebellion."*

The story of the 1967 riot, or rebellion, is a familiar one. In the early morning hours of July 23, police raided a blind pig on Twelfth Street, expecting to bust twenty people or so, but instead stumbling onto a party for a pair of soldiers just returned from Vietnam. Eight-five people were arrested: it took over an hour to cart everyone away. It was a hot summer night, and as the police worked, a crowd gathered, growing increasingly hostile. Some bottles were thrown. The cops took off, alerting the riot unit downtown. By eight that morning, over three thousand people had gathered on Twelfth Street.

After five days of unrest and a mobilizing of the National Guard and federal troops, forty-three people were dead and over seven thousand arrested. Nearly three thousand buildings burned. Governor

---

*Baker was not a military man; "General" was actually his first name. Beginning in the late sixties, he organized black autoworkers at Chrysler's Hamtramck plant as a cofounder of the Dodge Revolutionary Union Movement, or DRUM, and later the League of Revolutionary Black Workers. After being fired and blacklisted in 1973, he obtained a fake ID and got himself rehired at Ford (where he finally retired in 2003) in order to continue agitating from the inside. For more information on Baker, check out *Detroit, I Do Mind Dying*, an absorbing chronicle of radical seventies labor history by Dan Georgakas and Marvin Surkin. Baker also traveled to Cuba as a young man, where he met Che Guevara and played baseball with Fidel Castro. Me: "How was the baseball game?" GB: "Raggedy. We couldn't hang with the Cubans. We were a bunch of students! We weren't no ballplayers."

Romney was living in Bloomfield Hills, and he flew over the city in a helicopter to survey the chaos. Thirty of the forty-three dead had been killed by law enforcement. For many, despite the violence and the sight of tanks in the street, a heady revolutionary spirit was in the air, reflected more in the MC5 cover of "Motor City Is Burning" than in the John Lee Hooker original. Hooker's version ended mournfully, with a fireman telling him, *Look, get outta here—it's too hot*. But the MC5 finished the song by gleefully shouting, *Let it all burn . . .* * "I remember watching television during the riots," John Sinclair told me. " 'The tenth precinct has been pinned down by sniper fire.' We all said, 'Yes!' "

For Cavanagh, the riot—at that point, the worst in U.S. history—made the final act of his career, bookended by a failed Senate run and the collapse of his marriage, play out like classical tragedy. "If a guy put a gun to my head and asked me if *any* city in this country is manageable, I'd have to say no," Cavanagh told a reporter, while the fires still smoldered, in a moment of honesty that's still stunning today. He went on, "We did the textbook things here in Detroit. We did more than any other city in police-community relations, anti-poverty, inner-city schools, job training—the whole bit. I was sure of myself, got praised, and now I can't guarantee anything."

"Maybe cities can be governed," the mayor concluded. "But there has to be a different emphasis and a lot more money."

* * *

Even in Detroit, you don't hear about the 1967 riots as much as you used to. Looking back, there's an arrestingly dated quality to the contemporary responses. Observers worried over potential future uprisings, as if pyromaniacal mutiny might continue to spread like some new, incomprehensible youth-culture trend. In a used bookshop, I came across a copy of *The Detroit Riot of July 1967: A Psychological, Social and Economic Profile of 500 Arrestees*, a study by Sheldon J. Lachman and Benjamin D. Singer of the Detroit-based Behavior Research Institute, which probed respondents with questions such as "Will the

---

*And then there was Martha Reeves and the Vandellas' 1964 Motown hit "Dancing in the Street"—a call to urban dwellers across the country to prepare for a brand-new beat—used as a theme song at rallies throughout those insurrectionary summers by H. Rap Brown.

Negro Ever Have Everything the White Man Has?" "Is There Any Famous Negro Who Thinks Riots are a Good Thing?" and "Which Race Riots Have You Seen on TV?"

When I was growing up in the eighties, though, the riots were still invoked with the compulsive regularity of a fresh grudge. This was in the suburbs, of course, where the grudge was not always expressed politely, and where even today, blame for Detroit going off the rails harks back to that distant summer. Meanwhile, across 8 Mile Road, an entirely different oral history had been passed along. University of Michigan Professor Angela Dillard, a black Detroiter whose research focuses on radicalism in the African American religious tradition, told me, "The black middle class, in some ways, has good narrative about the riot. My uncles talked about how they stood on the border waving at the white people leaving, then bought their homes! It wasn't such a terrible thing when these people who had been terrorizing us for decades left."

As a kid, dragooned into working at my father's shop, I wound up spending more time in the city than most of my friends. Otherwise, family trips to Detroit were exceedingly rare, usually centering around a Tigers game, or a visit to Belle Isle to see the wild deer that used to roam in the more heavily forested parts of the island, my father slowing our Buick to a crawl whenever he spotted one and hissing "*Varda!** Look how beautiful."

Living on Service Street, I noticed how, at certain times of the week, downtown streets would be overrun by white people, at which point you'd realize there must be a game or concert on. For instance, Detroit Lions fans like to gather in parking lots near Ford Field, the downtown football stadium, several hours before kickoff time. By nine o'clock on a Sunday morning, when I'd step out to buy a newspaper, I'd spot the tailgaters bundled up like deerhunters, clutching coozied Miller High Lifes between mittened fists, their breath misting the chill air alongside the smoke coming off their grilled brats.

One Sunday, my brother Paul was going to a game with some coworkers, so I joined them for a breakfast beer and sausage in a

---

*Guarda in proper (non-dialect) Italian, imperative of *guardare*, "to look."

parking lot on Gratiot. A very pleasant carnival atmosphere reigned, the sort of communal gathering you didn't experience much in a driving city like Detroit. The crowd was overwhelmingly male and even more overwhelmingly white. When I finished my beer, I looked around for a trash barrel. My brother smirked and said, "If you want to, you can just crush the can and toss it in the middle of the parking lot. That's what they do here." He put his own empty can down on the ground, which seemed fussy and demure in the context, and I did the same. But it was true: lots of the other men were just tossing their empties. I wondered why the parking lot didn't look like the lowlands of a city dump, since a number of these guys had been drinking for hours before I arrived, and then I noticed that a handful of black men—homeless, or just hungry—were trolling the area with giant trash bags, gathering up the empties. In Michigan, cans and bottles can be returned for a ten-cent deposit.

A wave of exhaustion came over me, even though I'd only been awake for a couple of hours. The gulf between city and suburbs felt gaping and hopeless. Still, when one of the tailgaters asked about my reporting, I mentioned that things in Detroit felt different, better, knowing I risked scorn for being hopelessly naïve, a dupe. Predictably, the guy shook his head and said he'd been hearing that for the past thirty years. The main problem, he claimed, was leadership, that the city really screwed up by electing the worst people ever, that nothing would change unless you changed things at the top—a not uncommon assessment from white suburbanites, "leadership" often signifying "thieving blacks who demanded the keys to the shop, and now look what fucking happened." If there was national schadenfreude about the failure of Detroit, regional schadenfreude was even stronger, and it hinged in large part on race.

In that moment, I thought of certain aspects of United States foreign policy—the practice of isolating enemy states financially and then watching the leader whom we've labeled a tyrant act more and more like one when his regime begins to crumble under the pressure of the embargo. The leader and his state must fail in order to confirm the triumph of our own ideology. And if his people do not rise up against him, their suffering is, at least in part, their own fault. Here, Detroit was the rogue state, defying the bullying hegemony of a superpower that (in the eyes of many Detroiters) wanted to install its own hand-picked leader, making the transfer of any remaining natural resources that much smoother.

The Emergency Financial Manager law passed by the Republican-dominated legislature in Lansing and backed by the new Republican governor, Rick Snyder, granting the state's executive branch (i.e., Snyder himself) enormous power on a local level when municipalities faced serious financial crises, had heightened—and racialized—the perception of leadership being undermined. Emergency managers, past and present, had been appointed in majority-black cities (Pontiac, Highland Park, Inkster, Benton Harbor, Flint) and Detroit feared the possibility of an actual power-grab by outsiders. Thus far, the city itself had managed to hang on to home rule—although in the summer of 2009, a new financial manager, Robert Bobb, was granted near-dictatorial control over the Detroit public school system, one of the most racially polarized institutions in the entire metropolitan area.

The isolation of DPS began in the early seventies, when suburban opponents of busing—led by Oakland County Commissioner L. Brooks Patterson, who had made his name through demogoguery on the racially charged issue—fought the desegregation order all the way to the Supreme Court, resulting in the landmark *Milliken v. Bradley* decision severely limiting the state's ability to bus children across district lines. The ruling in effect ensured that Detroit's school system would be comprised of a concentrated body of poor and minority students. Patterson still runs suburban Oakland County, which comprises a large portion of metropolitan Detroit, having coasted to a fourth term in 2008 with 58 percent of the vote.

Meanwhile, Detroit's public school district now serves an almost entirely black population and has been one of the worst in the country for years, with a graduation rate of 25 percent, the lowest math and reading test scores in the forty-year history of the National Assessment of Education Progress and 73 percent of fourth graders lacking (in the NAEP's assessment) "even the basic skills that are the building blocks of reading." Unfathomable percentages of the city's children had essentially been written off as an acceptable level of attrition. What to do about Detroit's public schools had become a major and especially contentious part of the city's rightsizing debate, since many of the schools were not only failing but half empty, having been built when Detroit possessed more than twice its current population.

In 1999, the state first took over the school system, replacing the elected school board with an appointed body; when the state returned control of the district to Detroit in 2005, the schools were actually performing lower on key math and reading tests and the district had a $200 million deficit, which the outgoing state-appointed manager, Kenneth Burnley, attributed to declining enrollment, swelling teacher benefits, and cuts in state aid. In 2009, the Democratic Governor Jennifer Granholm reclaimed the school system, appointing Bobb, a former Washington, D.C., deputy mayor and city manager who'd also served as president of the board of education. The move was popular in the suburbs—Bobb being the sort of "leadership change" suburbanites generally praised. In the city, feelings were more mixed. Some Detroiters greeted Bobb as an educational messiah; others, including but not limited to members of the teachers unions, saw him in more Mephistophelean terms, yet one more outsider parachuting into town to figure out how corporate forces might profit from local misery. (In this case, the profit motive centered around the push to convert certain failing schools into private charters, as had been done in other troubled cities, most notably New Orleans.) The new emergency manager's opponents began mockingly referring to him as "Bob Bobb."

Still, there was no denying the system he'd been charged with fixing was riddled with corruption and violence, and something drastic needed to happen. The FBI was investigating a kickback scheme involving $57 million missing from the district budget. There were shady no-bid contracts; kids had to bring their own toilet paper to school. The principal of Finney High got his jaw broken after being punched by a student wearing brass knuckles. At Mumford High, two kids were shot on the first day of class; the year before, the school's new principal had resigned after serving only two months on the job, calling school violence "off in a different arena." Part of Bobb's mandate necessarily involved closing or merging schools, which could not help but be controversial. How far would kids be expected to travel to get to class? Would gangs from rival neighborhoods wind up in the same schools?

One of the dynamics at play in the media war over control of DPS was the unsubtle contrast between the school board and Bob Bobb.

The new emergency manager was a polished bureaucrat who spoke in tough-sounding platitudes; his opposition, meanwhile, came in the form of shouting inner-city parents and a board that included the dimwitted "Reverend" David Murray, who had legally changed his first name to Reverend as an adult,* and Otis Mathis, the board president who graduated from a DPS public school with a D-plus average, took fifteen years and a lawsuit against Wayne State University in order to receive his bachelor's degree (claiming in his lawsuit that an English proficiency test required for graduation discriminated against African Americans), was forced to resign after fondling himself in front of a female school superintendent, and whose emails, leaked to the *Detroit News*, suggested a literacy on par with the majority of his failing students:

> If you saw Sunday's Free Press that shown Robert Bobb the emergency financial manager for Detroit Public Schools, move Mark Twain to Boynton which have three times the number seats then students and was one of the reason's he gave for closing school to many empty seats.

An activist parent (and member of Mensa, per the article) told the *Detroit News*, "I know he's a terrible writer. Oh wow, I've seen his e-mails. His job, though, is to represent the community. His lack of writing skills is prevalent in the community. If anybody does, he understands the struggles of what it's like to go through an institution and not be properly prepared."

Bobb had been walking a tricky line since his appointment. To justify the sorts of upheaval of the status quo he had in mind, he railed constantly about how awful the district was, with some exaggeration, as in his widely reported discovery of "ghost employees" who'd remained on school payrolls for years, which was later proven untrue. At the same time, he needed students to remain enrolled in DPS. If parents

---

*Murray since technically became a reverend, though his "church" only had ten members. Child Protective Services removed four adopted children from Murray's custody, with one of the inspectors noting that Murray's home was filthy and foul-smelling, with broken windows and a large hole in the ceiling.

continued to jump from the sinking ship of the district—and why would they not, given how terrible it supposedly was—then DPS would lose all sorts of state and federal money, which of course it sorely needed. So as the 2009–2010 school year approached, Bobb and his minions—to convince parents to keep their children in the school system he'd spent all summer painting as one of the most corrupt in the country—rather perversely launched a half-million-dollar public relations campaign, with the goal being to get as many children's bodies as possible in the schools on the all-important "Count Day," when official head counts were taken to determine enrollment, which translated into per-pupil funding numbers.

The hard sell employed couldn't help but seem creepy, like the techniques of a used-car salesman or Las Vegas casino operator. To lure kids to Count Day, Bobb promised a free breakfast and lunch, along with raffles of goodies like laptops, iPods, and a 42" flatscreen plasma television. He also flew Bill Cosby to town, where the comedian (and former teacher) personally walked door-to-door to talk to parents about the district's virtues. (Though at times Cosby seemed to stray off message, in one speech announcing he would probably "look for a charter school" if he were raising kids in the city.)

Just before the beginning of the school year, Bobb staged a parade and rally in downtown's Campus Martius square. One of the parade floats featured Thomas Edison, from Michigan, though not a product of DPS, at work in his laboratory. Nodding to the demographics of the student body, the float designer gave Edison a black lab assistant, or equal partner, it wasn't quite clear—he wore a top hat and glasses and seemed to be cranking a phonograph. From a stage, Bobb and various DPS representatives, working together for the common goal of securing as much warm-body-money as possible, had the assembled children shout "DPS!" and wave their fists.

Bobb proceeded to enlist his new charges in the PR blitz being rained upon them, bullying the crowd with hoarse call-and-response questions that began innocuously ("How many of you agree that great things are happening in Detroit?") and became progressively weirder ("You wanna go into a building that's safe?" YEAHHHH!! "You wanna go into a building where the adults aren't stealing money?" YEAHHHH!!). The campaign's slogan, "I'm In," had been plastered on signs and T-shirts throughout the crowd. The logo featured a pair of blue doors, designed in a boxy, minimalist style that made me think of the World Trade Center. Actual blue doors had been set up on the stage, along with a sign asking "Are You In?" In a city with so many buildings in a ruinous state, entirely lacking windows and doors, this felt like an obvious reversal: just doors, with the rest of the home missing. Of course, the sight gag hadn't been purposeful, though someone might have considered the problematic symbolism of goading kids into stepping through a set of doors leading nowhere.

By the time Bobb left office in 2011, the DPS deficit had grown by another $100 million, though he'd shuttered fifty-nine schools and 30 percent of the workforce had been eliminated. On the plus side, the collapse of the housing market across the entire Detroit metropolitan area had allowed more and more families to send their kids to superior schools—by moving to the suburbs.

For those left behind in DPS, the school closings meant longer commutes, occasionally to charter schools, still the solution of choice for a number of education reformers like Bobb. Doug Ross, whose Urban Preparatory Academy charter had an exemplary track record, was made DPS's chief innovation officer, and would be overseeing ten planned "self-governing" public schools—which would receive full funding from the district but otherwise make autonomous decisions on budgeting, staffing, and curriculum—beginning in the 2012–2013 school year. It was an intriguing experiment, and one that might well pay off; proponents cited studies that favored granting talented principals as much leeway as possible. Still, whenever an experiment's subjects happened to be almost entirely poor and black, the notion took on an unavoidably queasy Tuskeegean ring, no matter how pure the intent. On the other hand, the district had already lost so many students to charters and other districts (via a "school of choice" program), only 48 percent of children in the city attended DPS institutions anymore. Experimentation, at this late stage, struck many as an eminently reasonable response.

* * *

There were a handful of exemplary DPS schools, the majority of them specialized institutions like Cass Tech. But the most remarkable success story had to be the Catherine Ferguson Academy, a magnet school for pregnant teenagers and mothers. Catherine Ferguson Academy boasted a 90 percent graduation rate; its principal, Asenath Andrews, required her students to obtain at least one college acceptance letter in order to receive a diploma. The school had built such a sterling reputation that students had actually been caught lying to gain admission, borrowing infants to pass off as their own or swapping out their urine with a pregnant friend's so as to produce a positive test.

The school's ninety-year-old building hulked on an otherwise barren stretch of urban prairie just north of Martin Luther King Jr. Boulevard. The student farm, where each of the girls tended her own vegetable plot and learned about everything from milking goats and baling hay to slaughtering livestock, included an apple orchard, chickens, rabbits, a horse, a beehive, a giant turkey, and an old red barn that appeared to have been airlifted directly from northern Michigan, though it was actually built by the students themselves. The farm took up several vacant lots behind the school, in the space where a football field would have been at a normal public school. Inside, the shabby hallway would have seemed unremarkable, save for the day-care workers tending to six infants seated in a long, multichild stroller made to look like a red bus. Nearby, a parking lot of single-rider strollers had formed in front of some lockers. A two-year-old in pink-ribboned braids wandered past, followed by her mother, cradling a second infant.

Principal Andrews, at six feet tall, with a broad, freckled face and silver-streaked hair that swooped dramatically up from her forehead, cut an imposing figure. Yet there was something soothing about her presence, a confidence at once utterly relaxed and (forgive me, but this really is the best word) impregnable. Such self-assurance lent her authority a casual, improvised quality; everything coming out of her mouth sounded like the words of someone who'd just happily alit upon a brand new thought.

Andrews grew up on Detroit's northwest side. She attended Mumford High School, the only black girl in her grade. There were five black boys; the rest of the kids were Jewish. She says she can't recall any overt racism, even though the neighborhood where she grew up was bounded by a six-foot-tall, foot-thick, half-mile-long concrete wall erected in the early 1940s by a local developer who wanted to build homes for middle-class whites and agreed to put up the wall in order to secure loans from the Federal Housing Authority, which considered such close proximity to a black neighborhood "high-risk." (Remnants of the wall still exist.) Andrews's family lived on the white side of the wall, but all of her cousins lived on the black side. Her parents both worked at Chrysler, like most people in the neighborhood. "It never occurred to me that I was less than," she told me. "I didn't think we were middle class, because I thought middle-class people wore suits to work. But my family had a middle-class income. Everyone I grew up with went to college, except for a boy named Craig, and he traveled around Europe instead."

Andrews attended Olivet College, a small liberal arts school a couple of hours west of Detroit, where she majored in psychology and art. She sold enough paintings to pay for her rent but decided by her junior year that if she ever had kids, she didn't want them attending public school, so she obtained a teaching certificate as well, just in case homeschooling would be necessary. Eventually, she came to believe the only real way to affect political change was through education, and she began teaching in the public school system. When she became the founding principal of Catherine Ferguson Academy in 1985, the six-week alternative-ed program was based out of a Salvation Army building. The district had designated all of the students as handicapped. Andrews described the original program as a "warehouse-segregation model," where students were taught things like cooking, typing, and bookkeeping. She began to lobby the district to lengthen the girls' stay, which improved their test scores. Then she fought to move the school to its current building, a former elementary school that had fallen into disuse.

"Look at the neighborhood," Andrews said. "There *is* no neighborhood. I campaigned for six months to get us in here. When they finally moved us, we had to share the space with bad boys and expelled kids. Because these were 'bad girls.' You know, bad boys hold up liquor stores and knock you over the head, and bad girls get pregnant. That's still the mentality. When I first came here, people were inviting me to teen crime seminars. I said, 'Hey! They didn't *rob* anybody. They had sex!'"

Andrews's telephone rang. We were sitting in her office. It was her sister calling. Andrews was having some work done on her house, and one of the contractors had apparently reached into a wall and got himself bit by an opossum. "No, I guess you shouldn't let him do that," Andrews said. She hung up. The opossum, a mother, had been holed up in the wall with a bunch of babies, and the contractor had wanted to seal the hole and let them die.

Andrews either didn't find the coincidence of having received this call in the middle of our interview amusing or she did but chose not to remark on it. In any event, she continued, "We had more teen mothers in the fifties than anytime since, but they all got married. The term 'drop out' didn't really exist until the midsixties, because it wasn't assumed you necessarily finished high school. You didn't have to. I heard the white girls went away or had special doctors. It was such a stigma to be pregnant and not get married. You didn't want anyone to go through that. By the time I got to college, we'd collect cigarette money if someone needed an abortion. You'd give your last."

I asked how she managed such an unheard-of college acceptance rate for a public high school. Andrews fixed me with a look and said, matter-of-factly, "I expect it."

I waited for her to continue, but she didn't. I said, "How is that not an overly simple answer? All of the special challenges—"

She cut me off and asked, "Did you go to college right out of high school?"

I said yes.

She said, "How come?"

This time I didn't answer. Of course, she had a point.

"You do things because that's what you *must* do," she said. Then she shrugged. She was wearing a pearl necklace over a periwinkle sweater. Often, though not this particular afternoon, she liked to pin unusually large corsages to her chest. We're talking flowers the size of a round sauceboat. This would have looked ridiculous on most women, but Andrews carried enough size, herself, to make it work.

"I mean, you don't have to be *smart* to go to college—George Bush was president," she went on, her dark eyes flashing. "These girls *know* they're important to me. Women do things for a lot of reasons. Most of them not for themselves. So you can use that for your own purposes."

* * *

Upstairs, in Mr. Drewery's stuffy world history classroom, six girls, looking as generally unenthused as your typical high school world history class, sat around four wobbly-legged tables facing a chalkboard crowded with a list of words: "Maginot Line," "Benito Mussolini," "Anti-Semitism," "Hittites." Since one of the girls was pregnant, Mr. Drewery let her sit at the desk closest to the window so she would be more comfortable. Another, not pregnant, wore a very short shirt and kept a single earbud of her headphones in her ear during class. I wasn't sure whether Mr. Drewery noticed, but did not snitch. A third girl, wearing a tight white tank top with FLIRT printed in pink letters across the front, her blond-streaked hair spilling out of a glitter Cedar Point cap, pulled a cell phone out of her bra and checked the time. There was a large, noticeable hole in the ceiling. Various pots and pans had been arranged on the bookcases to catch water from other leaks.

Mr. Drewery wore thick-framed black glasses riding low on his nose. He had sleepy eyes, a mustache and goatee, and a red lanyard with keys on the end dangling over his checked tie and white dress shirt.

"Miss Murray," he said to one of the girls, who had partially put her head down on her desk, "you're not your usual energetic self."

The girl sighed and said that last night she and her family had heard what they thought had been a loud series of thunderclaps, but it turned out to be guys on their roof, trying to break into the house. Her father had chased them off, but the police didn't arrive until two in the morning.

"I'm not sure why they didn't go into the abandoned house next door," Miss Murray said peevishly.

Outside on the farm, seventeen-year-old Tiffini Baldwin mixed soil and compost in a wheelbarrow. She had wild, frizzy hair pulled back into a ponytail and wore white work gloves and a blue hoodie. Nearby, a pair of goats rammed each other atop a woodpile. Baldwin had a two-year-old daughter named Nicole. She'd gotten pregnant at fourteen and kept it a secret as long as she could.

"I was just bawling in the nurse's office," she recalled. "I wasn't thinking about the baby. I was thinking about me, and I was worried about my family, particularly my mom. 'I can't be pregnant. Tiffini? The honor roll student?' I was in denial. I just wanted it to go away. By the time I told my mom, it was too late to get an abortion. I was going to put her up for adoption. I actually met the adoptive parents. But I couldn't go through with it."

Baldwin said her mother worked in human resources and her father did maintenance work for McDonald's. As she spoke, she added scoops of perlite to the soil, which she said helped it absorb water. When the wheelbarrow was filled with exactly eleven shovelfuls, she pushed it toward the apple orchard. We passed a girl in a pink hoodie weighing a goat on a scale. A turkey behind a fence spread its tail feathers like a peacock. Inside the red barn, someone had written on a dry-erase board, in slightly childish handwriting, "Please milk Emily halfway. It is painful for her if she does not get milked. If you have trouble massage her udders or hold warm cloth on her udders for a minute. Thank you. Your welcome."

"Excuse me, goat," Baldwin said to a runty white goat named Snow White. Glancing at me, she said, "This must be really exciting, talking to a girl mixing compost."

After school, Baldwin planned to become a nurse, "in order to live comfortably," she said. Baldwin also hoped to indulge more creative passions. "If it was up to me, I'd pursue writing, but I have a daughter," she told me. The father wasn't around much. "If he would just come over once a week, I'd be happy," she said. I asked if he was also in high school and she shook her head. "When we met, he *told* me he was seventeen. But he was older than that."

As Baldwin struggled with the wheelbarrow, I offered to help, but she grinned and shook her head. "If Ms. Andrews catches you out here helping me—she's superfeminist. So, hah, I'm good."

In a couple of months, Baldwin would be joining Andrews and some of the other students on a field trip to South Africa. She'd never even been to Canada before. Baldwin asked if I had kids. When I said no, she said, "I don't mean to sound like one of those parents who say, 'As soon as you have a child, *everything* will change.' But as soon as you have a child . . ." She didn't bother to finish the sentence. "I just knew I had to go to college. I didn't grow up dirt poor. But I want

Nicole to have a better life than me. All this stuff?" She rubbed her dirty gloved hands together, meaning the farm. "I don't really care about this stuff. But you do learn to take pride in your work. Students built this whole farm. *Pregnant girls* did this."

Baldwin was pretty, with dimples and a slightly nasal voice. She wore thick brown-tinted sunglasses. "I don't want to say all moms, but all teenage moms think about, 'What would I be doing if I didn't have a kid?' You do miss life before. I get nostalgic. If you're a pregnant teenager, no choice you make is a good choice. I'm happy with my decision now, but I wasn't sure at first. Ms. Andrews's thing is you're not dependent on a man. Like, *that's* what happens when you're around 'em." She sighed and then laughed. "Don't get me wrong," she went on. "I love America. Free this, free that. But it's a two-faced country sometimes. It contradicts itself."

A chicken squawked in the distance. Then I heard a police siren. We walked past a row of rabbit hutches and a fenced pond where a fat white goose stood watching us on one leg, the other held up like a palsied limb, and honked softly. Principal Andrews had wandered outside and cast a cold eye on Snow White. Earlier, when I'd asked her about the farm, she'd frowned and said, "I don't like animals."

Now, she said to Baldwin, with just the hint of a smile, "If that goat comes in this school, you fail."

* * *

In 2012, when the threat of financial insolvency had made all of Detroit's government a candidate for state takeover, the city held a series of contentious public meetings on the subject. The most inflammatory remarks came from Malik Shabazz, a local activist and founder of the New Marcus Garvey/ New Black Panther Nation*, who evoked 1967 when he stood up and said, "This is white supremacy, and we will fight you. Before you can take over our city, we will burn it down first."

I'd met Shabazz in his capacity as cofounder of the Detroit 300, the crime-fighting group that patrolled dangerous neighborhoods. Physically enormous, Shabazz had a personality to match, obviously

---

*Not the same New Black Panther Party or Malik Shabazz vilified nationally on Fox News and other right-wing media outlets in connection to an alleged voter-suppression scandal.

relishing his own oratorical skills in a way that is common among actors, preachers, and politicians. Shabazz had been all three.

One night, I stopped by the New Black Panthers headquarters to chat. The building stood on an unlit, deserted stretch of Fenkel Street on Detroit's west side. Shabazz was wearing a grey hoodie and oval glasses, which he kept perched on his forehead, and he chain-smoked compulsively. The headquarters was a junky looking storefront, with an old-fashioned domed hair-dryer in the back of the room and folding chairs and VHS tapes (with hand-written labels like "400 Years of Lynching") piled everywhere. Shabazz had two televisions running on mute, perched up so high they looked like closed-circuit monitors; he seemed to be copying a Malcolm X speech from one tape to another, though we didn't discuss this. A sidewalk sandwich board, propped in a corner, offered:

Audio and Video Tapes

Books

Oils

CDs

Crack Houses Shut

Detroit has been the biggest majority-black city in the United States since the 1970s, and remains so today, even in its shrunken state. Shabazz gives voice, albeit in militant language, to quite common concerns regarding designs on Detroit by a hostile white power structure. "There's a plot to take over Detroit," Shabazz says. "White folks built up the suburbs in haste as the browning of the inner cities took place, and now they desire to take this city back. Detroit is Chocolate City, the Mecca, the Jerusalem, the Medina of problackness and black conscious thought, in many ways. Detroit gave birth to the African American middle class, the Nation of Islam, the Shrine of the Black Madonna. Brother Malcolm was here. So much has come out of Detroit."

The latter half of Shabazz's claim is uncontroversial fact. Detroit has been known as a strong black city for years. By the nineteen-sixties, despite the rampant discrimination, all of the relatively high-paying manufacturing jobs in Detroit had resulted in a high proportion of black home owners. Shabazz himself is part of a long radical black tradition that came out of the city. Malcolm X grew up in Lansing, and after his release from prison, he worked as a minister at the Nation of Islam temple in Detroit.* The Nation was started in Detroit by a door-to-door peddler and life-long hustler calling himself Wallace Fard;† when Fard fled the state in 1932—after one of his followers, Robert Harris, stabbed another man to death at a home altar as part of a weird sacrificial ceremony, leading Detroit authorities to crack down on what became known as a dangerous Negro cult—he handed over the reins to an autoworker named Elijah Poole, who reformed his own hard-drinking ways and changed his name to Elijah Muhammad. Over thirty years later, on Easter Sunday 1967, the increasingly radical Reverend Albert Cleage Jr. changed the name of his Central Congregation Church to the Shrine of the Black Madonna, eventually adopting the Moniker Jaramogi Abebe Agyeman and preaching a revolutionary black liberation theology, famously promising to "dehonkify" Jesus. Shabazz, after falling into a life of drug use and gangbanging as a teenager and young adult, turned his life around when someone gave him some Malcolm X tapes and convinced him to begin attending services at the Shrine.‡ "I heard that little yellow brother speaking fire," Shabazz says, referring to Cleage. "I was afraid for his life."

To this day, though, the black radical most emblematic of Detroit remains Coleman A. Young, the city's first African American mayor.

---

*Twenty years earlier, Malcolm's father, Earl Little, was found dead near a streetcar track, most likely murdered by the Black Legion, a violent, dark-hooded Ku Klux Klan offshoot. In the 1920s with half of Detroit's 1.2 million residents foreign-born, and poor Southern blacks and whites also crowding the young metropolis, racial and ethnic tensions flourished, and Detroit became the Black Legion's unofficial national headquarters and prime recruiting ground. (The hate group also inspired the 1936 film *Black Legion*, starring a young Humphrey Bogart as a Detroit auto worker lured into committing behooded hate crimes after being passed over for promotion in favor of a Polish coworker.)

†Though Fard's birth name remains in dispute, it seems more than coincidental that his adopted prophet's name is only a vowel away from Ford, the most famous and successful businessman in the world when Fard began preaching. (Fard recommended his followers read Henry Ford's autobiography alongside the Koran and the Bible.)

‡Shabazz did not have an easy childhood, its difficulties compounded by a mother with a drug problem and a parade of boyfriends and husbands. "Some of them I liked, and some were just no good, low-down dirty Negroes," he says. "One of the stepdaddies started forcing me to do drugs or whatever." I asked how old he was. "Six," Shabazz says. "That's all I want to say on that." His mother ended up participating in the murder of a later husband as part of an insurance scheme. She's currently serving a life sentence in prison. Shabazz was in his early twenties when this happened.

No Detroit political figure in the modern era casts a greater shadow than Young, who was elected in 1974—Cavanagh's successor, Roman Gribbs, a law-and-order Democrat, having lasted only a single term—and remained in office for the next two decades, the longest mayoral reign in the city's history. Even if he'd never gotten into politics, Young would have left future biographers with a story to tell. He grew up in Black Bottom, on Antietam Avenue, which runs a block south of Service Street. The opening line of Young's 1994 autobiography, *Hard Stuff,* describes his earliest memory as being woken in the middle of the night by the bells of St. Joseph's Church.* His father, a hard drinker and dedicated gambler who had attended Alabama A&M on the GI Bill, eventually opening his own tailor shop, had been light-skinned enough to pass, which he did in order to take certain whites-only jobs. For this reason, Young writes, his father considered his skin color both blessing and curse—the latter because it often privied him

---

*He goes on to basically spend the rest of the short opening chapter teasing out similarities between Detroit and the old church, the latter a tenacious final remnant of a neighborhood long destroyed by urban renewal, and "somehow . . . Detroit," too, "like St. Joseph's Church, has managed to survive the schemes to bring it down." *Hard Stuff* is a wonderfully readable autobiography, in large part because Young's cowriter, Lonnie Wheeler, does such a fine job of capturing the mayor's distinctive high-low manner of public speech, at once rarefied and ornately cussed, for example: "This much is apparent: Detroit will never be the city it once was. By virtue of compounded and confounded federal policies and of the unsympathetic cycles of social and industrial evolution—of such damn things as decentralization and white abandonment and the Toyota Corolla . . ." Or even better, this passage, the music of which merits quoting at length:

> The popular way to explain the decline of Detroit—that is, the one so ardently talked up within certain white circles and the media, if I may risk being redundant—is to pin it all on me. The reasoning goes something like this: Detroit has had nothing but problems since the white people got the hell out, which goes to show that black people can't run anything by themselves, much less a major city, especially when it's in the hands of a hate-mongering mayor like the one who's been entrenched there for twenty goddamn years. . . .
>
> This, as one might imagine, is a school of thought to which I take exception. . . .

As with the church bit above, Young (or Wheeler, but you get the sense this is coming straight from Young) is also fond of portentous imagery. For instance, in the next chapter, describing his family's departure from Huntsville, Alabama, via train, for the promised land of Detroit, "on a rainy day in 1923," the five-year-old Young espies a dead mule lying on its back beside the railroad tracks, just as the train is pulling out of the station, "his feet sticking straight out like the legs of a kitchen table on its side"—ominously foreshadowing both the Great Migration's large-scale snuffing of a rural, Southern way of life and the further hardships to come in the fabled free North.

to the unexpurgated feelings of white people. "It caused him," notes Young with characteristic bluntness, "to hate them uncommonly."

Young himself experienced cruel and mundane prejudices as a boy: having his application to a Catholic high school ripped up in his face after the headmaster realized he was not Japanese but black; being turned away from the Boblo amusement park during an eighth-grade trip, when one of the guides, spotting kinky-looking hair beneath his hat, jerked it off and informed him that the park was for whites only. ("I honestly was not prepared for that," Young writes of the latter incident. "And I was never the same person again.") He worked as a shoeshine boy; read Du Bois; began working as a labor and civil rights activist after being fired from Ford (it was during this period that Young missed taking part in a major strike while he was off cavorting with a secretary, prompting an older union man to tell him, "Son, the human race is perpetually involved in two struggles— the class struggle and the ass struggle"*); flew during World War II with the Tuskegee Airmen, the elite, all-black B-25 squadron; returned to Detroit and began working at the post office, which was really just a way to begin organizing for the United Public Workers union (and become a thorn in the left side of the UAW's Walter Reuther, to Young a conservative throwback†); found himself subpoe-naed by the House Un-American Activities Committee, where his heroic, combative testimony became legend, in particular his verbal tussles with John Wood, "the motherfucker from Georgia who headed the committee" (Young's words, in *Hard Stuff*), in whose district only 2 percent of blacks had ever been allowed to vote, and with the com-mittee's counsel, Frank Tavenner, a Virginian.‡ Young wound up scor-

---

*This wise man also warned against mixing the two struggles, advice Young occasionally ignored, as evinced by his fathering of an illegitimate child during his fourth term of office, when he was in his early seventies.
†When word of the 1948 assassination attempt on Reuther reached a union meeting at a tool-and-die local, Young immediately wanted to know if the shooting had been fatal. Upon being informed that, no, Reuther would survive, Young said, "Too bad they didn't kill that mother-fucker," provoking a fistfight.
‡During his testimony, Young schooled Tavenner on pronunciation (Tavenner: "You told us you were the executive secretary of the National Niggra Congress—" Young: "That word is 'Negro,' not 'Niggra.'" Tavenner: "I said 'Negro.' I think you are mistaken." Young: "I hope I am. Speak

ing a regional hit record when a local label released a spoken-word recording of his testimony.

Then, after serving three terms in the state senate, he ran for mayor against John Nichols, the white police commissioner. In his campaign Young promised to disband of STRESS,* a deeply unpopular police operation created during the Gribbs administration in which under-cover officers served as lures for would-be muggers and ended up fatally shooting a staggering number of black Detroiters. (Young also prom-ised to fire Nichols if elected.) The numbers undergirding his victory turned out to be a grim statistical illustration of the region's forked path, with 91 percent of white Detroiters voting for Nichols and 92 percent of black Detroiters backing Young. At the time, the city was still just under 50 percent white, so Young won by only 14,000 (out of 450,000) votes.

"On election day I became godamn mayor of Detroit," he later wrote. But the truly frank analysis came a few lines later, when he acknowledged the reason for his win. "My fortune was the direct result of the city's misfortune," Young wrote, "of the same fear and loathing that had caused all of my problems and Detroit's problems in the first place. I was taking over the administration of Detroit because the white people didn't want the damn thing anymore."

In his acceptance speech, Young fell back on one of the tropes of the genre, warning criminals to leave town because a new sheriff had arrived. "To all dope pushers, to all rip-off artists, to all muggers . . . It's time to leave Detroit," he said. "Hit 8 Mile Road. I don't give a damn if they're black or white, or if they wear Superfly suits or blue uniforms with silver badges. Hit the road." Whites, and the media, reacted to what seems now like a patently unremarkable statement as if Young were a tribal chieftan ordering his most savage warriors to invade a

---

more clearly") and on the connection between Jim Crow and red-baiting (Young: "I consider the denial of the right to vote to large numbers of people all over the South un-American . . ." Tavenner: "Do you consider the activities of the Communist Party un-American?" Young: "I consider the activities of this committee, as it cites people for allegedly being a Communist, as un-American activities." Tavenner: ". . . I understood from your statement you would like to help us." Young: "You have me mixed up with a stool pigeon").
*Stop the Robberies, Enjoy Safe Streets.

peaceful neighboring land. While this reading of Young's speech strikes me, at least, as an astoundingly obtuse, almost certainly deliberate misinterpretation, its effect on the public perception of the mayor was immediate and devastating—and must be placed in the context of the day, when the fight between the city and the nascent suburban bloc felt nothing short of existential. In Detroit, Young and his new black majority had taken the reins for the first time and had giddy hopes for a renaissance, one in which they would finally share in the riches and create their own version of the American Dream, while just across 8 Mile an exponentially expanding population of whites saw themselves as displaced persons, refugees of a race and culture war forced to build dissident strongholds, where the true way forward would be demonstrated. For both sides, there seems to have been a zero-sum attitude toward resources, growth, and the overall development of the region. It was not unreasonable to think that the city, already increasingly irrelevant to the concerns of the suburbanites, who were building their own factories and office buildings and shopping malls and sporting arenas, might soon actually cease to exist in any recognizable form.

And if you believed Young's telling, the government did everything short of sending him exploding cigars to bring him down— only being a domestic enemy, the FBI was marshaled into service instead. Young became a target of federal investigations almost from the moment he took office, and though none of the charges ever stuck—on his death in 1997, he left an estate of $500,000, not exactly Boss Tweed money—several of Young's highest-profile appointees violated the public trust over the years, most prominently his longtime police chief and close friend William Hart, who was convicted, during Young's final term, of embezzling $1.3 million from an undercover-police fund. Hart was brought low by a deputy police chief named Kenneth Weiner, the son of a former Young accountant, who had started several businesses with the mayor, including one selling gold South African Krugerrands.

Young may very well have been dirty. But it doesn't require an outrageously conspiratorial bent to wonder if, only a few years after J. Edgar Hoover's well-documented targeting of MLK and the Black Panthers, a prominent black politician with as avowedly radical a past as the mayor's* might not have been subjected to specially zealous scrutiny.

What remains undeniable, of course, is Detroit's continued decline over the Young years—from the Devil's Night fires to the skyrocketing murder and unemployment rates to the crack cocaine epidemic—this, despite a handful of not-insignificant victories, including integration of the police department (and of city hall in general), a promotion of minority-owned business through increased government contracts, and a politically dexterous budgetary maneuver (involving voter-approved tax increases and state-level horse trading) that prevented the city from going bankrupt in the early eighties.

Young also certainly understood the concept of playing to your base. People tend to look at "white flight" as a prima facie bad thing—and that's true if you're talking about the flow of capital out of the city or more high-minded ideals of cohabitation and a united, color-blind populace. But for blacks who'd long been denied the right to move to certain neighborhoods and take certain jobs, who had been brutalized by a police force that felt more like an occupying army, a reasonable response to white "flight" might also be "Good riddance!" In the same vein, could a mayor who won office with almost zero support from those fleeing white voters have been expected to lure them back to the city, where they would promptly attempt to vote him out of office? This is not to say making whites feel unwelcome in order to maintain a black majority was somehow Young's endgame, an urban Democrat's twist on the GOP's Southern strategy. In fact, Young deliberately maintained a so-called 50/50 white/black government appointment policy, even as the changing demographics failed to reflect such a split—Young being a canny enough politician to understand he'd have to cut deals with a white regional business elite, not to mention the statewide government.

Still, as Young's cowriter noted in the introduction to *Hard Stuff*, the new demographics of the city "left the mayor in the uncommon position of simultaneously representing both a city and a race."

---

*Even as late as *Hard Stuff*, Young was disdainfully writing about "bleeding heart, pansy-ass" liberals, noting that "the change I seek for the world around me is a radical one."

Maynard Jackson was elected the first black mayor of Atlanta the same year as Young, and his more easygoing, accommodationist approach—and Atlanta's widely different fortune—makes for a tempting projection of an alternate possible destiny had Young not been so ornery. But Jackson's electorate included a prospering African American middle class, fostered by the city's growing economy and several historic black universities. Detroit, meanwhile, had a yawning underclass, poorly educated and mired in poverty. And so Young faced the same negative feedback loop any mayor, black or white, raging or conciliatory, would have likely faced: a steady loss of jobs and residents that had started long before he took office, leaving behind the poorest and least employable, which meant an ever-dwindling tax base, which meant increasingly diminished city services (including the sort of policing made especially necessary by such concentrations of poverty), which meant the city became ever more unlivable, thereby driving away more residents and businesses, thereby further eroding the tax base.

Perhaps if Young had been more of a visionary, he might have found some way to staunch the bleeding. But with the election of Ronald Reagan—needled throughout the 1980 campaign by Carter loyalist Young, who described the future president as "Old Pruneface"—federal disinvestment in urban centers exacerbated the struggles of big-city mayors across the country. And Young made plenty of mistakes of his own, throwing his support behind pointless boondoggles (the People Mover monorail) and ill-conceived moneymaking schemes (his tireless push for downtown casinos, which didn't pass until he'd left office) and rolling over for General Motors when the company threatened to pull a major factory out of the city unless space was cleared for a "state-of-the-art" robot plant. In the latter case, Young employed eminent domain—the same mechanism he decried for destroying his beloved Black Bottom neighborhood—to level Poletown, handing more ammunition to his critics, who pointed out that, of all the locations in the city he might have chosen to build the new plant, he'd settled on one of the last composed largely of working-class whites.*

There's no doubt that Young was a flawed mayor, and perhaps even

---

*The eminent-domain fight became a national cause, bringing to town the likes of Ralph Nader, whom Young described as a "publicity-grubbing prick."

the wrong man handed the wrong job at the wrong time. But the wild, disproportionate hatred of Young by white suburbanites was telling in ways that had nothing to do with the mayor's alleged malfeasances. With hindsight, it's difficult to understand how he managed to become so fearsome, with his cotton-mouthed, almost courtly speaking style and jowly stuffed-animal features, the twinkle in his eye perpetually giving his game away. (Like Bill Clinton, he was the sort of politician who brought to the class struggle the same skills he'd developed for years in the ass struggle.) Even today, there's an unsettling fervency to the hatred of Young among certain white ex-Detroiters, who will tell you *Coleman Young ruined this city* with such venom it's impossible not to see Young as a proxy for every black Detroiter who walks the halls of their old high schools or sleeps in the bedrooms of their childhood homes.

As for Young, by his final years in office, Detroit had become his fiefdom, and he developed an arrogance, which, for the first time in his life, struck many as more defensive than offensive. Detroit's obvious failings could not be fully acknowledged, in part out of political calculation but also, surely, for deeply personal reasons—for how could a figure as talented and exceptionalist as Young *not* feel a profound sense of sadness and regret, *not* be driven slightly mad, by the sight of his beloved city falling into ruin all around him? He had bucked the system and even changed it. But he had not been able to save his hometown. At his final press conference, Young declared Detroit's best days were still ahead. Did he believe it? Or was it just his way of saying, *Can't get any worse than this, folks.*

* * *

The most intriguing news from the 2011 census data wasn't the drop in Detroit's population, which, while steeper than expected, was nonetheless relatively unsurprising, but rather the new racial porousness of 8 Mile Road. While middle-class black flight from the city had been taking place for years, primarily to Southfield, the numbers had escalated dramatically over the past decade—obviously, as the 200,000 resident population plunge in Detroit indicated—and the migration patterns no longer seemed limited to specific suburbs. By 2010, Southfield was 70 percent black; the number of black residents in Warren jumped from 4,000 to 18,000; in Macomb County, the black population tripled to become 9 percent of the overall demographic makeup.

In a funny way, the recession had helped this integration along. With the collapse of the housing market, many white suburbanites had no choice in the matter: they simply couldn't leave, even if they wanted to. Perhaps Detroit's suburbs were experiencing an upside to the downturn, the incompetence of the Bush economic team having inadvertently managed the equivalent of Eisenhower's sending troops into Little Rock—forced integration through economic collapse!

There was friction, to be sure. As crime statistics shot up in the wake of the recession, there were alarming reports of carjackings in Grosse Pointe, armed robberies of fast food restaurants in St. Clair Shores, a shooting at my childhood mall. The expected slew of racist comments followed on the websites of community newspapers like the *Macomb Daily*. Fascinatingly, the Associated Press reported on similar tensions breaking out in Southfield—only here, they were occurring between longtime middle-class black residents and lower-income homesteaders who could suddenly afford to move out of Detroit as suburban rents and home prices fell. According to the article, the city had enacted "aggressive blight enforcement" laws after black Southfield residents began complaining of "newcomers from Detroit" who failed to maintain their property, walked and played basketball in the middle of the street, and "allow[ed] their children and teens to walk city streets at all hours."

The stresses of integration also seemed to be cutting along both sides of 8 Mile. Back in Detroit, the white population had actually *grown* for the first time in sixty years. The uptick was very slight— rising from 9 percent to about 13 percent—but enough for some black Detroiters to take note of all the young white people riding around on their bikes, raising chickens and goats in the middle of the city, and overrunning old dive bars that used to be frequented by middle-aged black transvestites. Typical gentrification worries about shifting power dynamics came into play, along with open talk about "outsiders" disrespecting "the community," how these kids walked around as if they owned the place.

"I've been thinking about the psychology of fear," a black Detroiter in her fifties told me. "It's interesting how white people can move into a neighborhood and walk down the street and think it's okay. Or go skateboarding at night. Or throw open all their windows. What makes them think they can do that?" She delivered the lines like a comic bit, almost, but she also seemed properly amazed. "Black people, we feel like we have to put bars up, be all huddled up in the dark," she went on. "White people are able to change the dynamic. Do they *demand* better? Walking down the street, do they bring expectations that everything will be okay, and that if they call the police, police will come? Do muggers think, 'Shit, this might be more trouble than it's worth?'" My friend chuckled. "This is funny in a way, because of course lots more white people are terrified of Detroit and won't set foot down here. This is a subset of white people. So it's interesting, all of these levels of misunderstanding. You sort of can't win."

U.S. Energy Secretary Steven Chu joins local dignitaries (including GM CEO
Ed Whitacre, Governor Jennifer Granholm and Senator Carl Levin) to celebrate
the first Chevrolet Volt battery coming off the assembly line at GM's Brownstone
Battery Plant. [Jeffrey Sauger, courtesy of General Motors]

7

MOTOR CITY BREAKDOWN

A new word was needed to express the trance, the fearful concentration with which all men awaited the approaching Automobile Show.

—MATTHEW JOSEPHSON, *Outlook*, 1929

A FEW WEEKS BEFORE the 2009 North American International Auto Show, the heads of the Big Three auto companies drove to Capitol Hill to make their case for a financial lifeline. It was their second appearance before Congress since the economic collapse, which had conspired with an ill-timed spike in gas prices to expose the carmakers' overleveraged, wildly mismanaged business model as unsustainable, built on sand. Not so different, really, from what the bankers had gotten themselves into, except—and this was Detroit's bad luck—the villains of Wall Street had yet to become household names, and their crimes would remain fantastically opaque. You didn't have to be Paul Krugman, on the other hand, to viscerally comprehend the shortcomings of Chrysler and General Motors. And so, with our elected representatives secure in the knowledge that their constituents wanted blood, the CEOs found themselves served with a public flogging befitting tobacco lobbyists.

Ford was still doing okay; the argument from GM and Chrysler, on the other hand, went, "Look, we screwed up, but if you let us fail, an entire Midwestern ecosystem of parts suppliers will go down, too, and that can't be helpful at a time when the U.S. economy is teetering on the brink of a full-scale depression, now can it?" Congress had just passed the Troubled Asset Relief Program, though, bailing out the banks to the tune of $700 billion, so there wasn't much appetite for further governmental largesse. Republicans from Southern "right to work" states, where the factories of foreign automakers happened to be located, were proving especially unmoved by Detroit's sob story. But back in Michigan, the very willingness of our notoriously arrogant corporate titans to prostrate themselves on C-SPAN spoke volumes about the dire straits in which the industry—the heart of Detroit's old way of life—found itself. At the Auto Show, the question on everybody's mind was not how Chrysler and GM might be saved, but whether they could be saved at all.

* * *

I hadn't been to an auto show since I was a teenager. My main memories centered on the bikini-clad booth models and getting to see the car from *Knight Rider*.* But in keeping with the New Austerity, the 2009 show was decidedly toned down. Spending taxpayer money on gaudy displays would have been bad form, so the show's planners promised a back-to-basics, "cars on carpets" approach. The trick for the automakers became figuring out how to simultaneously convey confidence and humility (not a typical trait associated with the Big Three), to acknowledge the troubles without making the industry's biggest party of the year feel like a wake. To that end, the purpose of the Auto Show was not simply to introduce the latest model of Silverado; it was the opening salvo of a very public, extraordinarily high-stakes publicity campaign. The automakers were selling the idea of their own relevance, and they had to convince Washington, the media, and the American consumer that they could adapt, making

---

*Later I realized that I'd actually seen the car at the much flashier AutoRama (a totally different event).

themselves nimbler and greener and building cars people might want to buy. The usual futuristic concept-car prototypes were on display, but the main thing showcased was entirely speculative—the idea of a future with Detroit in it.

In this regard, the automakers faced a very particular problem: the average consumer despised them. There were the decades of substandard products; the pathological myopia of a business model based on gas-guzzling SUVs and eternally low fuel prices; the pioneering outsourcing of jobs begun in the eighties; the preposterously overpaid executives, with their maddening, sclerotic passivity in the face of their industry's demise. And those were strictly macrolevel concerns— notice I haven't mentioned the Pontiac Aztek. Mustering public sympathy for such self-inflicted wounds was, in the words of a Detroit advertising veteran, "one of the toughest tasks not in automotive history but in marketing history."*

* * *

Growing up in metropolitan Detroit, attending the auto show was basically mandatory. It made no difference if you liked cars or not—I didn't—or if your family worked in some capacity for one of the automakers. We didn't own foreign cars; no one in our neighborhood did. No matter how badly they screwed up, the Big Three continued to exercise a psychological hold on residents, due to their place of importance in the city's history and a sense that, for all their faults, they had once made Detroit great and might do so again. For this reason, local support for the auto industry, which seemed only to intensify as the carmakers' fortunes continued to plunge, was more than just home-team loyalty. It was existential. When I moved away and bought a used Corolla, my dad, in his thick accent, noted mockingly, "They must be good cars—all the *smart people* buy them."

The first Detroit auto show was staged in 1899 by William E. Metzger, a former bicycle salesman who had become the city's premier (well, only) automobile dealer. According to the *Detroit News*, he

---

*The veteran, Pete DeLorenzo, writes the website *Autoextremist*. His father, Anthony, ran General Motors' public relations department from 1957 to 1979.

displayed four cars that year—two powered by electricity and two by steam—along with trophies from African big-game hunts and fishing tackle and other sporting equipment that might broaden the show's appeal. The cars were placed on rollers connected to crude speedometers, in order to demonstrate to skeptical customers how fast they could run.

By the late 1890s, magazines such as *The Horseless Age* had begun chronicling the expanding new market of motorcar enthusiasts, a growing but decidedly niche concern comprised of mechanically minded hobbyists who'd built upon the bicycle boom of the earlier part of the decade. Some weekend tinkerers, others more business-minded entrepreneurs, this far-flung brotherhood included Karl Benz in Germany, Armand Peugeot in France, the brothers Charles and Frank Duryea in Massachusetts, and Ransom Olds in Lansing, Michigan. The latter, obtaining backing from a millionaire owner of a copper mine, in 1899 shifted his operation to Detroit, where the Olds Motor Works became the first factory to mass-produce automobiles in the United States.

As Robert Conot points out, the northeast, with its established bicycle works, could have just as easily nurtured its own Motor City, but for the internal combustion engine winning out as the preferred mode of powering the new vehicles. The electric car batteries of the early twentieth century had proven too heavy and in need of constant recharging, while steam-powered cars would never be practical in the drought-prone western states. Gasoline engines, on the other hand, played to the strengths of Detroit's already considerable industrial base. The city had long been the carriage, ship-engine, and railroad-car capital of the United States, making for a deep talent pool to draw upon. The Detroit River, meanwhile, provided easy access to the natural resources (iron ore, copper, lumber, abundant in northern Michigan and surrounding states) necessary for automobile construction, and also facilitated the distribution of the finished cars.

Finally, the success of Olds Motor Works, and shortly thereafter Ford, began to create its own center of gravity, with an eventually irresistible pull, attracting like-minded talent in the manner of Hollywood or Silicon Valley, Nashville or Wall Street. The hard-drinking

Dodge Brothers,* who eventually opened their own factory, started out building transmissions for Ransom Olds. An obsessive machinist named Henry Leland, also in Olds's employ and already nearing sixty at the dawn of the twentieth century, went from building Oldsmobile engines to founding Cadillac Motors. The rakishly mustachioed French racer Louis Chevrolet made his way to Detroit (via New York) to start his own car company. Much later, Walter Chrysler, the gearhead son of a train engineer, came from small-town Kansas to be the works manager at Buick. When today's Detroit boosters talk of creating "entrepreneurial hubs," their dream scenario would look something like this wildly energetic period of the city's history, when the proximity of such skill and ambition and visionary moxie proved so profitably combustible.

By 2009, the show, having been staged everywhere from Beller's Beer Garden to the state fairgrounds to the Billy Sunday Tabernacle tent, had settled at Cobo Hall, the downtown convention center, where, inside, the expected rituals were still taking place. If you've never been to an auto show, these rituals mainly involve adults climbing in and out of vehicles they will not be allowed to drive, which always seems deeply unsatisfying, not unlike a visit to a strip club. Inside a car you cannot drive, there is not much to do. Most people give the steering wheel a firm, ten-and-two grip and wiggle their spines against the unfamiliar seats; occasionally, they try the radio. Outside the vehicles, hard-core motorheads, almost all men, photograph the new models from various angles, occasionally popping a hood to snap a close-up of an engine. A new Mustang turned on its side attracts a throng of guys who stare at the underbody in awe, as if they are peeking up a skirt. You are not allowed to sit inside the higher-end vehicles, like the Bentleys and Aston Martins. Sometimes the scent of new car is so powerful I wonder if they've figured out a way to enhance it artificially, like they do with the smell at Cinnabon.

Perhaps to signal a level of seriousness at the 2009 show, the booth girls were almost uniformly brunette and they all wore the

---

*During a bar fight, John Dodge reputedly once beat a man with two wooden legs to the ground, using the man's own cane.

same basic business attire (tight black pants, tops and blazers, stiletto-heeled black boots), a look I thought of as "Naughty Vice President of Marketing." The crowds were relatively sparse, so that the bright lights and forced cheer of the booth attendants felt creepy and desperate. In terms of square footage, the Big Three still dominated the main floor, but their displays had the least frills, with Chrysler making an especially depressing showing. In the past, Chrysler had been known for its over-the-top stunts during the show's press preview: hiring cowboys to herd ten dozen heads of cattle down the streets of Detroit to promote the new Dodge Ram, or driving a Jeep off a stage and through a plateglass window. But now, Chrysler didn't even introduce any new models ready for market, and their cars were modestly arranged on a thin gray carpet that bunched in places. Older models like the PT Cruiser were given wide berth by attendees, as if someone had spotted a dead body inside.

The foreign manufacturers, not chastened by crisis, allowed themselves a bit more flash. Volkswagen's display was multileveled, white and gleaming, with an Apple store brightness that made your eyes hurt. Honda's signage featured a humanoid robot that I assumed was some sort of jokey mascot until one of the representatives explained that last year it had conducted the Detroit Symphony Orchestra. Meanwhile, the U.S. Army, one of the only concerns still hiring in Detroit, had constructed a climbing wall in the food court, where camo-clad recruiters paced the floor.

In a sign of the times, so many automakers had dropped out of the 2009 show—Nissan and Porsche among them—that BYD, a Chinese car company traditionally stuck in a basement annex, was able to move up to the main floor. BYD entered the Chinese car market in 2003 and planned to begin selling in North America in 2011.* The company started out making rechargeable cell phone batteries and had put out extravagant claims for its electric cars—their batteries supposedly run for 250 miles and can be recharged to half power in ten minutes—about which U.S. analysts sounded both skeptical and nervous.

The biggest change at the show, everyone agreed, was the admis-

---

*This target date was later delayed to the final quarter of 2012.

sion, however belated, of the limits of the internal combustion engine. It was impossible to overstate how huge a deal this had been for Detroit. I could remember a childhood trip to AutoWorld, the ill-fated automotive-history-themed "fun" park meant to save Flint, Michigan (and famously mocked in *Roger & Me*), the centerpiece of which had been a three-story V-6 engine displayed in a rotunda like a giant statue of Buddha in a Bangkok temple. If someone had been asked to build a scale representation of the importance of the engine in Detroit history, this one would have been just about right.

But by 2009, all the major car companies were stressing their eco-warrior bona fides, setting aside prime real estate for their hybrids and concept electrics. An inordinate number of these vehicles were unsubtly painted some chlorophyll shade of green. The new Cooper Mini was housed inside a giant fake ice sculpture, because nothing says the oppo-site of global warming like a giant fake ice sculpture. Animated ads in the Lincoln display, meanwhile, showed the cars growing out of a leafy vine, as if future trips to an auto dealership would be more like picking organic produce at a farmers market. Toyota went a step further, pass-ing out little Prius-shaped flyers that actually had wildflower seeds embedded in the paper, so you could figuratively plant a Prius in your Earth Day victory garden. Toyota also passed out red paper swag bags bearing the message "Recycle This Bag." (Ford's plastic, flag-bedecked bags, by contrast, recommended shoppers "Buy American.")

In the basement, an entire artificial forest had been constructed, and people waited on line to be driven around a track in one of a fleet of hybrid vehicles. It felt like the National Public Radio version of Six Flags. I half expected Terry Gross to be driving my 2010 Ford Fusion hybrid, but instead I got a chirpy Ford salesperson. We slowly drove off, soon shaded by the plastic trees and creeping past a little water-fall. All of this was surely meant to be soothing, though something about the poky speed and utter silence of the car began to feel sinister, like intimations of a future where our robot cars won't let us drive too fast or tailgate or listen to loud hip-hop with lots of bass.

Cynicism regarding the car companies' sudden green epiphanies flowed abundantly, especially in light of Detroit's continued and vocif-erous opposition to any sort of reasonable national fuel-efficiency stan-dards. Charles Kettering, a groundbreaking auto industry engineer, once gave a speech warning about the finite nature of oil and proposed making lighter cars with more fuel-efficient engines.* This was in 1925. The technology was there, but Kettering's omen fell on deaf ears. Now, like T. Boone Pickens slapping windmill arms on his oil derricks and claiming to be Al Gore, the automakers' showy new appeals to the Sierra Club demographic seemed unconvincing.

I began to notice a striking discrepancy at the auto show between the green PR blitz and civilian interest. People milled near the hybrids with a detached curiosity, the same way you might check out the albino calf at a state fair but not necessarily write about it in your journal when you got home. The sports cars and the big polluting trucks still seemed to generate the most excitement. Over at Ford, scrums of large men surrounded every F-150 pickup, testing out the rear bed flaps with their feet and marveling at the new "smart" technology that would let you know if you'd forgotten one of your tools at home. As I wandered past Chrysler, a gelled spokesmodel was talking up the special features of another truck.

"That's right, guys," he told his audience. "Satellite TV!"

* * *

The real hand-wringing over the future of the auto industry was taking place at the Renaissance Center, where *Automotive News*, the local trade publication, held its annual World Congress, a four-day conference for auto insiders. The theme: "Global Strategies for Challenging Times." To get to the conference, I rode the People Mover, an elevated tram that runs through downtown Detroit in a three-mile, one-way loop. The city used to have an extensive trolley system, but it was purchased by National City Lines, a front company formed by GM, Firestone, Standard Oil, and other firms with automobile interests, after which the trolley tracks were ripped up and replaced with buses. The People Mover began running in 1987 and seems, in its utter uselessness, as if it might have been built by another secret auto industry cabal, as a way of mocking the very idea of public transportation. The monorail cars are automated and driverless, like trams at the airport or an amusement

---

*He invented, among other things, the electric self-starting ignition, the "Rocket 88" V-8 engine, and leaded gasoline.

park; occasionally, walking along a barren downtown block, you might glance up and notice a pair of empty cars passing above your head at a haunted crawl. In the People Mover, I rode by the Gem Theatre, where I worked one summer as a cocktail waiter (I remembered standing outside one afternoon as two of my coworkers showed off their respective bullet wounds), past Joe Louis Arena, where I saw my first concert (Springsteen, *Tunnel of Love* tour), and then the Joe Louis Fist. Louis worked briefly at Ford, pushing truck bodies onto the assembly line for fifty-five cents an hour, a job that quickly convinced him to return to the boxing ring. "I figured," he said, "if I'm going to hurt that much for twenty-five dollars a week, I might as well go back to try fighting again."

In the Marriott ballroom, speaker after speaker approached the podium, which was silver and gleamed like a hood ornament, to soberly address the challenges of the current market. The crowd could not have been friendlier, with the grimness of the times resulting in a chummy survivors' bonhomie, even among rivals. After a while, the room was so filled with positive vibes, it began to take on the air of a support group.* UAW president Ron Gettelfinger (who retired in 2010) apologized for his annual salary of $155,000 in a folksy Ross Perot twang. GM president Fritz Henderson (fired by late 2009) said nothing about his own $1.8 million salary, though during a Q&A with the moderator, he was pushed to admit that GM would run out of cash well before March 31 that year if a second round of bailout money didn't come through.

Those who followed offered no greater reason for hope. Frank Klegon, Chrysler's executive vice president of product development, exuded such barely concealed desperation, you got the impression he might personally try to sell you a car. Even his PowerPoint presentation felt half baked: one page had only the word *Innovation!* over a photograph of a Dodge Ram pickup.

---

*Though perhaps this had always been the case. In *The Reckoning*, David Halberstam's rollicking door stopper of an account of the decline of the Detroit auto industry in the seventies and early eighties, a former *Car & Driver* editor characterizes the Big Three as "one big company with three divisions, in which everyone played it safe and no division tried something new unless it was reasonably sure that the other two were going to try it as well." Another journalist tells Halberstam the automakers possessed a "shared monopoly."

Likewise, Jon Lauckner, a vice president at GM, who was wearing a red, white, and blue tie and an American flag pin, should probably not seek a second career as a motivational speaker. When the moderator asked, somewhat jokingly, if designing cars for use on the Autobahn resulted in making a better car, Lauckner responded, "Better is a value judgment. I don't like the word *better*."*

* * *

The headline speaker on the final night of the conference was Ralph Gilles, Chrysler's thirty-nine-year-old design chief, considered one of the most talented designers working in the industry today. In 2004, he styled the elegant and much-loved 300C sedan, described in the *New York Times* as "gangster chic" and "swagger[ing] into the full-size sedan market . . . like a mob underboss." The hippest guy in a roomful of blue suits, he was also one of the only black faces in the house—of Haitian descent, he was born in Long Island but raised in Montreal—and his keynote slot, coming just one day after Obama's inauguration, was perhaps meant, on some level, to give the conference a subliminal dose of audacious hope.

I had visited Gilles in Auburn Hills, a tony Detroit suburb considered the sticks when I was a kid but since turned densely residential as more and more people fled farther from the city proper. It was also the home of Chrysler's world headquarters, a gigantic complex the size of a shopping mall; my PR escort told me it was the second-largest office building in the world, after the Pentagon.

Gilles said he had loved drawing cars since he was a kid. After dropping out of college and working at a hardware store, he applied, on a whim, to the College for Creative Studies, an art and design school in Detroit. His decision to apply was so last-minute and half-considered, he had only a week to assemble a portfolio and was surprised when the school accepted him. After graduation, he received offers from a number of car companies but chose Chrysler because, he said, "I'm an underdog person. Also, at the time, they were doing K cars, so I thought, 'Man, they're gonna need a lot of help.'"

Ironically, it was Gilles, working for the most beleaguered of the

---

*I wouldn't either if I made the Chevy Malibu.

automakers, who offered a reason to believe that Detroit might find a way forward. He was a reminder that Detroit, after all, was built by visionary entrepreneurs. Before I met Gilles, I wandered through the nearby Chrysler Museum, three floors of classic models, from the early art deco Chrysler Airflow to sixties muscle cars like the amazingly named Dodge Fury. Here, you realized why so many early rock and roll songs were about hot rods—back then, there was a good chance they would be sexier than your high school girlfriend. Because people identify with their cars to a degree they don't with almost any other material possession, Detroit once knew, better than anyone, how to infuse a mass-produced consumer product with lust and danger, high gloss and ineffable, darker undercurrents.*

Even today, there aren't many hipper applications for an engineering or industrial design degree than building a car; the Chrysler Design Studio had the creative energy, and edgy talent pool, of a video game lab. And the disembodied car interiors Gilles showed me hinted at the sensual appeal of the museum pieces next door. He insisted the company's new ethos would be about perfecting niches rather than chasing volume: "less cars done better." At this point, Chrysler had just announced its coming merger with Fiat, though the ink had not yet dried on the deal. Gilles seemed to be laying the groundwork for a way in which consumers might come to see Chrysler, thanks to the new partnership with the Italians, as some kind of European luxury product.

"I'm an X, but my kids are millennials," Gilles said, "and the good news about millennials is they're not brand loyal. They'll skip around as long as the product is good. Boomers may have had an American car in the late eighties or early nineties and they'll probably never buy another one again. But there's a whole new group of people coming, so it's our chance to address that. I know where the perception's at. We have to create products so delicious, so mesmerizing, people forget all that stuff and say, 'I have to have this.' People have short memories. It wasn't too

---

*One of the most amusing byproducts of this era of Detroit car styling remains the solicitation in the 1950s of poet Marianne Moore by the Ford Corporation for possible new "dramatically desirable" model names. Moore's correspondence with the company includes such (sadly never used) suggestions as Anticipator, Intelligent Whale, Thundercrest, Silver Sword, Resilient Bullet, Andante con Moto, Varsity Stroke, and Mongoose Civique.

long ago that Apple was a write-off. Then the right product comes along."

*　*　*

Gilles was not alone in hoping a Steve Jobs–like visionary would come along and create the iPod of hybrid electrics. Over at General Motors, engineers had been developing a car that perhaps could fundamentally alter not only the perception of the domestic automakers but their very DNA: the Chevy Volt. The most hyped vehicle to emerge from Detroit in decades, the Volt was eventually politicized by right-wing opponents of both global warming science and the auto bailout, for whom it became a moving target (*barely* moving, they'd say) and perfect distillation of Obama's penchant for overreach. Debuting in late 2010 to rave reviews in the automotive press, the Volt was meant to be General Motors' answer to the Toyota Prius. Like the Prius, it was a hybrid, running both on battery and a small gasoline engine, but the Volt's technology took a great leap forward, in that its gas engine would never be used to turn the wheels of the car—it was merely present to keep the battery going if the power began to run out—and so, since the battery could last forty miles, the average commuter, who traveled far shorter distances, would not burn any gasoline. Overall, the car would have a fuel efficiency of 100 miles per gallon.

The Volt's chief engineer, Andrew Farah, worked at the GM Tech Center in Warren, a fading east side suburb, where I met him. The tech campus was huge, and in winter, with its vista of gray skies, snow-covered fields, and blocky, grimly functional buildings, the place felt like an industrial park in Volgograd. Farah had thin wire-rimmed glasses, salt-and-pepper hair, and a pen sticking out of his blue shirt pocket. We slipped on plastic safety goggles and he took me into the battery lab, where batteries were tested at a variety of temperatures inside thermal chambers that looked like meat lockers.

In the world of hybrids, the quest for the perfect battery is everything and remains a daunting technological challenge. Engineers have to maximize driving distance and overall life span—the batteries must be able to survive a Detroit winter just as easily as an Arizona summer—all while keeping costs reasonable. At the moment, the lithium-ion battery has emerged as the most efficient. At the Volt lab, the batteries, covered in black plastic shells, were T-shaped, about the right size for crucifying an eight-year-old. There were two hundred individual cells inside each battery. Farah pulled out a cell to show me: it was roughly as big as a trade paperback, but only the thickness of a few pages.

Farah grew up in Flint, where all of his family's neighbors worked for GM. He studied computer engineering in college, but when he graduated in the early eighties he didn't find working on PCs interesting enough, so ended up joining the automaker. "I preferred the idea of sticking a computer in something and making it do something for people," he said.

In the nineties, Farah worked on GM's EV1, the purely electric car produced in limited quantities for three years before its controversial removal from the market. The EV1 inspired the documentary *Who Killed the Electric Car?*, which implied deliberate self-sabotage by GM and reinforced the idea of the venality of the car companies. Farah explained that the car had fallen short of basic market demands. It was tiny and expensive, with a short range and no backup when the battery ran out, and therefore had an inherently limited appeal—a dune buggy for rich people. I asked if there was a point when Farah realized the EV1 was not going to work. "Well, technically, it *worked*," he said quickly, a hint of engineer's pride creeping into the peevishness of his tone. "It had a lower coefficiency of drag than a fighter jet! Was there a point we realized market desires for the EV1 weren't going to be there? Oh, yeah. I'm sure there was, for somebody." He paused for several beats, then continued, "Maybe even for me."

Farah had felt such a personal commitment to that project, its cancellation meant he was very hestitant when GM called him about working on the Volt. He'd transferred to a European division by that time and wanted to know the company's level of seriousness. They assured him it was real. "And I have to say, it has been," Farah insisted. "One of the reasons we're coming to market so quickly is because we have the full support of the company." He claimed that all of the problems with that first wave of electric vehicles were being addressed with the Volt. "You can end up with a battery on wheels, which people don't want. I have to think about what segment of the population will want this car. Is it only these ultragreen types? Hopefully not, because there are not enough of them. Soccer moms? Probably not. But there is a big space in between there, a little more to the green side, but you also get utilitarian people and early-adopter techies."

After the EV1 experience, Farah was acutely aware of the challenge. "If you want to get to the mass market and really drive a change in the population, you have to do it without making people feel like we're asking them to run around without a shirt. The change can't be that big. It has to be something they can deal with."

And yet the sheer scale of what needed to change for the auto industry, and Detroit, to look like a going concern could make your head hurt, especially when it came to something as fundamental to our lives and economy as vehicular transportation. As Kristin Dziczek, an analyst at the Center for Automotive Research, an Ann Arbor–based independent think tank, pointed out to me, even the most incrementalist steps toward greater fuel efficiency had to be "coupled with a more sensible energy policy from the government, because otherwise, with my new forty-five-mile-per-gallon car, I'm just going to drive more. People might start to choose automobiles over air travel. You can't do this on the backs of the auto industry alone."

Automakers loved this market-based defense: while gas prices remain low, consumer demand for inefficient vehicles does not change, and therefore it's not their fault for responding to that demand. (It's the Milton Friedman 101 version of "Stop me before I kill again!") Of course, for years the carmakers opposed any environmental legislation that might affect their industry, with the help of lobbyists and friendly legislators like Michigan congressman John Dingell (and complicity from the UAW). As recently as 2008, GM's vice chairman Bob Lutz called global warming "a total crock of shit." As Jim Kliesch, a clean-fuel expert at the union of concerned scientists, told me, "The average fuel economy of vehicles produced today is roughly the same as vehicles produced in 1987. The automakers have demonstrated they would rather apply other technologies that improve amenities—you know, putting DVD systems in the backs of chairs and whatnot—because they can get a higher profit margin out of that than from putting the money into fuel economy. Their research at the time showed consumers didn't care about fuel economy. So we've gone nowhere on the fleet average in two decades."

* * *

The auto bailout that passed later in 2009, over the objections of congressional Republicans, came with numerous strings, all being manipulated by an Obama-appointed "car czar" who forced tough modernizing and belt-tightening measures on a recalcitrant Detroit. The result—significant union concessions, radically altered corporate structures, Chrysler's merger with Fiat, and all three domestic automakers (including Ford, which never took any loans in the first place) posting profits for the first time in years—handed the president's economic team a tangible achievement and made the Big Three seem like twenty-first-century corporations with viable business models.

The dependence of the auto industry's comeback on underemployment, slashed benefits, and corporate profits mirrored the larger economic "recovery" in a predictable and depressing way, but the city was buoyed by the prospect of the carmakers actually turning a corner. Restored profitability, while not exactly trickling down to the average worker, still seemed like a sign of *something*, as did the on-time arrival to market of the Volt. Even more unbelievably, Chrysler—Chrysler!—had aquired a patina of hip, at least in advertising circles, thanks to a celebrated 2011 Chrysler 200 commercial featuring the rapper Eminem, filmed driving through the city to the opening chords of his hit song "Lose Yourself." Downtown Detroit is shot in a gauzy and melodramatic noir mistiness, and in a brilliant final touch, the ad heralds the new Chrysler line as being "Imported from Detroit," at once tweaking the historic quality- and bourgeois-cachet gap between the Detroit automakers and their foreign competitors and playing up the notion of Detroit as an alien, potentially hostile world, technically but not exactly part of the rest of America.

The Volt, meanwhile, debuted to sluggish sales, prompting temporary halts in production, and then faced an early recall after catching fire during a rollover test. Also, its cost, $41,000, minus a $7,500 federal tax credit, was prohibitive for the average driver. Still, *Motor Trend* named the Volt its 2011 Car of the Year, and enthusiasts reportedly became hooked on the car's slick electronic interface, which made the avoidance of gas stations—the display informed drivers whether the engine was using only the battery or had switched over to fuel—as compulsive a challenge as an iPhone game. For the most obsessive of these new drivers, reported *New York Times* columnist Joe Nocera, "it could be months between fill-ups." (When a lawyer from New Jersey bragged to Nocera about getting 198 miles per gallon, another Volt owner interrupted, "Is that all?")

By 2012, the Volt had been named European Car of the Year—the first time a car designed and produced entirely in the United States had won the award—but the honor would not help rehabilitate the car's reputation on the right, now that it had bizarrely joined *Piss Christ* as an artifact from the culture wars. Conservative pundits like George Will and Rush Limbaugh held the car up for ridicule, while Darrell Issa, a Republican representative from California, denounced the Volt as "a demo project funded by edict," conjuring images of framed portraits of Obama glowering over Stalinist battery-cell assembly lines. Newt Gingrich, being Newt Gingrich, took the criticism to its most absurd extreme during the GOP primary when he decried the Volt's impracticality by pointing out you couldn't fit a gun rack in the car.*

At this point, even Bob Lutz—"global warming is a crock of shit" Bob Lutz!—began to defend the Volt out of sheer paternal loyalty, despite being a lifelong Republican. Michigan, meanwhile, had decided to double-down on the potential of the new technology, hoping it would translate to jobs. Governor Jennifer Granholm supported numerous tax incentives to lure battery manufacturers to the state, to mixed early results. A123 Systems in Livonia, for instance, created 3,300 jobs, but required $250 million in federal stimulus money and another $125 million in incentives from the state.

Despite the conservative misinformation campaign, though, the Volt's sales were inching up; by June 2012, GM had already matched its sales numbers for the entirety of the previous year. Even more important, the Volt had spurred the competition to step up: an electric

---

*Newt Gingrich being Newt Gingrich, this claim proved false, though the Venn diagram of Volt and gun rack owners probably offers up a slim overlap.

version of the Ford Focus was slated for a quick debut, with electrics in the works from Toyota and Honda.

As for the electric car being the future, well, the verdict remains fuzzy. In March 2011, for instance, CNN reported some very good news for the auto industry that remained, potentially, very bad news for the portion of the auto industry that cared about our collective carbon footprint—namely, a rise in truck sales of *32 percent* over the previous year. As the Big Three had been making their much-touted comeback, their top-selling vehicles were all SUVs and pickups—for GM, the Silverado pickup; for Ford, the F-series of pickups (though sales of the Ford Explorer SUV also shot up 139 percent); for Chrysler, the Dodge Ram pickup and the Jeep Grand Cherokee SUV. These sales showed no signs of slowing down, even as gas prices once again began to rise.

"Keep in mind, we reset our expectations," Paul Ballew, the chief economist at Nationwide Financial, told CNN. "Five years ago, three dollars a gallon was, 'Oh my goodness.' Now it's more of a norm."

A crowd gathers outside Detroit's Cobo Center to pick up applications for federal aid to low-income residents. Approximately 60,000 people showed up over the two-day period, though assistance would only be available for 3,400 families. [Daniel Mears/ *Detroit News*]

8

COMEBACK!

Or, What Will Become of the Workingman in Detroit?

JOHN ZIMMICK, THE PRESIDENT of United Auto Workers Local 174, parked his black GMC Canyon pickup truck in the lot of one of his shops, a metalcrafting factory in the west side suburb of Romulus. Zimmick wore a gunslinger's-length black leather jacket, blue jeans, and a forest green sweater pulled tightly over his low-slung paunch. He was middle-aged, on the shorter side, with facial features at once sharp (aquiline nose, narrow, appraising eyes) and rounded (the rest of his face) and a vowel-flattening Michigan accent bound to a dry-throated chain-smoker's baritone. Zimmick handed me a manila envelope and a briefcase. The briefcase turned out to be a gift box of World's Finest Chocolate designed to look like a briefcase. After grabbing two KFC carryout bags from the back of his truck, Zimmick craned his head suspiciously in the direction of my car.

"This ain't foreign, I hope," he said. It was not.

"Good," he replied, and we headed into the plant.

It was a chilly morning in 2011, two years after the auto industry's second bailout and some months into its vaunted comeback. The factory comprised four warehouse buildings arranged on two sides of a service drive, which in turn wended its way through an entire office park of similar light-industrial manufacturing plants, the signage of many of these buildings bearing cryptic acronyms (EWI, DRS, NWC), most of them smaller auto parts suppliers of the sort the Big Three and their allies warned would topple in a domino slide of bankruptcies if the U.S. government dared allow GM or Chrysler to go out of business. Zimmick asked that I not reveal the identity of this particular facility. He personally worked about seventy hours a week, acting as the direct service rep for thirty-one of Local 174's approximately one hundred plants.

Inside one of the factory's buildings, twelve-foot-square sheets of solid white foam material had been stacked like drywall next to a garage door. An outsized drill hanging from the ceiling would be used by pattern makers to cut the foam sheets into molds according to customer specifications. These molds would then be packed into what looked to me like an enormous dirt-filled garden box, though the earthy substance was actually something called "green sand." The newly molded sand would eventually be covered with molten 835°F zinc from a pair of bubbling vats. The final mold, after cooling, would then be taken to one of the buildings across the street and squeezed like a retainer into the mouth of a two-story stamping press and used to punch out (say) the metal side panels for the latest Toyota truck body.

Just beyond the presses and up a short flight of stairs, we entered the plant's designated union office, a cramped and shabby space: cheap wood paneling, rolling desk chairs with stained fabric and broken spines, a faded American flag and various informational flyers (e.g., "Your Rights: Family and Medical Leave Act") decorating the walls. Ray Grimble, one of the shop stewards, sat behind a cluttered desk typing something on an antique PC. Grimble had a mustache and a slightly feathered hairstyle and wore a navy-blue sweatshirt. When I asked how long he'd worked at the plant, he replied, "Twenty-three years," then added, "Let me put it this way: too damn long." But he said it with a congenial smile, Grimble possessing the sort of ingrained pleasantness that struck some people as particularly American and was ascribed most often to residents of midwestern and southern states.

Grimble was a patternmaker. He'd grown up in Inkster, and though his wife, Lisa, worked as an adjunct professor of English, much of his immediate family had been employed in some capacity by the auto industry: both parents at stamping shops (his father, until his retirement, at this very plant), his grandmother at GM's Fisher Body facility, his brother ("a big-time computer geek") in the CAD (computer-aided design) department of Ford. When he was a kid, his parents had only one car, so after school they'd always hurry over to pick up his father at Dearborn Stamping, where he was working at the time. His interest piqued by the big machines, Grimble got into the business himself. The first ten years were "pretty decent," he told me. "It's been steadily downhill after that. I've seen lots of shops go out of business. I've had friends my age have to move back in with their parents because they couldn't make it. Two Christmases ago, everyone at dinner from my wife's side of the family was like, 'You know about any snowplow work for me?'" Grimble had been elected steward that fall. "I just got tired of all the bullshit," he said. "You can only take so much. Hopefully, my input can make a difference."

Nodding at the KFC bags, he said to Zimmick, "I see you took care of Marv." He was referring to Marv Townsend, the shop's chief steward.

"I took care of you, too!" Zimmick exclaimed.

Grimble looked around the room and said, "Where is she?"

Of all the Detroit-area UAW locals, Local 174 holds a place of pride in union lore, owing to its connection with Walter Reuther. The seminal labor activist got his start in the UAW as president of Local 174, which he founded in 1936 with a $350 loan from a Communist buddy working in one of the Cadillac plants. The local was amalgamated—meaning, its membership had been drawn from dozens of various-sized factories and shops, as opposed to workers from a single massive GM or Ford plant. It represented an area of west side metropolitan Detroit described by Reuther biographer Nelson Lichtenstein as "a sprawling field of parts and assembly plants," places like Federal Screw, Timkin Axle, and Michigan Malleable Iron. Reuther began Local 174 with seventy-eight registered members; by the end of that first year, after the successful resolution of his first big sit-down strike at the four-thousand-employee Kelsey-Hayes Wheel Company, membership had exploded to three thousand—over the course of only ten days! Eight months later, the union had thirty thousand members.

This flourishing dovetailed with the thrilling success of the Flint sit-down strike, begun on December 30, 1936, which forced General Motors to broker a deal with the UAW for the first time and gave workers across the country, not just autoworkers, a glimpse of the power of organizing. Reuther, meanwhile, had the audacity, in May 1937, to make a move on Ford's Rouge facility, heretofore entirely off limits to UAW organizing. The city-sized plant was "both physically and psychologically insulated from union influence," writes Lichtenstein, "surrounded not by the West Side's friendly ethnic neighborhoods but by a sprawling set of highways and parking lots under Ford control." Still, with its hundred thousand employees, the Rouge proved an irresistible target. While attempting to cross the Miller Road overpass leading into the complex, Reuther and three other UAW leaders were brutally attacked by forty security goons directed by Harry Bennett, Henry Ford's thuggish enforcer. Reuther was repeatedly slammed to the concrete and kicked in the head, before being thrown down a flight of stairs. Unfortunately for Ford, a *Detroit News* photographer captured the beatings in a series of shots that would win the Pulitzer Prize.

After the so-called Battle of the Overpass, Reuther's legend was born. He would go on to become one of the iconic figures of the twentieth-century labor movement, the historic concessions on health care and other benefits wrung by Reuther from the Big Three playing no small role in the creation of an American middle class. The title of Lichtenstein's biography is drawn from a quote by American Motors president and future Michigan governor George Romney: "Walter Reuther is the most dangerous man in Detroit, because no one is more skillful in bringing about the revolution without seeming to disturb the existing forms of society."

Zimmick and his members remained well aware of the historical significance of Local 174. A framed black-and-white photograph of Reuther and his wife, May—both killed in a plane crash in 1968, en route to the UAW retreat in northern Michigan—hung on the wall of the little office. And yet, as everyone knows, the fortunes of unions in general, and the UAW in particular, have fallen precipitously since those glory days. Although still one of metropolitan Detroit's biggest locals, 174 has seen its membership drop to about forty-two hundred from over ten thousand members only four years ago, before the recession and numerous plant closings and layoffs decimated its ranks.

The reason for this afternoon's house call was a mediation, the factory's management standing accused of using temp workers on

Sundays and holidays without offering the hours to union members, who contractually are supposed to receive first dibs and who would also be paid double time, based on hourly wages much higher than temp pay. Such petty shenanigans on the part of management seemed less about cost cutting than provocation, an intentionally maddening form of psyops. Still, Zimmick was fired up about the proceedings and their potential outcome. "The last contract was hard," he told me. "Everybody got raises. Everything seems to be going well. But management is going to try to get away with things if they can. It's always a struggle. Our advantage is, we have a lot of eyes around this place."

"The clause states they're not supposed to use temp employees over a thousand hours," Grimble added. "They've done pushed that issue way beyond."

"We're asking for full pay at double time for everybody who would've worked," Zimmick said. "And if they wanna sit there and be stubborn without even giving a counter, we'll say, 'See you at arbitration.' Do you want to go to D.C. in May?"

Grimble was trying to get the fax machine to work. "What's the cause?" he asked.

"Unfair trade agreements. We're going to challenge the Chamber of Commerce. Tom Donohue"—president and CEO of the Chamber—"is a real pain in the ass. He's never seen protests yet. We'll raise a little hell. There'll probably be a 150, 200 members going. It's not officially UAW, though. The second floor of the hotel will be the naked girls and the Jell-O shots. I'm president, so I'll stay on the first floor. Can't have cell phone pictures of me with a beer bong."

I couldn't tell whether Zimmick was joking or not. Before I could ask, Marv Townsend showed up, along with two other shop stewards, Fred Kus and Len Kreimes. As the men, none of whom could be described as slender, entered the office, its unoccupied square footage was reduced with fleet dispatch. They all removed orange foam earplugs and thick plastic safety goggles, except for Townsend, who left on his goggles for a while. Kus had a gray-flecked beard and looked like an outlaw biker, though not as much as Kreimes did. Before grabbing a paper plate and helping himself to fried drumsticks and mashed potatoes, he handed Zimmick a thick computer printout detailing the number of hours worked by all of the temps. Many, it turned out, had well exceeded the thousand-hour limit, at which point they were supposed to become union members; some had worked as many as seventeen hundred hours. The top union worker at the factory made $25.09 an hour; temps could be paid whatever the job market was willing to accept, which, in this job market, could amount to $10 an hour, or even less.

Zimmick greedily flipped through the pages, loosing a wicked laugh. "I like it," he said. "Oh my goodness. It's the Golden Goose. They're making money on this shit. Nice job, Fred."

Townsend, the only black guy in the room, had close-cropped graying hair and a mustache and had been working at the factory for seventeen years. He and Kreimes actually started a week apart. Townsend said he moved to Detroit from Mississippi after he got out of the service in 1975. His first job had been working at a barrel factory, cleaning out the big drums. All of his coworkers had been ex-cons. "They'd just got out of jail or prison, and that was the only work they could find," he told me. "They were good workers, though. That was a fun job." He paused to bite into a biscuit, then said sadly, "I used to love coming to work here. Loved it."

The company had been started in the sixties, in the garage of the founder's home, at first strictly servicing the automotive industry but eventually expanding into making parts for boats and motorcycles, which had proved disastrous, at least according to the stewards. "Way I look at it," Grimble said, "you can't sell cars, you're not selling boats." Still, the company had bounced back of late, in part because of new environmental regulations requiring semitrucks be more fuel efficient; the company had been contracted to make special brackets for the trailers to help achieve these ends. "So now we're doing real good," Townsend said, before quickly correcting himself: "*They* are. We're surviving." It was an old story: when times were tough, the union had agreed to concessions in order to save jobs. But concessions had a way of quickly settling into permanence, at least until the next round of concessions.

> GRIMBLE: "They got everybody so damn scared, nobody wants to say anything, because they're afraid their job's going to go away."

ZIMMICK: "They have an advantage. The deck is stacked against us real heavy in this economy."

TOWNSEND: "The company says maintenance is not, it's not . . . what? What did they say y'all wasn't?"

KREIMES: "We don't make money for 'em."

TOWNSEND: "Right!"

KREIMES: "Overhead. We're overhead. We got the same amount of maintenance guys we had seventeen years ago and we've added three buildings."

ZIMMICK: "Tell you what, though. The past few months here things have changed for the better. I've been getting phone calls. People like working here."

GRIMBLE: "People like working here? You mean *new* people? Because they're just glad to have a job. If people had been here when times were good, and then they went bad, and then the company stepped on you, *those* people sure aren't calling you."

ZIMMICK (PENSIVE): "No. And these new guys, they'll get their turn, too, down the road, I'm sure. They're fair about that!"

TOWNSEND: "We've been sold out. Who owns this country now? I was watching the news yesterday. In Indiana they got a freeway with a bridge on it, and they had to keep repairing it, so they sold it to Australia. Who done own us? Our workforce, man, they come out and say, 'Americans don't got no more pride in their work.' We got a lot of fucking pride! They just don't understand how it is to come to work and people are depending on you, and you make sure all of your jobs are taken care of, and you're working ungodly hours to keep the customer happy, you do all of this, and then at the end, they reap all the rewards."

KREIMES: "They don't even come back there and give you an 'Attaboy.'"

The mediation took place in a conference room in the front office. Zimmick glad-handed the management representatives, including a top executive with slicked-back hair wearing an open-collared suit. Introducing the executive, Zimmick told me, shamelessly, "Now *this* is a brilliant guy. If you're looking to interview someone who knows about manufacturing, you need to talk to him." The executive arranged his face into a cheesy grin, seeming at once involuntarily pleased by the compliment and yet determined to convey, via an air of ruthlessly circumspect professionalism, both the fact of his being onto Zimmick's flattery and the nonexistent odds of my ever getting any face time with anyone in the executive suite.

Zimmick said I would have to wait in the lobby during the mediation. I followed him into the front-office break room, which he entered with impunity, implicitly putting himself on equal footing with the bosses and the suits. "They got the best coffee here," he said, fixing himself a cup. A pair of management guys sat at a long table eating lunch. Zimmick shot them a mischievous look and exclaimed, "Sushi? You can definitely pay all our grievances, then." The management guys chuckled self-consciously.

Stepping outside for a quick cigarette, Zimmick lowered his voice and said to me, "I know you saw those two guys sleeping when we walked through the plant." I hadn't, actually, and felt derelict for being so easily distracted by the big machines, but I nodded silently. "I don't represent everyone," he said. "I call it like I see it. Unions get a bad name for a reason. Now these two guys, that's a circumstance, because of the hours at this place, they might've had permission to sleep. But I ain't got time for a guy who goes in and steals from the company. That's stealing, even if it's hours. If they come to me and say, 'Well, John, you can save my job, right?' I'll say, 'Yeah. Once. One time.' That guy may hate me after that conversation, but I don't care. You're on your own. You do this again, don't call me."

Zimmick made his way back to the conference room and I took a seat in the lobby. Display cases showed off gleaming examples of the company's handiwork: a slick one-piece production hood, an aluminum dash cluster panel. After a few minutes, I opened my satchel and pulled out a book I'd been reading, a very funny jeremiad by the writer Jack Green against the literary critics who had (in Green's opinion) failed to intelligently review William Gaddis's great experimental novel *The Recognitions* upon its publication. Only after I removed the book from my bag did I notice its title, *Fire the Bastards!* I decided to put the book away and finish it later.

After nearly an hour, Zimmick and Townsend emerged from the conference room looking tense. Zimmick gave me a tight little nod as they passed through the lobby. When I joined them outside, Zimmick was taking a drag on a cigarette and nervously shifting his weight from one foot to the other in the crisp January air. He seemed even more edgy and intense than he'd been prior to the mediation. The ruling was being debated as we spoke. "They know me, and they know my arbitration record," Zimmick said, summoning the blustery confidence he'd expressed earlier in the afternoon. "I guarantee you, they're in there saying to management, 'John Zimmick's gonna stomp your ass!' They're gonna have to dig in their pockets."

Townsend remained perfectly still, other than for the occasional arm motion required to bring his cigarette to his lips.

"You heard me," Zimmick told me, nodding at Townsend. "I just gave my chief steward my word."

Townsend didn't reply or shift his gaze, fixed on one of the buildings across the street, in our direction.

Zimmick gave Townsend an anxious look, then cleared his throat and added, "Marv had words with the mediator. Some things were said he didn't like."

What sorts of things, specifically, I wondered.

Townsend said, "Lies," finished his cigarette, and went back inside.

Zimmick did not remark on Townsend's mood. He said, "They came up with an excuse about how they'd offered our guys those hours before they brought in the temps." He shrugged and continued, "We'll be okay with whatever they come back with."

Zimmick was not a natural politician. He had yet to master the art of feigning sincerity while saying the opposite of what he actually believed. Instead, like a rookie bad liar trying to brazen his way though a line of bullshit on sheer balls, he would just lock eyes with you, as if daring you to call his bluff were proof enough.

Zimmick gave me a hard stare. I didn't say anything. We reentered the lobby.

* * *

The same week of the mediation, it was reported that in 2010, Ford and General Motors had earned $6.6 billion and $4.7 billion respectively. These numbers represented the highest annual profit for either company in more than a decade, an improvement by Ford of 141 percent from the dark days of 2009. Even Chrysler posted a "modified operating profit" of $763 million in 2010.* Overall, a certain conventional wisdom had clearly begun to settle in:

AUTO SHOW 2011: DETROIT CELEBRATES
INDUSTRY'S BIG COMEBACK
(*Detroit Free Press*)

SNYDER HAILS AUTO INDUSTRY'S
REBOUND
(*Detroit News*)

FORD WORKERS' PROFIT-SHARING
CHECKS EXPECTED TO TOP $5,000
(*New York Times*)

DETROIT AUTO SHOW: INDUSTRY
GETTING ITS VA-VA-VA-VOOM BACK
(CNN.com)

As with Wall Street's early "comeback," though, the celebratory tone struck many on the ground as premature and perhaps overly indebted to a definition of "coming back" that focused on corporate profit, which, contrary to the wishful thinking of supply-side economists, was often obtained at the expense of working people—hence the oxymoronic "jobless recovery." In the case of the auto companies, this new profitability had been spurred by a variety of convergent events: gas prices dropping back to normal (i.e., artificially low) levels, Americans feeling comfortable making larger purchases again as recession fears temporarily ebbed, Toyota suffering a public relations disaster after certain of its models turned out to have defective brakes, perhaps even sufficient improvement in the quality of domestic cars and trucks to affect consumer choices.

But there was a telling punditocracy disconnection when it came to Detroit's stark example of the human cost differential between simple corporate profit and more general social welfare. The writer Malcolm

---

*This is a profit modified to not include pension liability, taxes, and interest.

Gladwell, for example, published a thoroughly entertaining takedown of Obama car czar Steven Rattner in the *New Yorker*, using Rattner's own self-serving memoir to dismantle the myth of his outsized role in the heroic rescue of General Motors and Chrysler.* The highlight of the article probably came with Gladwell not only pointing out that Rattner visited Detroit just *once* while overseeing the restructuring of GM and Chrysler, but that he actually bragged about this fact in his memoir.†

And yet, in his gleeful undoing of the myth of Rattner, Gladwell heaped promiscuous praise on ousted GM president Rick Wagoner, who, it's true, seemed indicative of the double standard the Obama administration applied to corporate welfare recipients on Wall Street (who were allowed to keep not only their jobs but their bonuses) and their counterparts in Detroit (Wagoner being "the head that was rotting," in Rattner's words, atop GM's otherwise resuscitable body). Still, Wagoner's "tremendous" (Gladwell's words) accomplishments supposedly included slashing the workforce from 390,000 to 217,000, opening plants in China (GM announced it would be the first of the Big Three automakers to import Chinese-built cars to the United States, beginning in 2011), and renegotiating contracts with the UAW, creating a two-tiered system in which pay for new hires plummeted from between $28 and $33 an hour to between $14 and $17 an hour. Wagoner was also praised for essentially shifting pension obligations related to health care off the books. (Not surprisingly, Wagoner's own pension of $23 million remained untouched after his forced departure.) The loathsome *Wall Street Journal* editorial writer Holman W. Jenkins even applauded Wagoner for his "steady, long-term gamesmanship perhaps unique in the business world"—a "gamesmanship" requiring the fortitude "to wait patiently for a generation of UAW workers and retirees to succumb to their smoking-related

---

*In late 2010, Rattner, a Wall Street private equity investor who specialized in acquiring distressed companies on the cheap and "fixing" them before making a tidy profit on the stock rebound, settled a lawsuit with the state of New York for $10 million following a kickback scandal involving his private equity firm and the state's pension fund.

†"We knew we could function most efficiently by staying put in D.C., yet we realized from the outset that we'd have to make at least one trip to Detroit to avoid more criticism from the heartland. By early March, we could delay no more. All the same, we were determined *not to waste more than a day*" (italics mine).

illnesses so GM could again become a normal company, with something like normal labor economics."

Back in 2009, several months before the bailouts had been
announced, Professor Gary Chaison, a labor specialist at Clark University, had prophetically told me, "What they're calling 'restructuring' really translates into job losses—reducing models, closing plants.
It won't be the auto industry of yesterday. It will be a global industry,
where a very large share of the operations and profits will take place
overseas." So, yes, the companies had made themselves more profit-
able through a process of "reinvention" that, in many cases, involved
simply reducing payroll and cutting the salaries and benefits of union
members lucky enough to have survived the latest round of downsizing. "A lot of the guys I know who got laid off are back to work now,"
Ray Grimble told me. "But they're not making nowhere near what
they had been making. That's how the companies are making their
money now. The middle class is almost gone. A guy can't support his
family at fourteen bucks an hour."

* * *

In 1932, Diego Rivera and Frida Kahlo spent several months in
Detroit living at the Wardell Hotel on Woodward Avenue while
Rivera painted a mural at the Detroit Institute of Arts. Edsel Ford,
Henry's son, at the time the nominal president of Ford Motor Company (though his aging father still pretty much ran things from
behind the scenes), paid Rivera just over $20,000 for the commission.
Rivera and Kahlo arrived in Detroit at the peak of the Great Depression. The automobile industry, booming just a few years earlier, had
been hit particularly hard. Unemployment in Detroit had risen to 50
percent, with two-thirds of the population living below the poverty
line; just a few weeks before the famous international art couple's
arrival, police officers and members of the Ford Company's private
security team had fired on laid-off workers agitating for unemployment compensation outside of the Rouge plant, killing five men.
Nevertheless, Rivera, a Communist, had romantic visions of "the
dawn of a period of new splendors for the [North American] conti-
nent and for mankind," in the words of his biographer Bertram
Wolfe—a "free union of the Americas" wedding "the industrial pro-

letariat of the North with the peasantry of the South . . . the factories of the United States with the raw materials of Latin America . . . the utilitarian aesthetic of the machine with the plastic sense that still inhered in the Amerindian peoples."

After spending weeks having the run of the Rouge and other factories, climbing into turbines and incessantly filling his sketchbooks, Rivera began painting what he would later describe as his greatest work, the *Detroit Industry* murals: twenty-seven separate frescoes on all four walls of the museum's templelike courtyard, depicting both the awesome scale of the modern factory floor and an iconized Marxist fantasia of working-class solidarity and collective toil. For visitors today, the room still feels like a holy space, albeit one filled with imagery more bizarre than even your typical Catholic reliquary. Rivera drew inspiration from creation myth, Aztec statuary, the Mexican *retablo* (painted tin votive art), Soviet propaganda posters, the ceiling of the Sistine Chapel, and Charles Sheeler's photographs of the Rouge (taken one year earlier).

Though the piece is dominated by workers bent like galley slaves over various stations of the assembly line, with the monstrous stamping presses and blast furnaces seething in the background, there's also a creepy fetus (Kahlo had just suffered a miscarriage, the inspiration for her own canvas *Henry Ford Hospital*) and a panel depicting the vaccination of the child Christ (painted to resemble the recently kidnapped Lindbergh baby) and another pair of panels, flanking an entryway like caryatids, depicting, respectively, a brawny high-pressure-boiler operator holding a hammer, his work glove decorated with a red star, and Henry Ford poring over a blueprint.* Local religious leaders, editorial writers, museum patrons, and politicians condemned the perceived revolutionary nature of the artwork, but to his credit, Edsel Ford defended Rivera, and the *Detroit Industry* murals emerged from the controversy intact, unlike Rivera's next major commission, at the Rockefeller Center in New York, which was destroyed after the artist refused to remove a portrait of Lenin from the work.

Rivera's murals remain a favorite stop for Detroit-area schoolchildren on field trips. I must have visited the Rivera Court, as it's called,

---

*At a dinner party, Kahlo mischievously asked Ford if he was Jewish.

many dozens of times. It's the one room in the museum you make sure to pass through on every visit, even if simply to luxuriate in the space for a quick, rejuvenating moment. But somewhat incredibly, the first time I ever really sat and stared at the artwork for longer than ten minutes or so came shortly after I moved back to the city, when one of my favorite singer-songwriters, Vic Chesnutt, performed an evening concert in front of the courtyard's South Wall. Normally, there's no seating in the room, aside from a handful of benches set deep in a few corners, but for Chesnutt's performance, the museum had set up rows of folding chairs, and so during his set, I'd had the opportunity to study the mural for as long as I liked, as I'd never done before. One thing I noticed was that, despite all the manual labor taking place in the frescoes, you couldn't actually see many of the workers' hands, at least not in the foreground of the South Wall, where gloves or heavy machinery or the close-packed bodies of other men almost entirely obscured just about every laborer from the wrist up. Yet on the uppermost panels of the mural, an octet of enormous, bare, disembodied hands hovered over a volcano, clutching at the air and shaking angry fists.

Chesnutt's own hands occasionally drew the eye as well, tugging spasmodically at his baggy pants and inert legs—he had been paralyzed in a car accident decades earlier—or else adjusting a lever on the side of his wheelchair with a frantic repetitiveness that seemed like the effects of an involuntary tick. I'd noticed his hands the last time I'd seen him play, several months earlier, at a Carnegie Hall tribute to his fellow Georgians R.E.M., where he had managed to transform the band's maudlin antisuicide ballad "Everybody Hurts" into something raw and fractured and beautiful, his own vulnerability nakedly on display on the hallowed New York stage. About a month after his performance in Detroit—on Christmas Eve, actually, just over a hundred years to the date from Henry Ford's first successful experiment firing up a motor in his tiny kitchen—I read on Facebook that Chesnutt had taken his life at his home in Athens, Georgia.

Chesnutt's performance was also the first time I'd noticed, in the middle distance of Rivera's South Wall mural, the small group of civilians in street clothes observing the workers from a catwalk, part of some factory tour, which I'd always considered (such tours, that is) a relatively recent construct, but of course in the twenties and thirties

Fordism fascinated the public, and witnessing the bustle of the miniature city that was the Rouge would have been as exciting as a visit,
in more recent years, to Cape Canaveral for a shuttle launch. One of
the tourists, a stern-looking old man in a fedora, broke the fourth wall
of the painting to glare directly at the viewer, one bourgeois spectator
locking eyes with another from opposing shores of a river of working-
men. Only later did I realize he was standing apart from the others,
and that he was actually supposed to be a foreman, which gave his
look a different sort of pointedness. *Is there a reason*, he seemed to be
asking, *why you're not working, too?*

* * *

Ford still offered tours of the Rouge facility, so one afternoon a couple
of days after I met John Zimmick, I drove out to Dearborn and
bought a ticket at the Henry Ford Museum. I was the only one to board
the tour bus when it arrived; likewise, I found myself sitting alone in
the theater where, prior to taking an elevator to the catwalk overlooking the factory floor, visitors watch an informational film about the
Rouge, the so-called First Wonder of the Industrial World, which,
to my surprise, acknowledged the Battle of the Overpass alongside the
expected touting of Henry Ford's canny perfection of vertical integration and the assembly line (though Ford's long-standing and deeply
personal hatred of unions received somewhat of a gloss).* Upstairs, a
video warned us against waving at workers on the factory floor or
otherwise distracting them.

The first thing that struck me about the Rouge, or at least the
Dearborn Truck Facility, the portion of the Rouge we were allowed to
see on the tour, presumably spit-shined for public consumption, was
the lack of chaos, how *orderly* it all seemed, especially compared with
descriptions from the earliest days of the plant (e.g., Ferdinand's futile
struggle in *Journey to the End of the Night* to resist the "furious din" that
"shook the whole building from top to bottom. . . . [I]t's hard to despise
your own substance, you'd like to stop all this, give yourself time to
think about it and listen without difficulty to your heartbeat, but it's too

---

*"Although Henry did not like it at the time, this new partnership of labor and management
would prove to be one of the company's greatest assets."

late for that. This thing can never stop") and the grimy, documentary photographs and films dating from the same era.

From the catwalk, you could peer down onto the open floor and watch each point of the assembly line where workers put together the popular F-150 pickup truck. The colors of the bodies were White Platinum (white), Royal Red (burgundy), and Blue Flame (an almost neon blue). At one part of the line, just the front sections of the trucks, riding on individual palletlike stands called skillets, according to a placard, slowly rolled past a woman in a red sweatshirt, who stuffed something foamy-looking behind the seats, and then past a balding guy wearing a Red Wings T-shirt with a spider tattoo on his left forearm, who screwed in the headlamps using a pneumatic drill hanging from a long air tube, and then past another guy, who sat on a chair at the end of a long, swiveling arm, almost like the arm of an adjustable lamp, only moving sideways, allowing him to slide into the backseat to screw in some part I couldn't quite make out and easily slide back out again all by pushing himself on this cool arm-seat. At least this particular techno-logical advancement seemed like a vast improvement for the workers—actually encouraging employees to sit down on the job!—something you'd assume certain bosses just on principle would deny, perhaps even insisting on having the guy laboriously climb into and out of every backseat, regardless of its cutting into productivity.

Video monitors at various points along the catwalk displayed faces of Ford workers cheerily explaining, in layman's terms, the spe-cifics of the work taking place at the particular station below. Accord-ing to one of the docents on hand, these were actually actors portraying Ford workers. At Windshield Installation, the actor-worker on the video, "Kevin," introduced visitors to Bumper and Blinker, his robot-arm coworkers—or "teammates," as "Kevin" called them—an espe-cially lame attempt to anthropomorphize away the general Rouge tourist's unease at the idea of salt-of-the-earth assembly line employ-ees being displaced by automation, said unease no doubt stirred by the frankly eerie cleanliness and absence of heaving multitudes at what was, after all, supposed to be the First Wonder of the Indus-trial World.

The assembly lines advanced at a strolling pace, just slightly faster than the part of a rollercoaster ride where the cart goes uphill. There were also truck parts dangling on conveyors all around me. Suddenly a shadow would wash over the catwalk, and glancing up, I'd see a truck body pulled along by car-wash-type chains on a track running above my head. The calm banality of the plant seemed unexpectedly peaceful at first, but then I began to feel unsettled by the constant, creeping movement everywhere, which, alongside the natural sounds of the factory, by no means cacophonous, though constant and slightly disorienting—the sharp needling whir of pneumatic drills, the hollow clanking echo of hammered metal, the occasional shrill safety alarm—combined to produce a sense of slow-motion vertigo.

The lines made me think of slow-moving digestive tracts, and the factory as a whole began to remind me of one of those medical school illustrations of the human body in which the skin is removed and you can see all of the body's veins and arteries and internal organs, or else of an ant farm, or else of the "enormous dollhouses, inside which you could see men moving, but hardly moving, as if they were struggling against something impossible," again, Céline, only without the impossible-struggle part. I wondered what the people below me might be doing, if not this, if heavy manufacturing *did* go away. Subsistence farming? Would that be more rewarding? Some kind of service job? I wondered if the original factory tour, the one depicted by Rivera, rather than celebrating a shared myth of American productivity, reveled in porno-graphically watching brute labor.

Unfortunately, pundits and elected officials on both sides of the political spectrum seem to have reached a consensus, most often phrased as, "Those jobs"—meaning, the hundreds of thousands of manufacturing jobs that have disappeared over the past decades—"are never coming back." This verdict is delivered as tough love, a harsh truth akin to the unpleasantness of air travel or the inevitability of death, something accepted by grown-ups as part of life. Market forces, like the weather, can be studied, perhaps even crudely predicted, but to attempt to buck or control the invisible hand would be hubris. You might as well shake your fist at a tornado. Those jobs are gone; they had to leave; *they're never coming back.*

Autoworkers had also appeared in an earlier, rock-video-style film of a F-150 pickup's construction, where a long row of them gave the camera a thumbs-up as the truck breached the figurative birth canal at the end of the assembly line. The Big Three had long used its employees as convenient props, skimping on their pay, health care, and safety whenever possible, yet more than happy to trot them out as a means of humanizing faceless and unpopular megacorporations. Come contract negotiation time, of course, the UAW members became greedy, lazy, fantastically overpaid. But as extras in a Chevy commercial, they were Just Like You, schlubby and hardworking Real Americans making an authentically American product.

* * *

One of the most interesting legacies of Fordism has been its effect on Henry Ford's own idealized notion of labor. As Ford biographer Steven Watts notes, the sort of repetitive, machinelike grunt work being done in plants like the Rouge was largely the opposite of the specialized craftsmanship that so informed Ford's concept of a Protestant work ethic, in which satisfaction in the production of something with one's own hands provided a substantial part of the reward. Now, work required extracurricular compensation, in the form of high wages for the time, yes, but more importantly in the creation of consumer culture, whereby workers could treat themselves after a week of dehumanizing labor by purchasing the very mass-produced crap they and their fellow proletariat had played an otherwise interchangeable role in building.

Fordism, at its outset, drew fervent admirers from the left, though many of today's leftist utopianists would be happy to see the auto plants, if they can't be wholly remade as windmill, high-speed rail, or solar panel factories, just disappear. But "saving" Detroit's traditional economy requires at least a partial embrace of an ethically fraught industry. Urbanists like Craig Ruff may want a Detroit repurposed as "the world's greatest bio-urban hub," but lots of people in the UAW simply want their old jobs back.

This split makes for interesting levels of cognitive dissonance. Along with calling for things like universal health care and a broader social safety net, which would undoubtedly ease the transition from a strong manufacturing base, the pipe dream most often touted by the

sensible liberal policy maker in places like Michigan, at least econom-
ically speaking, is certainly not the Chamber of Commerce–enraging
tariffs supported by people like Zimmick and a handful of outlying
public figures (generally dismissed as fringe) like Dennis Kucinich
but rather a wholesale conversion of the economy away from dirty
industrial jobs. For possible replacements, people look to former manufacturing cities that have successfully reinvented themselves as hubs
of technology (Seattle), higher education and general hipness (Pittsburgh, Portland), and the arts (Glasgow)—sidestepping the fact that
in a state where one adult in three reads below the sixth-grade level,
calls for the "reeducation" of workers to help them adapt to a new
brainiac economy amount to the feeblest of platitudes.

Many of the outsiders who made their way to Detroit in the wake
of the auto industry's near collapse came bearing suggestions of how
the region might replace those jobs that were never coming back.
Newt Gingrich called for stimulating new investment by making the
city of Detroit a tax-free zone. In business circles around town, buzz-
words like "tech incubators" and "entrepreneurial hubs" entered the
lexicon. Experts cited all of the research highlighting the ways in
which diversified local economies thrived, while the single-industry,
large-scale paternalism of old faded away.

Wayne State University's TechTown, funded in part by General
Motors, was meant to stimulate "job growth and small business creation by supporting entrepreneurs and developing companies in
emerging industries including advanced engineering, life sciences and
alternative energy"; likewise, Detroit-based Bizdom U, created by
Quicken Loans founder Dan Gilbert, was an intensive four-month
training and mentorship program designed to foster budding local
entrepreneurs. All good and necessary moves, but still, it remained
tricky to see how the jobs created in these tech hubs would help the
people left behind by the vanishing factories.

In the summer of 2010, a number of Detroit media outlets reported
on another piece of positive economic news. From a column in the
Detroit News:

Tim Bryan took his company to Bangalore, India, in 2002. Now,
he's moving it into the new Third World alternative: Detroit.

At the foot of Woodward, adjacent to Campus Martius, Bryan is steadily hiring information technology professionals to work in GalaxE.Systems Inc.'s new Detroit hub.

The New Jersey–based firm is leasing at least two stories of a 25-story office tower that's otherwise almost vacant—a star-crossed building that in the 1960s was built to be the dazzling headquarters for First Federal Bank of Detroit.

Detroit, though, offers some of the low-cost benefits of doing business in the Third World. The rent at 1001 Woodward Ave.—between $14 and $17 per square foot—is rock-bottom for a major city.

Detroit's labor costs have dropped so far, even for technology workers, that Bryan tells his Fortune 500 clients they'll pay only 5 percent more to work through Detroit than to send their business to Brazil.

The reality is that Bryan flies in one to three days a week to work with 20 employees in a skyscraper originally built for thousands. To Detroit's latest clutch of business visionaries, this is what opportunity looks like.

Bryan was interviewed in outlets all over the city, greeted unanimously with the sort of accolades one would expect to be handed to a man bearing a giant check. By the following spring, he had 110 employees, and a new slogan: "Outsource to Detroit." Detroit's working class had now been so thoroughly pummeled that the city was grateful to be considered competitive with the Third World. This passed for good news in 2010.

* * *

About thirty minutes after the mediation resumed, Zimmick reemerged from the conference room, this time beaming and back in upbeat campaign mode. The ruling had gone in the union's favor. In a compromise, the company had agreed to pay out eight-hour paychecks to the union members who'd been improperly denied the opportunity for Sunday and holiday overtime. Since the union members hadn't worked, they were awarded what Zimmick called "rocking chair" money (meaning straight time, rather than overtime, paychecks), but Zimmick had never really expected overtime pay to begin with. Moreover, the settlement was not precedent-setting, so if the company tried pulling a similar maneuver in the future, he could take the evidence of the first deal straight to an arbitrator, who would almost certainly grant the union a full payout. Victory had put Zimmick in a generous mood. "This was a mistake," he said of the company. "I saw that today. They weren't trying nothing crafty."

I followed Zimmick back to his office, a short drive away. Local 174 was housed in a tan brick building next door to a post office sorting center. Under Reuther, 174 had been the first UAW local to purchase its own building, an Odd Fellows Hall on Maybury Grand Street in Detroit. The local had moved to its current location in 2001. Zimmick took me into the banquet room and showed me a WPA mural, transferred from the old building, celebrating the history of the UAW, including the Battle of the Overpass. There was also a lounge area with billiard tables and a long, curved bar. We pulled up a couple of stools. It was only about four thirty, so the place was empty and the lights were off. Zimmick sat on the very edge of his stool, keeping his feet on the ground, one of his knees bobbing incessantly. He did not remove his leather jacket. A hand remained in his pocket, as if he held a concealed weapon and felt safer with his finger on the trigger, prepared for the first sign of trouble.

Zimmick had not come from a union family. "My ma tended bar," he said. He'd never known his father, sent to jail for smuggling weapons over the Mexico-Arizona border when Zimmick was still an infant. Mostly, he was raised by his grandfather, a cab driver. Zimmick joined the UAW in October 1988, while working as a salt lab operator at Commercial Steel Treating in Madison Heights. "I ran the salt pots," Zimmick explained, unhelpfully, when I inquired about the duties of a salt lab operator. (Subsequent research revealed it has something to do with hardening steel parts in baths of molten salt.) After clashing with management, Zimmick decided to run for shop chairman and won. Then he began clashing with the heads of Local 174, who eventually told him, when he needed a case to go to arbitration, "You don't get to go. You guys don't vote the right way." Zimmick said, "That's the way it's going to be?" He put a team together and learned parliamentary procedure at Wayne State University's Labor Studies program. In 2007, he ran for president of Local 174, narrowly lost, convinced the UAW to overturn the election results because of voting-day shenanigans pulled by the existing leadership, and, after a second vote was held, won handily. Three years later, his entire slate was reelected without opposition.

As we sat at the bar, not drinking, just talking, the light from the outside grew dim and Zimmick's mood seemed to darken concurrently. The high of the afternoon's successful mediation was fading, especially as I probed Zimmick on the current state of his union. "The middle class really is going away, and I don't have the answers for it," he said, sighing. He talked about the need for the labor movement to regroup, to hit the streets, to pressure the political leadership to renegotiate trade agreements, though he admitted no one in Michigan was talking about such things—his only guys, really, were Kucinich in Ohio and Virg Benero, the Democrat who'd run for governor of Michigan and been defeated by Rick Snyder, a millionaire venture capitalist who had previously run Gateway Inc., a company that outsourced thousands of jobs while Snyder served on its board of directors. With membership taking such a massive hit, Zimmick had given himself and all of his officers a 50 percent pay cut. "I could go back to the steel plant and make more money with overtime," he said. He told me stories about laid-off members he knew who'd committed suicide, gone to jail on purpose, become strung out on heroin. The drug business was the only one booming in metropolitan Detroit, he said. Zimmick often spent the night on a cot he kept at the local if he worked late and didn't want to drive all the way back to Madison Heights, where he lived. He said he didn't have many friends.

"We've been beat," Zimmick continued. "Absolutely lost this battle. People talk about the comeback of the auto industry." He snorted. "American *cars*, now that's true. The quality is the best in our lifetime. But the workers aren't feeling it at all. It's called 'lean manufacturing,' and they cut corners everywhere they can. Temps are rampant. People are *used* to having nothing. That's the difference. They're grateful to be temping for eight bucks an hour now. 'Wow, I have a job for the first time in eight years!' It's so sad. There needs to be a wake-up call, or a revolution. But they do it to you gradually, just carve out little pieces over time, so you don't notice. That's how it works in this country." I mentioned the frog in the pot of slowly boiling water,

Abandoned Highland Park police station.

[Yves Marchand and Romain Meffre]

and Zimmick, nodding, added cryptically, "If you have an elephant on a dinner table, you're not going to eat it in one sitting." Correctly reading my silence as confusion, he went on, "You're going to carve it every day, little by little. Until it's gone."

Our talk suddenly felt boozy and confessional. Perhaps the mere act of sitting at a bar long enough naturally brings out such moments, even if there's no alcohol. "Big business, big corporations have just destroyed us," Zimmick told me. He stared at the surface of the bar, like a drunk contemplating another round he couldn't afford. "They won," he said.

9

AUSTERITY 101

No MATTER HOW DEXTROUS or well-intentioned our elected officials, any plan to reinvent Detroit, or even adequately address the city's most fundamental crises, required the one thing Detroit lacked most of all: unimaginable amounts of money. As John Mogk, the Wayne State law professor and urbanist, pointed out, Detroit's major recent success stories have been obtained in large part through spectacular levels of capital investment. "If you reach back to the sixties," he said, the housing development of Lafayette Park "has probably experienced a billion dollars a mile in public and private investment. Midtown"—which includes the university and hospital districts—"in the two miles from the Fox Theater to Grand Boulevard, has probably experienced a billion a mile over the past ten years."

Mogk contrasted this healthy area of Detroit, which he calls the Core, with the other 130 square miles of the city, which he calls the Heartland—historically the strength of Detroit, a city never known for its downtown as much as for its industrial plants, strong neighborhoods, and high levels of home ownership. The Heartland, Mogk noted, has been steadily deteriorating. "And that's where all the problems are," he says. "And the only part of that whole area that's received anything commensurate with the level of investment in the Core area has been the Poletown Plant and the Chrysler Jefferson Plant. So, as Core Detroit becomes more closely linked with the suburbs, Heartland

Detroit is drifting off on its own. To focus on what's happening in the Core area really creates a false sense of future hope. If you look at the income distribution in the city and ask me if the Heartland is coming back, well, are you kidding me? Cities are not built or rebuilt for low-income residents. It would be nice if they were. But that just doesn't happen."

As municipalities across the globe stare down varying levels of financial catastrophe, the notion of increasing investment in failing communities such as the Mogk-defined Heartland has become folly, with the terms of debate instead shifting almost entirely to discussions of debt reduction and austerity. The received, morality-tale version of the salvation of the auto industry, often recounted in the form of a self-help recovery narrative, in which the mulish executive-suite occupants were forced to hit rock bottom before making the "hard choices" necessary for survival, has more recently been applied to ever more insolvent governmental entities, which have been painted as the functional and moral equivalents of GM or Chrysler, that is, bloated and inefficient bureaucracies unwilling to change with the times, get tough on labor, and become "lean" and "competitive." Like the Big Three, we were all being told that our cities and states—along with their citizens and public servants—needed to discard childish illusion and accept that aspects of American life had changed forever.

In this context, the Michigan legislature adopted the Emergency Financial Manager law, which deficit hawks cast as a top-down, stern-father means of enforced frugality, necessary for irresponsible charges who had proved incapable of making, and abiding by, a budget. The fact that most of the cities facing possible EFMs were, like Detroit, contending with all of the problems associated with concentrated poverty (including the absence of any sort of real tax base) tended to be glossed over, though it was hard to see how any of this could end well: cities like Detroit already barely delivered on the most minimal of public services, and the idea of forcing even more cuts, somehow rooting out "waste" in the system, moved beyond the vague shared-sacrifice campaign slogans employed by politicians across the spectrum and began to enter the realm of field amputation.

For those who wish to observe the effects of austerity measures taken to their natural extreme, one local Galapagos-scaled ecosystem worth studying is Highland Park. Located about six miles from downtown, Highland Park is technically not part of Detroit at all but its own separate municipality. (Though one surrounded on all sides by Detroit, so central on a map of the city it practically marks a bull's-eye.) In the aftermath of the Great Fire of 1805, the federal government had given Michigan territorial officials permission to sell state property in order to fund the rebuilding of Detroit. Part of the unloaded land, a patch of mostly swamp, passed through the hands of a series of developers who hoped to turn the place into a viable township. As developers are wont, they seized upon one of the most appealing aspects of the local landscape—the few hills punctuating the marsh—to come up with the prototypically suburban name of Highland Park.*

One of the would-be developers was Judge Augustus Woodward, who proposed naming the village Woodwardville. But his plans didn't go anywhere, and nothing much happened with Highland Park until Captain Will H. Stevens, a one-eyed veteran and former Colorado prospector, managed to get the swamp drained, making the land inhabitable, if not yet desirable. When Henry Ford relocated to Highland Park in 1906 to radically expand his production capability, the area surrounding his new factory was predominantly farmland. There were also modest shoe and wagon factories, a general store, and a blacksmith's. The site of Ford's world-changing Model T plant had once been a hotel resort and spa, with mineral baths and a neighboring harness racing track. In 1910, the year the factory opened, the population of Highland Park was 425. By the following year, it had grown to 4,120, and by the end of the decade, it had become 46,000.† Highland Park

---

*The plot was eventually leveled when development truly got under way, so today the area is no higher than anywhere else in Detroit.

†In Highland Park, Ford not only perfected his notion of the assembly line—the number of Model T's produced annually at the plant soared from 82,000 to two million in the course of a decade—but also announced the doubling of his workers' daily wages to an unheard of five dollars. John Reed, the radical journalist and future author of *Ten Days That Shook the World*, wrote after his visit to Highland Park, "The Ford car is a wonderful thing, but the Ford plant is a miracle. Hundreds of parts, made in vast quantities at incredible speed, flow toward one point. The final assembly is the most miraculous thing of all." In Aldous Huxley's *Brave New World*, Year Zero of the AF (After Ford) calendar aligns with the year the first Model T rolled off the Highland Park assembly line. "Like the New Testament story of the loaves and fishes," writes Ford biographer Steven Watts, "Ford seemed to be creating material sustenance for thousands of people by a superhuman process. His fellow citizens responded with a kind of worship. . . ."

resisted annexation by Detroit at the behest of Ford, the city's largest corporate citizen, as part of a blatant tax dodge. The tiny Polish enclave of Hamtramck, also surrounded by Detroit, pulled a similar move around the same time to create a tax haven for its Dodge plant, robbing Detroit, even in those boomtown years, of revenues from two of its most productive factories.

As recently as the fifties, Highland Park, called the City of Trees, boasted one of the area's most desirable addresses. Even after Ford decided he needed more space for his manufacturing operation and decamped to the Rouge plant, the city remained the world headquarters of Chrysler, founded in Highland Park in 1925.

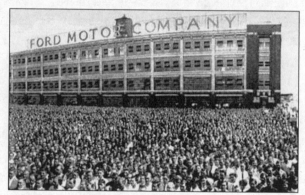

Ford's Highland Park plant, ca. 1920

By the early nineties, though, Chrysler chair Lee Iacocca had announced that the company would be moving to Auburn Hills, some fifty miles north of the city. With the departure of those final five thousand Chrysler employees, Highland Park lost a quarter of its tax base and 80 percent of its annual budget. Having spurned Detroit's advances during Ford's heyday, Highland Park now stood abandoned by its onetime corporate suitors for younger, prettier suburbs. There was occasionally talk of Detroit absorbing Highland Park, but that was just wishful thinking, Detroit at this point having zero interest in adding more crime, blight, and desperately poor people to its own mean buffet of urban pathologies.

Today, driving north on Woodward Avenue, you'd never notice having crossed from one city to the other. You pass a combination fish market and takeout restaurant ("U Buy, We Fry"), and the Gold Nugget Pawn Shop, and Mo' Money Tax Returns, and a Babes N Braids, and a place called Cherokee's Hot Spot where you can get your ears or nose pierced or pick up some exotic dance wear ("Plus Sizes Available," notes a sign in the window), alongside numerous other long-shuttered apartment complexes, municipal buildings, and storefronts (including the rubble of a florist).

Yet Highland Park, officially the poorest city in Michigan, manages to tidily pack all of the problems of Detroit into just three square miles. In fact, fantastic as it might seem, the city is actually in much worse shape than Detroit proper, the one place Detroiters can gaze upon and say, "Man, *those* guys are fucked!" One afternoon, wandering around Highland Park, I must have accidentally stepped back over the border, because when I asked an older gentleman raking his lawn about Highland Park's city services, he appeared deeply offended. "This is *Detroit*," he snapped. "I don't know anything about Highland Park. I don't go over there." We were two blocks away.

In other words, Highland Park is the Detroit of Detroit. In 2011, the Bing administration floated the possibility of closing eighteen of the city's twenty-three public library branches; Highland Park's entire library system has been closed since 2002. Detroit has shed more than half its population since the 1950s; Highland Park, over the same period, has lost four-fifths of its citizens. In Detroit, the streetlights are notoriously spotty, and there has been discussion of reducing their number by nearly half; Highland Park owed so much money to the electric company that it agreed to entirely decommission all lights on residential streets—which meant not only switching them off but physically removing the posts. (Residents have been asked by city officials to leave on their own porch lights as crime-prevention measures.) Detroit's police force remains woefully understaffed; Highland Park fired its entire police department in 2001, outsourcing patrols to the Wayne County Sheriff's Department. Since its revival in 2007, the Highland Park PD has been headquartered in a ministation at a strip mall, where the jail is a makeshift chain-link cage.

When I visited the Reverend David Bullock, head of the Highland Park chapter of the NAACP and pastor of Greater St. Matthew Baptist Church, he told me, "I always say to people, 'You want to see what Detroit's going to look like when the auto industry leaves? Come to Highland Park.' It's Detroit writ small."

* * *

One day, my brother Paul called to tell me about one of his coworkers at Children's Village, the juvenile detention center where he worked as a therapist. This particular colleague, Marvin Vaughn, held a staff position; his duties ranged from moderating group activities to restraining kids who became violent. The name Children's Village took on a more sinister shading when you realized certain of the villagers had been accused of stomping random homeless guys to death or shooting people during violent carjackings. (Paul wasn't allowed to talk about his clients, but the highest-profile cases always turned up in the papers.) Marvin, meanwhile, had a second job, in Highland Park, where, in addition to his full-time position at Children's Village, he moonlighted another thirty hours each week as a firefighter.

Marvin would often drive straight from Children's Village to Highland Park and spend the night at the firehouse. (Those overnight hours were billable, which was how he managed to work seventy-hour weeks.) Per capita, Highland Park had an insanely busy engine house, averaging 150 fires each year: apartments, party stores, vacant homes, most probably arson, though this was always tricky to prove. When Paul told Marvin about my book, he suggested I swing by on Angel's Night.

I headed over to Highland Park around eight. It was unseasonably humid for a late October evening, nearly seventy degrees. On Oakland Avenue, I passed a couple of citizen patrollers in a gray Cadillac creeping along in the left lane at well below the speed limit. A yellow light, the sort an undercover detective in a seventies cop show would attach to his unmarked car if he needed to give sudden chase, flashed from their roof, its languid blink rate having seemingly been set to match the speed of the vehicle. It looked like the lead car in a funeral procession, if everyone else who might've attended the funeral had also met unexpected and horrible ends.

Marvin had given me directions to the firehouse earlier in the day, but we'd had a bad phone connection and I assumed I'd misheard the address, because the only thing in the vicinity appeared to be an industrial park of cheap prefabricated warehouses. After circling for twenty minutes, I finally called Marvin back, and he told me to drive into the park, the former site of Chrysler's world headquarters. Following a circuitous road past nondescript auto-parts factories (Magna Seating, Johnson Controls), I reached the edge of a cracked, weed-strewn parking lot, where I spotted a tiny blue sign reading Fire Department. On the far side of the lot, bordering a set of train tracks, an unmarked warehouse building stood, so anonymous and isolated you'd think it housed toxic waste material or a fleet of garbage trucks. A tall, full-figured guy wearing a Highland Park Fire Department sweatshirt emerged from a side door and waved me over.

You could see how Marvin's size would intimidate a misbehaving juvenile offender, but everything else about him exuded a laidback, almost goofy affability. Marvin had grown up quite poor in Picayune, Mississippi, before his dad, following a well-trod African American migratory pattern, landed a job with Pontiac and moved the family to the metropolitan Detroit city of the same name. Marvin was in his midthirties, married, no kids yet, though his wife wanted some. There was a throat-clearing quality to his way of speaking that made it sound like at any moment he might suddenly burst into a raspy chuckle, and his voice darted up a couple of octaves whenever he became excited. Tonight, he wore a pair of thick-armed glasses that looked like they should be tinted. He also had a single patch of gray hair near the middle of his head, about the size of a large birthmark.

A dirty secret of union towns like Detroit was how the historic battle for fair overtime pay, combined with the shrinking of benefits and real wages, had resulted in the strange phenomenon whereby, in the midst of deliriously high unemployment, the lucky people who'd somehow managed to hang on to their jobs might actually wind up overemployed, either via copious overtime—this worked out well for management, as overtime remained cheaper than covering the benefits of an entirely new hire—or, as in Marvin's case, snagging second, lower-paying jobs, simply to maintain something approaching the middle-class lifestyle to which they'd grown accustomed.

Marvin led me around back, through the wide-open bay doors. The Highland Park Fire Department, it turned out, was being housed—stored?—inside a warehouse. Marvin explained that the department's poorly maintained former headquarters had been declared an environmental hazard by OSHA, so they'd come to occupy this temporary location. That was six years ago. Past a row of aged fire trucks, a white McDonald Modular Solutions trailer had been set up as an office. In front of it, an old stuffed couch and a pair of recliners, all scavenged from various curbs by the firefighters, had been arranged around a television set. A rack of oxygen tanks lined one of the walls like bottles of wine. Next to the trucks, the rest of the uniforms stood at the ready: boots on the ground, with thick, flame-retardant pants and suspenders already attached, so the firefighters could step right into their pant legs and yank up their suspenders with a single motion. The prepared uniforms drooped down over the boots like melted fireman candles.

Firefighters milled in the dim light, chatting and eating. The ceiling of the warehouse rose nearly two floors above us. In a distant corner, I could make out a gym consisting of free weights and benches people had brought from home or picked up at garage sales. It had been a quiet night so far. Nearby, a blue plastic barrel with a handwritten sign taped to it read

POP
CAN$

Beverage cans in Michigan were returnable for deposits.

The firefighters had actually been evicted from their old firehouse while Highland Park's finances were being controlled by the state of Michigan, under the auspices of an emergency manager. Rather than bring the old firehouse up to code or build a new one, the city had been paying several thousand dollars per month to heat the cavernous space each subsequent winter. Thanks to a proposal written by one of the department's junior firefighters—on his own time and initiative, with no grant-writing training*—Highland Park received a $2.6 million federal FEMA grant for a new building. But after two years, the grant money still hadn't been spent. Officials blamed the historic designation of the old firehouse, which made it difficult to tear down, though sources inside the department ascribed the delay to political infighting and shadier efforts to funnel the grant money to other city projects. Questions have also been raised about the way in which the architectural firm that contracted to design the new firehouse won its bid.

In the meantime, the firefighters had made do. "We call this the Village," Marvin said, leading me to the back of the warehouse. "One guy came up with this idea, because the trailer doesn't hold us all." In a dark corner, the firefighters had nailed together planks of raw plywood, constructing a multilevel warren of individual cells, a cross between a children's box fort and the sort of slapdash partition undergraduate roommates might throw up in a dorm. They'd built twenty-six rooms in all; a Jolly Roger flag hung from the roof. Two of the firefighters, apparently preferring al fresco accommodations, slept in tents. Marvin pushed open the door to his room.

"It's small, but everyone's got their own humble abode," he said. The space was about the size of a large walk-in closet, with barely enough room for a twin bed and a television set. A framed photograph of a fierce-looking house fire hung next to the TV.

"Were you there?" I asked.

Marvin nodded and said, "It's the fire devil holding on to the house—see it?" He stabbed the flames jutting from the roof with a thick finger. Sure enough, they resembled a cartoonish demon's head, and you could even flesh out the pair of fiery arms reaching down to hug either wall of the place. "It's not cropped or anything," Marvin said.

---

*Beyond some assistance from his sister, a high school English teacher in rural Clio, who helped edit the narrative portion of the proposal.

Marvin had started out as a firefighter in Pontiac. "Before that, I was a junior engineer," he said. "Sucked! I tried nursing. Sucked! I said, 'I need something exciting.'" Eventually, a friend told him, "You want to see some real fires? Come down to Highland Park." At the time, Republican governor John Engler had just modified the residency rules in Michigan, allowing city workers to live outside the community employing them, so Marvin was able to transfer to Highland Park without moving there. None of the Highland Park firefighters I met actually lived in the city, except when they slept at the warehouse.

An average night found eight firefighters on duty. Normally, this level of staffing would be more than adequate for a city of Highland Park's size. But considering the firehouse often saw multiple structure blazes over the course of a single evening, the place eked out its defensive duties with an absurdly skeletal crew. One of Marvin's lieutenants, Eric Hollowell, told me about a time when eleven houses burned in one night. Hollowell's entire seven-person unit—one of the eight firefighters on duty must always remain behind to answer incoming calls—had been in the midst of combating the first three fires, a trio of neighboring houses, when they got word of several more fires breaking out at the opposite end of the block, forcing Hollowell to split up his already overstretched crew. (Normal procedure would call for three trucks—about fifteen people—when responding to a single residential fire.) Not long after that, a resident approached Hollowell at the scene and informed him of another abandoned house that had caught fire, on the next block over. Hollowell had to let that one free-burn for an hour. He couldn't spare any more guys.

One of the fire trucks came from Texas, used; another, also used, from Arizona or Georgia, no one could remember which. All were ancient by fire engine standards, twenty years old, leaky. One had a five-hundred-gallon tank that, by the end of an average night, would lose three-fifths of its water; another's ladder, so rickety, had everyone afraid to climb it.

"You know how we communicate at fire scenes?" Hollowell asked me.

A part-timer named Chuck, sitting nearby, glanced up and muttered, "You telling him everything?"

Hollowell continued, "We only have three radios. We communicate by voice. Once people are inside a building, I have no way to know if they're okay. Chuck is driving our main truck and he doesn't have a radio. If people are called to another scene, he can't communicate."

Chuck, nodding glumly, admitted, "It's like in baseball: all hand signals."

Then he did an imitation of a catcher flashing dispatches to the mound.

* * *

Angel's Night had been slow, so Marvin invited me to come back to the station on another occasion. Even by Highland Park standards, the week of my return had been a rough one. A two-hundred-unit apartment complex had burned several days earlier, one of the residents dying after leaping from a second-story window. "Definitely arson," a firefighter who wished to remain anonymous told me. "Either an insurance job or some kind of retaliation."

When I showed up, several of the men had arranged their folding chairs in the mouth of the bay doors, facing the train tracks. They all looked crispy and adrenaline-deprived. Even Marvin, outwardly jovial as ever, had exhausted, vacant eyes. The night before, there had been only two fires, but afterwards, Marvin hadn't been able to fall back asleep. "Every time gas prices drop, we see an increase in fires," he noted. A Bluetooth device blinked from one of his ears. He delivered the line matter-of-factly, like an observational comic doing a bit about airplane food.

Hollowell sat nearby, chain-smoking and drinking coffee from a thermos. A trim black man with a cleanly shaved head and a wispy mustache, he wore a blue Highland Park Fire Department polo shirt tucked into dark slacks. Hollowell was thirty-seven. He'd grown up in Highland Park, just a few blocks from the warehouse; so few houses remained on Hollowell's old street, one of his coworkers told me, "I call that block We Lost It." Hollowell's mother had been a teacher at Highland Park High. His father died when Hollowell was only ten years old. An electrician, he'd been doing work in a friend's basement as a favor and stepped into a puddle of water, not realizing someone had cut the power back on.

Hollowell had always thought being a cop would be a cool job, that or the military, and began working as a cadet-in-training at the police department when he was fifteen. By the time he turned twenty-one, he'd already seen close to thirty homicides. The job started to get to him. He'd been fired upon by people openly selling drugs from their porches, and he took to strapping on his gun before going out to cut the lawn.

"Actually, if I was outside at all," he emended. "I could be sitting on my porch and I'd have a gun on the table next to me with a rag over it. The city was riddled with dope."

Hollowell related all of the above in a muted deadpan. I'd be tempted to describe his affect as hard-boiled if not for his habit of coaxing reactions from his listener by pulling some manner of exaggerated face.

A train flew by. Hollowell lifted his hand and waved at the conductor. He told me he'd transferred to the engine house as soon as word of an opening came down.

Hollowell's colleague Sergeant Nate Irwin wandered outside and planted himself in another chair, bringing his cigarette and coffee mug. Hollowell told Irwin about my book.

Irwin gave me an appraising look. "You going fiction or nonfiction?" he asked.

Non, I said.

He snorted. "No one's gonna believe it."

Hollowell and Irwin could be characters in an eighties Hollywood buddy movie about firemen. Irwin, a thirty-two-year-old white guy, had grown up in Royal Oak, which, back when I was a kid, had been the "hip" suburb (record stores, vintage shops, a bondage outfitter). His head, shaved cleaner than a brush cut, retained a sandpapery stubble, and Irwin clearly derived therapeutic pleasure from pensively rubbing it while discussing the particular hardships of his career path. Having worked in Highland Park for over ten years, he'd armored himself with a jaded air similar to Hollowell's.

"How did I end up here?" he asked. "Well, you watch the news." He meant that, like Marvin, he'd been drawn by the action. "And then," he said, lighting another cigarette, "after a few years, you can't leave, for multiple reasons: (a) you don't want to, and (b) no one will take you." The reason for (b), oddly enough, had to do with the amount of field action one quickly accumulated in a place like Highland Park: a captain at a suburban department, who might see a handful of fires each year, wouldn't necessarily be eager to hire a young guy with so much more experience.

Highland Park and Detroit get so many fires, of such spectacular variety, that firefighters from around the country—Boston, Compton, Washington, D.C.—make pilgrimages here. Some monitor the police scanners and just turn up at the scene, snapping photos and shooting video. A decent enough photograph might make the pages of one of the trade (*Fire Chief* or *Firehouse*), where a cover shot could fetch a thousand bucks. "We're YouTube legends now," Irwin noted wryly. One firefighter from the Bronx visited twice every year. He'd told the Highland Park guys the Bronx had become boring. Most of their buildings were occupied now, and it just wasn't popping like in the old days.

The sky had turned a mauve color. On the service road of the industrial park, a stream of cars began to depart; a late shift at one of the parts shops must have ended. From inside the warehouse, we could hear the echo of a television commercial for Liberty Mutual Insurance. *What's your policy?* the announcer asked. A slight, pleasant breeze stirred up.

"It's probably something free-burning somewhere, sucking up all the oxygen," Hollowell said.

A firefighter named Chaplain sat nearby, occasionally answering a phone and taking notes on a pad. I hadn't paid much attention to him until I realized he was talking to someone who seemed to be requesting an ambulance. Hollowell noticed the curious look on my face and said, "This is our 911." He meant that Chaplain—a lone guy sitting in a folding chair answering a phone—was the 911 operator for the entire city of Highland Park. When the call was completed, Hollowell said, "Chaplain, who have you got tonight waiting for the EMS?" Chaplain looked at his pad and said, "Two strokes, a heart attack, a guy who fell and cracked his head open." He said the first call had come at 5:56 p.m. and none had received EMS attention yet. I looked at my watch. It was after eight.

The city of Highland Park did not own an ambulance and had only one EMS truck. Many of the calls Chaplain had been fielding were repeat calls from people asking when the medics would arrive.

With the exception of Hollowell and Irwin, the other firefighters sitting out there—the diminutive, shaved-headed white guy who talked about his impoverished childhood, how when his mom got remarried, the family finally had enough money to buy Kool-Aid; the ripped Iraq vet, with tattoos of a machine gun and Arabic script running up and down his arms, who used to live in Detroit, but had moved across 8 Mile, to suburban Ferndale, "just to get city services," he said, adding, "I mean, my fiancée is pretty tough. She can handle herself. But if you get someone on your front lawn acting crazy and you have to shoot 'em, that's no good"—all of these guys were being paid ten dollars an hour. Cops in Highland Park started at eight. Irwin and Hollowell both liked to use this fact to wind up their right-leaning chief, especially when it came to conservative demagoguing on the supposed overcompensation of the public workforce.*

"Unions, I mean, what's left?" Irwin asked. "The trades? None of those guys even have *jobs*. The only unions left are the ones they can't break: public safety, UAW, Teamsters, teachers."

Public safety officers in Highland Park were no longer unionized, which was how the city got away with compensating the cops and firefighters so pathetically. As with corporate structured bankruptcies, the city had been able to break its existing union contracts when, facing a $6.5 million deficit, the first emergency financial manager, Ramona Henderson-Pearson, took over the city's finances in 2001. A disastrous attempt by Henderson-Pearson and then-mayor Titus McClary to build a new suburban-style development within Highland Park was later investigated by the FBI.† Henderson-Pearson's

---

*The first time I visited the Highland Park engine house, they'd just had a benefit for a part-time firefighter who almost died when he'd been overwhelmed by flames while putting out a fire in a vacant house. "His hands, for all practical purposes, are gone," one of his colleagues told me. "That's for a guy who makes ten bucks an hour, no benefits."

†The neighborhood, called North Pointe Village, remains one of the eeriest in Highland Park, a miniature ghost town composed of 150 brand-new two-floor colonials with cheap-looking gray siding, most standing vacant and gutted, some partially burned. The majority of the homes had never even been occupied. They were so cheaply built, their basements almost immediately began leaking ground and sewage water, and certificates of occupancy couldn't be issued by the

successor, Arthur Blackwell II, was convicted of illegally paying himself a salary of close to $300,000 while serving as manager. Blackwell's successor, Robert Mason, was not convicted of any wrongdoing—though, to be fair to his predecessors, he served only for three months.

✳ ✳ ✳

Why were there so many fires in Highland Park? The high number of vacant houses, along with squatters and legitimate residents who pilfered electricity via jerry-rigged, easily combustible wiring jobs, pushed up the count, for sure. But Irwin considered most of their runs the result of arson. You could quick-claim a deed to a house in Highland Park for a thousand dollars and insure it for eighty thousand. If the house burned a month later, suspicious or not, it would be one fire among many, and best of luck proving anything, because until recently Highland Park had no fire inspector. Irwin had paid out of pocket to take investigatory courses at the fire academy. He'd also bought his own equipment.

Hollowell said, "Mark, he probably doesn't want to tell you this, but I'm going to: getting a license on your own like that is totally unheard of. Up until this point, fires were just not investigated in this city, at all."

Irwin, seeming embarrassed by the attention, leaned down to adjust the volume of a walkie-talkie next to his chair. "I have a hard time sitting around," he murmured. "I was just looking to do stuff."

"For fifteen years here, the fires have gone completely unchecked," Hollowell went on. "The city played games as if they were being investigated, but they didn't really do anything." Hollowell was convinced that the eleven-fire night hadn't been a fluke, that one of the arsonists had started the latter fires to taunt the firefighters.

Irwin, who was sitting with his legs crossed and black boots unzipped, finally warmed to the topic. "Investigating sucks," he said.

---

city. The developer sued the building contractor, who filed for bankruptcy; a group of backers in California who'd bought the homes as investment properties in turn sued the developer, who also filed for bankruptcy.

"Only 1 to 2 percent of arson cases end in prosecution, nationally. It's so difficult to prove. You're looking at all circumstantial facts. Before you even get into court, the DA is going to try to prove you're not qualified." He smiled. "The good thing about Highland Park is, that's hard to do, because we have lots of experience. But basically, if you can lie you can get away with arson. You know the foam in furniture, like a couch from Ikea, is made of low-grade petroleum. So if you can put your space heater next to your couch, it's as good as or better than gasoline. And I can't prove it was intentional. You'd pass a lie detector test. Not that I have a polygraph machine. Nor am I allowed to interrogate people. But every single case I get has accelerants, so there's not a problem proving incendiary. The problem is proving who did it. So I just keep trying and trying, hoping to find a fingerprint on a gas can one day." He smiled ruefully at his own Willy Loman impression. After a moment, the smile vanished and he added, "It gets depressing."

* * *

Another night, after most of the firefighters had drifted off to the Village, I was left alone to doze off in front of the television. A young firefighter I'd never seen before lay sprawled on the striped couch closest to the fan. I wondered why he hadn't gone to his room, and then we started chatting and I found out he was a volunteer. Having recently completed his fire training, the guy—I'll call him Donnie—was looking for a job, and so a few times a month he'd work a shift as a volunteer, hoping to make his presence known and increase his likelihood of being hired if a paying position opened up. I hadn't realized you could work an unpaid internship at a job requiring you to risk your life.

Donnie kept turning his head to one side when he talked to me, finally revealing that he was partly deaf in his left ear, on account of being carjacked. He said he'd been very stupid: he'd stopped for gas after dark. (In certain parts of Detroit, this qualified as "asking for it.") He'd seen the carjackers approaching and hadn't tried to resist, but one of the guys pistol-whipped him anyway and the gun had gone off near his ear, permanently damaging his hearing.

Donnie also told me that he was taking classes at Wayne State, that he thought Medicaid should fund abortions and that people on welfare shouldn't be allowed to have kids.

I said, "Huh."

Donnie said, "I might sound like an extremist, but that's the way I feel." Then he complained about how the downtown riverwalk, late at night, had become rowdy—how there were too many "ethnic" people there, if I knew what he meant. I was pretty sure he meant black people. If it had been another white guy saying this to me, I would have felt obligated to keep my face very still and not seem like I was agreeing with any racist insinuations. In the case of Donnie, though, I nodded ambiguously, almost imperceptibly, in a way that might lead one to believe I'd merely started to nod off, considering the lateness of the hour.

* * *

Hollowell told me I could ride along with him if a call came in. One evening, close to midnight, the alarm sounded. This time, I was alone on the couch, reading. Then I blinked and everyone was wide awake and suited up. Marvin, on dispatch, took the call. His voice came over an intercom, sounding disconcertingly serious.

"All apparatus respond to 40 Pasadena house fire," he said. "Police department is on the scene."

Irwin frowned. There'd been a fire on Pasadena the night before, directly across the street. Irwin thought someone must have gotten the address wrong—that, surely, the same house must have lit up again.

Hollowell and I climbed into his engine. "Sounds like a good fire," he said. Oxygen tanks set into the front seats forced me to sit forward in an awkward manner. The instrument panel was covered in dust and looked very old, like technology from another era. Different buttons that could light up read "Left Scene Light," "Right Scene Light," and "Retarder Applied." An axe with a yellow handle leaned between our seats like a manual gear shift.

Blasting his siren, Hollowell raced to Oakland, leading a three-truck convoy. We took a dramatically wide turn onto Woodward, hurtling down the center of the street, and I felt a boyish thrill. Hollowell had a sober look on his face.

When we turned onto Pasadena, I could see flames strobing from the porch of a brick duplex. As we got closer, though, it became clear that the home itself wasn't ablaze. Someone living inside had, inexplicably, started a fire in an oil drum on the covered porch—a wooden porch, so doubly foolish. The flames were practically tickling the underside of the eaves. Still, it wasn't a three-alarm call. As we exited the fire truck, one of the police officers, a blond woman, approached Hollowell apologetically. "When we rolled up, there were flames all the way up to the roof," she insisted.

The man who'd started the fire, wiry, in a white undershirt, appeared inebriated. He insisted he'd been burning wood to keep away bugs. When the police officers ordered him to extinguish the fire, he'd disappeared into the house, emerging with a single ice cube tray sloppily filled with water. Hollowell asked the man for his name. He grimaced and said, "She took it," nodding dismissively at one of the officers, before retreating inside to fetch more water.

The other firefighters were already beginning to climb back into their trucks. I looked across the street at the remains of the previous night's fire: a decent-sized brick home, its arched roof now partially collapsed.

Back in the truck, Hollowell grumbled about having been summoned for such a nonsense run. "The address on the guy's license was in Detroit—Burn Street!" he said, appreciating the irony on some level but not laughing. On the way back to the warehouse, we passed an old firehouse on Stordivan dating back from when Highland Park had three stations. That particular station place had been shut years ago and since horribly burned. Hollowell said the fire had happened when a man from Inkster who'd murdered his mother had carried her corpse to the empty station and torched it.

At the warehouse, Irwin said he thought there might be a connection between that night's episode and the fire across the street. But Hollowell shook his head. "I think that guy was just stupid. And high. He'll start up that porch fire again as soon as the police leave."

Hollowell's mood had soured. A few years ago, he'd moved out of Highland Park to a suburb north of 26 Mile. When I asked him what could be done with the city, he gave me a look and said, "Honestly? Level it. Tear it down and start over."

Marvin came out of his room to hear about the nonfire. When

they told him the guy said he had just been trying to keep away bugs, Marvin said, "Well, in Picayune, Mississippi, you *do* burn wood to keep away the bugs."

"This isn't Picayune, Mississippi," Hollowell said.

Marvin said, "No, it's not."

The family of murder victim David Morgan Jr., posing with his photograph before the trial of his alleged killers. [Patricia Beck/ *Detroit Free Press*]

10

MURDER CITY
Or, Just an Everyday Activity in Detroit

Years ago, while idly researching what I thought might evolve into notes on a novel about the city, I'd come across the story of an Italian immigrant named Benjamino Evangelista. Like my own family, he'd arrived in the United States around the turn of the last century (1904), not settling straightaway in Detroit but initially on the Eastern Seaboard (Philadelphia, in Evangelista's case), where Italians had already begun to cluster. He was nineteen and Neapolitan; he worked for the railroad, and later as a carpenter, and by the early twenties had made his way to Detroit, capitalizing on the city's boomtown status by expanding his own enterprises, first into home construction and then real estate.

But he also had a healthy side concern going as a religious prophet. Evangelista had been having visions for decades and became convinced he'd been chosen to reveal a complex plan. He began transcribing the things God told him in 1906 and eventually self-published the prophecy, which he titled, fantastically, *The Oldest History of the World, Discovered by Occult Science in Detroit, Michigan*. The book opens with a strangely nonchalant gloss on Genesis:

> Before the creation of God there existed nothing but air and water.
> Today we find land, men, animals, etc.

It's not clear if Evangelista was a madman or a scam artist, or some combination of both; as a writer of prose, though, he did not make the most graceful conduit for occult science, and much of *The Oldest History* is a slog, even by the standards of crackpot mythology.* The book was the first of an intended four volumes. By the time of its publication, Evangelista had changed his name to Benny Evangelist and begun to develop a reputation as a healer, fortune-teller, and local eccentric. Both his family physician and parish priest—he still attended mass and kept Roman Catholic iconography in his home—described Evangelist as insane, though the priest also suspected that the cult was likely a moneymaking ruse and that Evangelist, whom he described as close to illiterate, could not possibly have written *The Oldest History*.

On the morning of July 2, 1929, a colleague of Evangelist's named Vincent Elias stopped by the two-story frame home of the prophet to discuss some real estate business. There he discovered the bodies of Evangelist, his wife, Santina, and their four children, ages seven (Angeline), five (Margaret), four (Jean), and eighteen months (Mario). All had been stabbed or hacked to death. One of the children's arms was cut off at the shoulder. Santina Evangelista's head had been "horribly mutilated and nearly severed from the body," according to the *Detroit Free Press*. "The murderer worked with demoniac frenzy." Evangelist's body was discovered in his home office, slumped in a chair. His head lay at his feet.

Positing the killing might have "been actuated by religious mania," the *Free Press* writer portrayed Evangelist as a shadowy figure, the "'divine prophet' of a mysterious religious cult." The article continued, luridly, "Behind the tragedy was a grotesque background of religious insanity paralleling in its weirdness and barbarism any voodoo fetish of the West Indies":

> In a dingy, but electrically lighted room of the basement, the "prophet" had set up one of the weirdest "altars" ever uncovered in Detroit.

---

*A (trust me) representative passage: "Itol took his people to his temple and he said: 'Pray to our Bailan to save us.' But Bailan could not repair the damage of God. The temple was struck with lightning. One stroke of lightning hit Trampol and he dropped dead. When Itol saw his son he tried to help him, but he was already dead. Itol also was struck with lightning and died. The temple was mashed to pieces and the people killed."

Eight or ten wax figures, each hideous and grotesque to the extreme, and each presumably representing one of the "celestial planets," were suspended on the altar in a circle by wires from the ceiling. Among them was a huge eye, electrically lighted from the inside, which Evangelist referred to in his bible as "the sun."

The walls and ceiling of this "religious sanctum" were lined with light green cloth, which bulged out in places like the walls of a padded cell. In a window of the basement, which was on a line with and visible from St. Aubin avenue, a large card bore the words: "Great Celestial Planet Exhibition."

A man's bloody footprints led from Evangelist's head up to the bedrooms where his wife and children were murdered. But the case was never solved. Police theories alternately fingered mafia extortionists, a mad or disgruntled follower of Evangelist's, and a murderous Negro acolyte of Wallace Fard, the original prophet of the Nation of Islam. Neighbors described Evangelist as an oddball whose public incantations included "gazing toward and waving his arms at the sky." Otherwise, they said, he basically seemed like a nice guy.

The location of the former Evangelist home, at 3587 St. Aubin, turned out to be a short walk from my apartment. Heading east on Gratiot, I passed an old man in a motorized wheelchair riding in the street against traffic. Fortunately, the dearth of actual traffic made it unlikely he'd be struck by a car. I stepped over a toppled streetlight about fifteen feet long, stretched diagonally across the length of the sidewalk. Then I crossed the boulevard and turned onto St. Aubin, where I passed the warehouse of a sausage company, a flophouse, two entire blocks of unruly grass (aside from a single lonely home), the blocks after that—Watson to Erskine, Erskine to Pierce, Pierce to Scott, Scott to Hale, Hale to Mack—holding, respectively, one, one, zero, two, and three houses, with topographically unusual hummocks rising in the middle of certain of the lots.

The Evangelist home would have been on the west side of St. Aubin between Hale and Mack, but that entire side of block had gone, too. The mounds, most likely, were illegally dumped trash, since camouflaged by vegetation.

* * *

In the fall of 2010, some body parts were discovered in Upper Chene: two legs, with the feet still attached, and two arms, with the hands still attached. All four limbs—"unknown tissue," in the parlance of forensic experts—possessed notably clean cuts. The arms had been sliced off just below the armpit, the legs along the inguinal area of the thigh. They had not been hacked from the body with an axe or regular sort of knife but rather had been removed with an extremely sharp cutting instrument. The smoothness of the cuts reminded the Wayne County medical examiner of the rotating saws they used in the morgue.

It was quickly determined that the limbs all belonged to the same person, a sixty-one-year-old African American male named David Morgan Jr. Morgan's left leg had been found on the berm in front of 2281 Hale; his left arm in the front yard of 2281 Hale, inside the fence; his right arm in front of a house closer to St. Aubin, 2137 Hale; and the right leg in an overgrown alley across the street. The right leg turned up bent in an L-shape against a backdrop of yellowed grass, the foot still clad in a dirty white tube sock. The right arm formed an even more precise right angle, like a detached mannequin's limb.

A few days later, Morgan's torso was discovered several blocks north of Hale, in a field not far from the one where Pete Barrow threw his weekly blues concerts during the summer. The torso had been wrapped in a blanket.

Morgan's head was never recovered. His neck had been removed entirely with his head.

Two months later, after it seemed as if the case had gone cold, a pair of suspects were arrested: Kevin Howell, twenty-one, and Aaron Coleman, twenty-two. In the telling of the police, Howell and Coleman had been selling crack cocaine out of a home at Hale and Grandy. The young men became concerned when a second group of dealers set up a drug spot just a few blocks away, at Hale and Chene, and so decided to send the newcomers a message by killing one of their own customers and scattering his limbs around the rival drug house. Howell and Coleman also had a side business scrapping out abandoned homes for metal, so they owned the sorts of cutting tools necessary for the grisly job. The unlucky victim had been Morgan, a habitual drug user known around the neighborhood as "Barbershop Dave" because of the clippers he always carried with him, in order to perform impromptu haircuts for money.

Eighty years earlier, the Evangelist murders had taken place more or less across the street, on the opposite corner of St. Aubin and Hale. None of the coverage of Morgan's murder noted this uncanny convergence of dismemberments. In fact, compared with the Evangelist case, which received widespread and sensationalistic local news coverage at the time—and for years to come, as wild new theories about the possible killer emerged—the death of David Morgan Jr. barely registered. The following spring, to mark the outset of Howell and Coleman's trial, one of the dailies ran a story on Morgan. The reporter interviewed his siblings and grown children, who posed together for one of those depressing photographs in which the family of a dead person holds up a framed head shot of their departed loved one, as if they could be a missing person who might still be found alive somewhere.

When I arrived at the courtroom in the Frank Murphy Hall of Justice, I was surprised by the absence of any other journalists. I thought I'd pulled a boner and turned out unnecessarily early. Perhaps, I fretted, veterans of the crime beat never even bothered with that first day. But not a single reporter turned out for the duration of the trial. You'd have figured a gruesome dismemberment would have merited *some* small interest, but apparently the crime wasn't quite extraordinary enough by Detroit standards. What did you have to do around here to get some ink?

Actually, that same week, the big local crime story had been the twelve-year-old girl who'd tried to rob a suburban convenience store with a loaded gun.

* * *

In reality, despite the violence of the crime, Morgan had been the wrong kind of victim to merit much in the way of sympathetic, or even prurient, tabloid coverage: too old, too black, too poor, too addicted to crack. Likewise, his alleged killers, a pair of young, African American (alleged) drug dealers, had become such dully familiar types in the urban crime genre, it would take a lot more than a not-even-ritual dismemberment to transform them into Leopold and Loeb. I questioned covering the trial myself. The fact that the murder took place so close to my apartment had piqued my interest, as had the weird echoes of the Evangelist killings. But to illustrate the problem of crime in Detroit, I might have turned to any number of other cases.

For instance, at the same time the David Morgan Jr. murder trial was occuring, prosecutors in a different case were working out a homicide plea deal with a man named Chauncey Owens. The previous summer, Owens, though in his thirties, had gotten into a verbal beef with a seventeen-year-old named Je'Rean Blake Nobles. They'd been standing outside a massive party store on Mack Avenue and St. Jean where, behind counter-to-ceiling bulletproof glass, kids from the neighborhood could also buy soft-serve ice cream. It was two in the afternoon. Nobles had gone to the party store for an orange juice and happened to be standing out front. By all accounts, Owens hadn't liked the way Nobles had looked at him. According to a construction worker waiting for the bus, Owens had said, "Stand right there. When I come back, I got something for you." He'd returned a few moments later in an SUV, along with three other men, and shot Nobles twice with a revolver, killing him. As part of Owens's guilty plea, he agreed to finger another man in the car, his buddy "CJ"—Charles Jones—as the person who'd provided the murder weapon.

Killing a teenager in broad daylight for no discernible reason would not necessarily have stood out in Detroit but for what happened two days after the shooting, when the Detroit police came looking for Owens at CJ's house. Owens had been hiding out in the upper floor of the duplex home, but the police went in through the ground level, where CJ's seven-year-old daughter, Aiyana Stanley-Jones, asleep on the couch, was shot in the head. A film crew from a cable television reality show called *The First 48* was shadowing the police officers, leading to speculation that the cops had been recklessly playing to the cameras; a Detroit police officer had been shot and killed during a similar raid a week earlier, which might have also had an effect on protocol. After Aiyana's death, people began to question the judgment of Police Chief Warren Evans, who had increased the number of such paramilitary-style raids, and later that summer, when a video of Evans's own reality show pitch surfaced—titled *The Chief*, it showed him standing in front of the abandoned train station holding a shotgun—Mayor Bing relieved Evans of his duties.

While most discussion of reinventing Detroit centers on wonkish policy paper topics involving land use and the efficacy of Keynesian economic stimulus, the biggest obstacle to any sort of serious change arguably remains the problem of crime. Detroit's notoriety for violence and general mayhem scares off new residents and businesses and makes it exceedingly difficult to retain old ones. By 2011, as Mayor Bing was trying to maintain focus on positive, upscale-demographic-luring new developments, the members of the permanent underclass inconveniently refused to stop killing one another. In fact, the murder rate soared after the ousting of Chief Evans, handing Detroit its statistically highest homicide rate in more than twenty years.

Modern Detroit has always been considered a rough place. During Prohibition, the city's proximity to Canada made it the wettest in the United States—"a wide-open booze town,"* with liquor ferried or driven across the river, depending on whether it was frozen or not. "It was absolutely impossible to get a drink in Detroit," wrote *Free Press* columnist Malcolm Bingay, "unless you walked at least ten feet and told the busy bartender what you wanted in a voice loud enough for him to hear you above the uproar." The local board of commerce estimated the illegal liquor trade employed fifty thousand Detroiters by 1929, making it the city's second-largest industry, right behind automaking. As would happen later in the century with the prohibition of drugs, gangs flourished, with "individual entrepreneurs," according to Robert Conot, "[falling] by the way as syndicates were formed in emulation of trusts in legitimate industry . . . that would have done justice to General Motors." There were Jewish mobsters—

---

*In the words of visiting reporter Ernest W. Mandeville ("Detroit Sets a Bad Example," *Outlook*, 1925), whose descriptions of the wild proliferation of blind pigs sound like harbingers of the crack trade of the eighties and nineties. One of his sources estimated eight saloons on every downtown block, adding that enforcement problems stemmed from the fact that "a good many of the policemen are Poles, and drinking liquor to them is a tradition. They can't understand why liquor should be prohibited. . . . It strikes them as a prohibition of sugar for our coffee would strike us."

most notoriously, the Purple Gang—and Italian mobsters, and their turf battles turned Detroit into a war zone, with one of the highest murder rates in the country.

The seventies brought heroin crews like Young Boys Inc., the eighties crack gangs like the Chambers Brothers, who controlled half the dope houses in the city, netting an estimated $50 million annually. For the three-year period between 1985 and 1987, Detroit was the homicide capital of the United States, with triple the murder rate of New York City. Local law enforcement estimated there were more guns in the city than people. On average, a child was shot every day in 1986.

The Carter, the terrifying high-rise apartment complex run entirely by a drug gang in the movie *New Jack City*, is based on a real building in Detroit taken over by the Chambers Brothers after overly conspicuous lines began forming at their more traditional crack houses. As William Adler chronicles in his compulsively readable book about the Chamberses, *Land of Opportunity*, you could get five-dollar rocks of cocaine on one floor and ten-dollar rocks on another, with special areas set aside for smoking and prostitution.*

Violence ebbed in Detroit in the nineties, mirroring a national trend, but after the turn of the new century, murders started to creep up again. Long before Warren Evans, police chiefs in Detroit had been mounting their own versions of shock-and-awe, and by 2003, the Justice Department placed the Detroit Police Department under a consent decree for illegally detaining suspects and excessive use of force; a *Free Press* study showed Detroit leading the nation in fatal shootings by police officers for the eight-year period beginning in 1990.

---

*All manner of illicit drug activity continues to happen in plain sight in Detroit. One evening, a friend of a friend drove me to an unmarked warehouse building not far from downtown. Inside, the place looked like a regular garage, the only unusual feature being the conspicuous closed-circuit TV monitors, its cameras trained on the street outside. But behind a secret panel, my friend's friend had set up a massive grow-op, with several hundred marijuana plants flowering at various stages beneath rows of grow-lamps. ("This is not an easy business," the source told me, shaking his head. "I have to worry about so many things every day. Maybe some kid sees me come in here and decides to rob the place. Am I willing to kill someone for two hundred grand? Some of the people I grew up with, they'd kill someone for twenty grand. I'm not one of those guys anymore. But do you see the dilemma I face? I don't want to kill some kid over pot. But what would I do? You steal my shit, I can re-gangsta.")

Substantively, Evans's replacement, former assistant chief Ralph Godbee, didn't mess with his old boss's strategy, a data-driven, *Moneyball* approach to policing that called for stretching the city's miniscule budget by statistically targeting the most crime-ridden neighborhoods. Some wondered if Evans's aggressive tactics, however criticized, had been the secret of his success; but then again, the perpetual downturn in which the economy seemed mired might have made the spike in crime rates inevitable. Godbee, unsurprisingly, and not necessarily incorrectly, cited dwindling resources as his biggest problem.

"Between layoffs and restructuring, we're a thousand officers fewer today than in 2005," he told me in late 2010. "That's significant. The city is still 139 square miles. And you have a high level of people who move because they can afford to, leaving behind a disproportionate number of people who are fending for themselves with all of the problems that go along with poverty. This leads to, for lack of a better term, a perfect storm, where crime stays high even as the population is dropping." Godbee grew up in Detroit, the son of a brick mason; his father discouraged him from entering the police academy, afraid he would not continue his education, but Godbee wound up getting a master's degree and working his way up from street patrol, in one of the city's most dangerous districts, to become head of security for Mayor Dennis Archer and eventually chief.

He said that he hoped to build on Evans's approach by adding more community policing. The elimination of the state law requiring public servants to live in the city where they worked had an especially deleterious effect on cities like Detroit, in Godbee's view. "Now over 50 percent of our police department doesn't live in the city," he noted. Godbee himself owns a home practically across the street from my old high school. The neighborhood used to be nicknamed "Copper Canyon" because so many police officers lived there. Since the change in residency requirements, though, most of those officers decamped for the suburbs, and crime has soared.

One night while I was on a police ride-along with a Detroit Police Department gang-detail veteran named Harold Rochon, we were called to a reported shooting in this very neighborhood—actually, quite close to where my high school girlfriend used to live. Her parents took in severely disabled foster children for extra income, and a number of my rookie make-out sessions had taken place on a living room sofa across from a crib where a pair of encephalitic twins lay on their backs, occasionally moaning, the whole thing like a movie codirected by John Hughes and David Lynch. When I returned to my ex's neighborhood with the Detroit police, it was close to one in the morning. The woman who'd reported the shooting lived in a small brick home with bars on the door. The porch was just a bare block of cement that had steps attached but no railing or awning or any kind of furniture. About a dozen people were milling around outside. Most seemed to be in their teens or early twenties. The complainant herself was probably in her late thirties and wore a loose housedress. She said her ex-boyfriend had slapped her daughter, prompting her nephew and the daughter's boyfriend to roughly show him the door. He'd returned with two truckloads of men with guns and taken a couple of shots at the house.

"It was a red pickup truck," a spindly guy wearing a skullcap and a long jersey shouted, slurring his words like a ham actor pretending to be drunk. "Niggas in the back of that bitch shooting and acting crazy, man. Y'all be late as hell."

Another officer had already gone off in search of the offending vehicles, with no luck. Rochon told everyone to go back into the house and to call 911 if the men returned.

The woman became incredulous. "What if he shoot up the house? These niggas had *guns*. You know what I deal with? I deal with a baseball bat. I don't mess with no guns. But you don't touch my child. You don't touch none of my kids. And then you wanna go get your niggas on some bitch shit? Nah!"

Rochon's partner, attempting to reason with her, said, "If you're outside, it ain't gonna make it no better."

"Realistically speaking, bullets can go through a house," the daughter's teenage boyfriend pointed out, not unreasonably, I thought.

"You're more prone to be hit out here," Rochon said tersely.

The boyfriend said, "It's a fifty-fifty chance. I witnessed bullets go through walls with my own eyes. And hit people!"

"You need to go into the house," Rochon said, "or if you're that afraid, you need to go somewhere else for the night."

For some reason, the guy in the skullcap had extended his arms in an about-to-be-frisked position and called to the officers, "Want me to stretch out, too? I'm used to it!" Then he began cackling. One of the younger guys told him to shut up.

I'm not sure how I expected the police to respond, but I suppose I figured it would be something more buoying than, "If someone is threatening to shoot up your house, don't stand on the porch, and maybe leave for someplace safer."

Once again, though, Rochon ordered everyone inside, threatening to arrest any minors who continued to loiter. Then we drove off to the next call.

* * *

The two defendants, Kevin Howell and Aaron Coleman, were to be tried simultaneously, though they had different lawyers. In court, Howell, the taller of the two young men, wore glasses and a white dress shirt, its collar unbuttoned to reveal a white crew neck T-shirt. He had a chunky, pear-shaped build, and an Afro and fuzzy sideburns that might have passed for intentionally retro, had not his glazed eyes and generally sedated affect made any deliberate fashion choices seem implausible. Coleman, a little guy, had a wispy mustache and wore his hair in braids that fell to the back of his neck. His outfit was fairly ridiculous: a cream-colored dress shirt buttoned all the way to the top, but with no tie and the wrong size, the shirt billowing piratically out of his waistband when tucked, making you think of a little boy posing uncomfortably for a First Communion photo. Still, he had trained his face to betray no emotion other than an icy soldier's stare and, puffy shirt or no, he threw off an effortless menace.

The fact that no one else was covering the trial persuaded me to stick around and see how things played out. The story revealed itself as infinitely more tangled and needlessly tragic than even the incomprehensible grotesqueness of the crime in question might have portended. As evidentiary detail accrued, the circumstances leading up to the murder and its subsequent unraveling acquired both a depressing

banality and a sense of doom as foreordained as Greek tragedy—here, taking the form of an urban pathology so deep-rooted and inescapable it came to feel conspiratorial, a form of predestination.

It went like this: One night, Kevin Howell was hanging out with Monique Foster, his ex-girlfriend. Foster was a very attractive nineteen-year-old, petite verging on alarmingly thin, still looking much closer to the age she'd been when she met Howell, which was thirteen.[*] They'd dated for three years and had an infant daughter, and remained close even after their breakup. On the night in question, they were lying on Howell's bed at his mother's house on Grandy Street, where Howell still lived, just chatting about old times and what their daughter, Teresa, also on the bed, would be like when she got older.

Then, unexpectedly, Howell had turned to Foster and said, "Remember on the news, when the body parts were found?" The crime had taken place a few weeks earlier. Foster remembered hearing about some arms and legs being found in a field in the neighborhood but hadn't thought much of it.[†]

Howell suddenly became serious. "I did that," he told her.

Foster, startled, recoiled from the bed. When she turned on the lights and saw Howell's face, she could tell he wasn't joking.

He spoke in his normal ("mellow") tone. He said a guy came to purchase crack from him and asked if he could smoke in the house. Howell told him no, go next door, and that was where he shot the man and took apart his body.[‡]

The story would have ended there—Foster, though scared by the confession and unable to stop thinking about it, had not gone to the police—but for a series of bizarre unrelated events. About a month after Kevin Howell's confession, his older brother Brian was hanging out with Aaron Coleman, called "Mikey" by everyone around the

---

[*]So much so that, after she took the stand and answered her first question in a barely audible murmur, the judge had spoken to her as if to a child, saying, "Keep your voice up, honey."

[†]When the prosecutor asked if the news reports had given her pause, Foster replied, "No. Just an everyday activity in Detroit."

[‡]Foster also claimed (less credibly) to have been unaware Howell had been selling drugs. The prosecutor asked if anything else had been said. Foster testified, "That was pretty much all: he killed a man and dismembered his body. After that it was silence."

neighborhood, and a few other friends, including a guy named Jermaine Overman, who happened to be the only other person who knew something about the murder.*

Overman was a stocky but muscular twenty-six-year-old, handsome, with broad features and wispy hints of a beard and mustache. Cocky and performative, he was an old friend of Coleman and both Howell brothers. He also had a daughter with one of the Howell sisters, Sarah, whom he'd been dating for seven years. The day before the news about the body parts broke, he'd been out with Kevin and Mikey. They occasionally scrapped houses together, and that day after drinking gin and smoking weed by the river, they'd begun trawling Upper Chene in a van—Overman claimed he didn't know who owned the van, though he'd been the one behind the wheel—until eventually, at Howell and Coleman's direction, they pulled to a stop in front of the house on Hale Street where Morgan had been executed.

Overman said he thought the house had been chosen at random, for a scrapping job. It was after dark, and the place looked abandoned, "which," he said later, "people who do scrap metal, those are the houses we target." He didn't find it unusual when Coleman and Howell led him directly to the basement, either, since "gas pipes, lead pipes, furnace, copper wire: that's where everything of value is." Kevin had been laughing and joking around, acting goofy. But once they got downstairs and Overman's eyes adjusted to the light, he noticed what looked like a rolled-up sheet, or some other kind of covering, with a human head poking out of one end. Startled, Overman got himself out of the basement as quickly as possible, or so he later claimed. Rather implausibly, he also insisted Howell and Coleman said nothing about the body, not in the basement, not afterwards, though they'd definitely seen it and hadn't seemed surprised or upset by its presence.

Whatever actually happened, Overman, too, never alerted the authorities. Nor did he sever his ties with Mikey and Kevin. And so a couple of months later, at someone's apartment in the Martin Luther King Jr. housing projects, Overman found himself hanging out with Mikey, Kevin's brother Brian, and a few other friends. A gun had

---

*At least according to trial testimony.

appeared at some point—Overman professed not to know where it had come from—and Mikey and another friend, named Kevin Williams, started messing around with it, debating, specifically, whether or not it would be possible to kill two dogs with a single shot.

Eventually, they left the apartment in two separate vehicles. Their buddy Nathan Smith drove everyone but Mikey, who, alone in his own car, got pulled over by a cop.

"Oh, shit," Overman said. "I hope he ain't still got the gun on him." Brian Howell was sitting in the backseat next to Overman. He was two years older than Kevin, not quite as tall, but thin and fit, and he crossed a room with a swaggering insouciance.

Nate, glancing in his rearview mirror, said, "Mikey about to go down."

"No, not exactly," Brian said. "Because I got it."

He meant the gun, which he pulled out of his jacket. Nate, who had just gotten out of prison a week earlier, began to panic, as did Overman, especially when Brian waved the gun in his face in a reckless manner. Overman went to snatch the piece, and somehow, in the chaos, Brian accidentally squeezed the trigger.

"Everybody just got to freaking out," Overman said.

Brian had shot Kevin Williams, up front in the passenger seat.*

It was bad. Overman leaped out of the car, gun in tow and made his way back to his girlfriend's house, while Nate and the others raced to the hospital. Williams was already making disturbing choking sounds. "I jumped in the front seat and started slapping him, trying to keep him woke," Brian recalled later. But this did no good: Williams died en route.

After leaving Williams's body at the hospital, the friends reunited with Overman and decided to go to the police to explain what had happened. Overman didn't think it was a good idea to walk into a police precinct with a gun, so he hid it under a bucket he found in an empty field across the street from his girlfriend's place. The only other person who knew where he'd stashed the pistol happened to be Kevin Howell, who'd been home at the time.

---

*As Brian Howell testified, "My friend Jermaine Overman tried to take the gun away from me for some odd reason and it went off. I really doesn't know whose finger hit the trigger, sir."

When they arrived at the ninth precinct, it was 10:00 p.m., and despite their willingness to confess to a fatal shooting, the cops told them to come back in the morning. When the detectives finally got around to taking their testimony and asking to see the weapon, Overman led them to the bucket, but the gun was gone.*

Brian Howell was facing an extended prison sentence. His mother, Mary, had been talking about the case to one of the detectives, who made it clear that the production of the accidentally fired gun would be very helpful in ascertaining the veracity of her son's version of events. They weren't buying the bucket story. Mary Howell knew Kevin had been around when Overman had hidden the gun, and she pressed him on where it might be. Kevin kept saying he had no clue. She didn't believe him and was becoming convinced the gun must have had some darker history if he wouldn't come clean to help his brother. Kevin admitted she was right, but that's all he'd give up. His mother asked what the history had been. Kevin said he couldn't tell her.

Not long after this conversation, Mary Howell was talking to Monique Foster, with whom she had remained close. They were discussing the missing gun, and suddenly Foster began to relay the story of Kevin's confession. "My kids always knew: don't tell me nothing you don't want to me to know, or it's ending," Mary Howell told me later. "That day with Monique, when she started to tell to me about Kevin, I said, 'Monique, I advise you to stop talking now, because I'm not gonna sit on it.'"

Foster told her anyway. After Mary Howell stopped crying—"it took me about three hours to pull myself together"—she called the police.

---

*The judge, Michael Hathaway, briefly became hung up on the sheer illogic of Overman's bucket testimony. At one point, when Overman mentioned how the bucket had filled up with rainwater by the time the police got around to searching underneath it, Hathaway interrupted, nonplussed. Had Overman actually placed the gun inside a bucket without a lid? Briefly, they went into a debased Abbott and Costello routine—Hathaway: "So, the bucket is empty?" Overman: "No." Hathaway: "So you *filled* it?"—until it became clear that Overman had hidden the gun under the *bottom* of a *right-side-up* bucket. When Hathaway finally understood the mechanics of the bucket maneuver, he seemed more disgusted and baffled by the stupefyingly unwise choices of young people than at any other moment in the trial.

* * *

I visited Mary Howell one afternoon at her home on Grandy Street. Howell lived in a two-story wooden house with a peeling white paint job. One of the top-floor windows was partially boarded, and a blue tarp covered half of the A-frame roof. Only two other homes remained on the block, which looked like Greenwich, Connecticut, compared with the next block over, taken up entirely by the rubble of a three-quarters-demolished brick warehouse. One of the walls still standing read LAMINATED RECYCLING; closer to the Howells' place, an exposed second-story bathroom appeared to have survived aerial bombardment, only the pink toilet still clinging precariously to the edge of the crumbling floor. Mary Howell said the warehouse had been like that for at least three years. An activist woman, not from the neighborhood, had come around once, trying to ascertain which demolition company had left such an unholy mess, but as Howell had told her, shaking her head at this lady's naiveté during the retelling, *It was no one. The* community *did it.* By which she meant some entrepreneurial-minded fellows had showed up with chains and a truck one day and pulled the walls down themselves, carting away whatever they could sell.

"Brick farmers," Howell explained.

Howell was fifty-one years old, with nine children, ranging in age from thirty-one to ten. Throughout the trial, she sat with four of her daughters, each one physically larger than the next, Howell relatively svelte by comparison, short, busty, her hair straightened and combed back from her forehead. She never once removed her cobalt wind-breaker, even when she took the witness stand, which somehow added to the stoicism of her bearing. When I met her at home, we sat next to each other on the porch, on a couple of kitchen chairs with worn fabric seats. Part of the metal porch railing was held together with twisted pieces of wire. She didn't invite me inside. Through her screen door, I glimpsed a stilled box fan and a hardwood floor spattered with what appeared to be white paint. It was a gorgeous spring afternoon, the neighborhood exploding with bird noises. Howell's ten-year-old daughter, dressed like a princess on her way to a ballet lesson, had been sitting on the porch when I pulled up, and she'd literally danced inside to fetch her mother.

At some point, I mentioned how Mayor Bing was talking about downsizing neighborhoods like this one. Mary Howell said, "I wish he would. They trying to get rid of us. But look at it. What's there for us to stay for? I keep this lawn up." She nodded at the empty lot next door, neatly mowed, which did not belong to her. "But if they end up building a house on it, who wants to live next door to *this*?" she went on, gesturing at her own place. She said her family had lived in the house for nineteen years. Her sister, one of twelve siblings, worked in real estate and had managed to secure the property for a steal, eventually selling it to Mary Howell and her husband of thirty-three years, Bernard, who used to work at Ford and now did landscaping. Howell herself had been a secretary at the board of education, and later worked as a paraprofessional.

"Now there's no jobs out here," she said matter-of-factly, gazing at the empty lot next door where no one would want to live anyway, her hands steepled in her lap. "They say they're bringing jobs back, but those jobs are way out in Battle Creek, Ypsilanti. How can you get out there?" From inside the house, I heard something beeping steadily every few seconds. It sounded like a fire alarm warning you its battery had run low.

This is a court-reporting cliché but striking enough to note here: when Mary Howell took the witness stand to testify against one son in order to save the other, her face betrayed zero emotion. Her voice was unusually low for a woman's—husky, too, and unspeakably weary, though the deepness gave her testimony a stony and unwavering quality. It maintained that croaking timbre up close, seeming to almost vibrate out of her chest, like an echo from an underground cave. I thought of that *Our Gang* character with the impossibly deep voice for a child.

Howell approached me during a lull in the courtroom action. I was sitting in the lobby and she walked over and asked when my book was coming out, so she could tell her friends to pick it up.* We chatted

---

*Judge Hathaway had spotted me taking notes on the first day of the trial and asked, from the bench, whom I was writing for.

some. She still had on that blue jacket, but she spoke in a near-whisper. "That house was a drug house," she said. "My son wasn't involved in that. He's had mental health issues since he was one year old." I said it must have been difficult to testify. She blinked at me impassively and said, "Well, when I heard he might have done it, it wasn't hard. It was so horrible. I felt for the victims. Nobody deserves to die like that."

On her porch, Howell elaborated. She said Kevin hadn't started going to jail until he was eighteen, when he did two years on a drug charge. "Following in the stupid footsteps of his older brother," she muttered, staring straight ahead. He'd been in and out of mental institutions for his entire life. When he was a little boy, he'd started a fire in Howell's closet once. Another time, Howell turned her back for an instant while making cornbread and Kevin took the opportunity to stick his head in the oven. She said Kevin had been diagnosed as mildly retarded and schizophrenic.

Looking back, Howell admitted she'd "felt the vibes" on the day of the murder. She knew something was amiss, enough to ask Kevin, once the body parts had been discovered, if he knew anything about what'd happened. "Of course he said no," Howell said. I asked if Kevin had been upset with her for calling the police. "He know," she said. "He know he didn't have no reason to kill the man. He didn't even *know* him. He still won't come forward and tell where the man's head is. I said, 'If you get life, will you tell where the head is?' He tells me no, he don't know where the head is. He said Aaron Coleman was the last one with the head. But he did something so brutal to that man, I had to think, who would be next? Me? One of his sisters?" She sighed. "The way I feel, Kevin took a life. But he still have one. He just on the inside. His family could visit. His family could write. That man he killed, his family can't. If I'd ignored it, I'd be just as guilty as Kevin."

Something about Howell's squat, mother-hen build reminded me of my paternal grandmother. That, and her Coke-bottle glasses—you almost never saw lenses so outrageously thick anymore, magnifying the wearer's eyes in a way that hinted at some all-seeing oracular power. In the little village where my father's family came from, so much surname overlap took place that families also retained nick-names. My grandmother's family nickname had been *Rano*, local dialect for "frog"—*ranocchio* in proper Italian—apparently on account of the family's propensity for bulging, froggy eyes, so, in my grand-mother's case, it wasn't just the glasses.

"There's drugs and crime in every neighborhood," Howell went on. "That house right there?" She nodded at the lone house on the other side of Grandy, a tidy ranch with white siding. She'd lowered her voice, and I thought she was going to tell me the place was a drug spot. Instead, she said, "*All* the kids graduated and went to col-lege. You can't blame the neighborhood. It's up to each individual to achieve." I asked about her other children, and immediately regret-ted it. She fell quiet. Finally, she said, "Most of my kids are under mental health—disability. My second oldest daughter has a job. She's a housekeeper." Howell paused again, then said her youngest, the princess ballerina, talked about getting a teacher's certificate, though she didn't really like the idea of going to college. "She's still young," I said. Howell just hoped the girl would finish high school. "None of my kids really did nothing with their life," she said.

I didn't think of my paternal grandmother very often. She'd been dead for years, and as a kid I hadn't known her very well. We used to take family trips to Italy every couple of summers, to visit. We'd stay for a month, living in the upstairs apartment at my grandmother's house, which she would otherwise rent out to tourists. You had to yank a chain hanging from the ceiling to flush the toilet. It was an old stone building, and the kitchen had the funky smell of a cellar where someone had been curing meat. Every visit, a few days before we were supposed to leave, my grandmother would begin to cry. You could set your watch by it. My father's sister, my *zia* Rafaela, would slap her mother gently on the shoulder and tell her, *Ma dai, Bianca!* Those glasses, at such moments, would enlarge her sopping irises until you could imagine each of them filling its own drive-in movie screen. I couldn't get over how much Mary Howell reminded me of Nonna Bianca, and I could easily picture her own eyes redly swelling behind her lenses, just like my grandmother's, though the whole time we spent together there was never the slightest hint of tears.

* * *

On the sidewalk outside the Frank Murphy Hall of Justice, a sign listed the various items forbidden in the building, including Alcoholic Beverages, Ammunition, Aerosol, Bingo Markers, Boxcutters, Bullets (Anything Resembling), Curling Irons, Combs (Metal or Rattail), Drug Paraphernalia, Flatware, Noisemakers of Any Kind, and Whistles. When I arrived, there was a long, morning-rush-hour queue to get inside (all court spectators were required to pass through a metal detector) and I felt a sleepy camaraderie among the line waiters, most united in some form of direct or by-proxy opposition to the Man.

The courtroom was on the fourth floor. I found the windowless, climate-controlled space, with its minimalist, midcentury modern decor—blond wood benches, darker ribbed paneling on the walls, a recessed octagonal ceiling—cozily hermetic. Silver-haired Judge Hathaway also seemed of another era, looking as if he should be interviewing Dean Martin on a late-night talk show while chain-smoking on air; even his flat, slightly nasal accent had a faintly Carsonic purr.

Kevin Howell's mother and sisters lined the bench in front of me. As far as I could determine, Aaron Coleman had no family members in the courtroom the entire week. David Morgan Jr.'s sister and brothers and two grown sons occupied a bench running along the courtroom's far wall. One brother, a postal worker, stole into the room a couple of hours late every day, still wearing his blue postman's uniform and cap. Another brother, apparently a motorcycle enthusiast, had a shaved head and a long beard and wore a leather Harley-Davidson jacket, and whenever he walked stiffly by, you could hear the swishing of whatever sort of protective leather chaps he had on underneath his jeans.

Mary Howell's call to the police had resulted in the questioning of Monique Foster and Jermaine Overman and ultimately the arrest of Mikey and Kevin. Still, on the level of forensic evidence alone, the prosecution's case remained basically nonexistent. No fingerprints or DNA connecting the young men to the crime had been discovered. David Morgan Jr. had most likely died from a gunshot to the head, but since his head was still missing, there was no official cause of death, and the gun suspected as the murder weapon had disappeared from under a bucket. In fact, the abandoned home where Morgan's murder allegedly took place had mysteriously burned down forty-eight hours after the body parts were discovered on Hale Street. By the time the police arrived to search for Morgan's missing head, the condition of the house was deemed too structurally unsound to allow the cadaver dog to enter. The day after Morgan's torso was found, Coleman's alleged drug house also burned to the ground.*

Lacking a solid case, the district attorney had offered Howell a plea bargain, which would have entailed a 27½-year sentence in exchange for an admission of guilt. Howell not only rejected the offer but became so irate when his court-appointed attorney, Wayne Frost, brought up the plea during their first meeting, he refused to speak with Frost again until the morning of their first day in court.

Despite the problematic evidence, the two sides were utterly mismatched. The young, meticulously prepared prosecutor, Raj Prasad, a compact presence with a high, reedy voice, couldn't wait to lay a series of PowerPoint presentations on the jury. Frost, on the other hand, had a beleaguered air. He read haltingly from a yellow legal pad and did not call any witnesses of his own. Aaron Coleman's attorney, Brian Gagniuk, an almost comically baby-faced man† who nonetheless comported himself with a practiced and lawyerly flamboyance, was probably the most impressive of the bunch, but had a minor role thanks to the lack of any direct evidence against his client.

For the state, the most damning testimony came from Monique Foster—underlined when Prasad played back a jailhouse phone conversation between Howell and Foster. In the recording, Foster has obviously been weeping. "I hope that everything goes as you want it to go," she says, pausing between words to sniffle.

---

*A full arson investigation was never conducted on either structure fire, though one of the homicide detectives, when asked how frequently this sort of fire occurred in a neighborhood like Upper Chene, testified, "Houses like this? Many times. Almost daily."

†Before the trial began, I was standing in the hallway near a small group of Kevin Howell's friends when Gagniuk walked past. Jermaine Overman cast a skeptical look in his direction and muttered, "If I need a lawyer, I want an old nigga. That nigga look like Jim Carrey. That nigga look like he just got back from spring break."

Howell, belying his rather dim courtroom presence, sounds confident in his reply. "They subpoena you, they can't force you to testify," he tells Foster. "You ain't got to."

Foster says, "I don't know, Kevin."

Before she's able to continue, a computerized phone-company voice interrupts to say, "*Thank. You. For. Using. Evercom.*"

On the stand, Foster, dressed in high boots, tight black jeans, and a bright pink zippered sweatshirt, became visibly upset during her testimony. Foster admitted she'd only told the police about Howell's confession out of fear of losing her child. "They said I was looking at conspiracy and could get life," Foster said. "Honestly, today, I don't want to be up here. I love this man." She exhaled deeply, and her voice hitched. "I wouldn't be able to live with myself knowing I put my child's father behind bars."

Frost, during his opening argument, anticipated Foster's testimony and launched directly into an obfuscating Hail Mary pass, insisting to the jury, "The prosecutor wants you to connect dot after dot after dot. This was a guy trying to get back together with his girl-friend! He saw something on the news, and he was trying to act important. This is a different era, ladies and gentlemen. Listen to the music they sing now. He was simply bragging the way they do in rap music now. I'm pretty sure they [rap artists] don't actually kill police officers just because they sing about it."

Before closing arguments began, Hathaway considered the case against Coleman, who had not been directly implicated in the killings by anyone except the prosecutor. Monique Foster never claimed Kevin Howell said anything about Coleman's participation in the murder or dismemberment; Jermaine Overman had simply described Coleman as being present the night they'd entered an abandoned home and seen a dead body; Brian Howell, in his testimony, would only say Coleman had been selling crack.

Prasad endeavored to argue that, regardless who committed the murder, the dismemberment would have required at least two people.

Judge Hathaway frowned. "The dismemberment apparently occurred after the murder," he murmured. "But I don't know if that's a two-man job. I really don't."

Prasad chuckled in an unsettling way and said, "When I say it's a heavy job, judge, I mean it's a heavy job. That torso alone weighed fifty-eight pounds."

Gagniuk, Coleman's attorney, stepped forward and announced, "Last Tuesday, Your Honor, I cut down five trees. It was a two-person job, but I did it myself. I have pictures on my phone to prove it. It was probably not the best idea. But I did it."

Once this debate exhausted itself, Hathaway dismissed the charges against Coleman, but he continued to express reservations about the overall logic of the prosecution's case. "It just doesn't make much sense as a motive," he said, rubbing his temple as he stared down at his notes. "They wanted to kill a random guy buying drugs from them?"

"The unfortunate analogy," Prasad countered, "is *The Godfather.*"

"So they killed one of their *own* customers?" Hathaway asked. "It just doesn't make sense as a way to drive the competition out of the neighborhood. I still don't quite get the motive, at least as presented."

Prasad smiled nervously and acknowledged, "It might not be the *best* way to do business."

"Why wouldn't they do it to one of the competitors if they really want to reenact *The Godfather*?" Hathaway continued, apparently not quite understanding Prasad's reference, which clearly had been meant to recall the scene where one of Don Corleone's enemies, the recalcitrant Hollywood producer Jack Woltz, wakes up, horrified, beside the decapitated head of his beloved prizewinning racehorse.

Prasad diplomatically replied, "I understand that."

Hathaway shook his head and said, "I understand expecting reason from people who have never evinced reason in their lives is like whistling in the wind."

Jury deliberation began on a Thursday and continued the following morning. I shifted back and forth between the courtroom and lobby, waiting alongside the victim's family and Howell's mother and sisters, the two sides respectfully steering clear of each other, but without a trace of discernible hostility. Morgan's sister, Gwen Thomas, was smartly dressed in a navy blue suit and a large beaded necklace. She said her family was originally from Detroit's east side. She lived in the suburbs now, where she ran her own marketing and public relations firm. As she spoke, she mostly kept her gaze focused on a binder in her lap, where she was rearranging some papers for work. "My brother was a product of the sixties," she told me. "Now athletes take drugs, they go into treatment. Back then, they didn't know. He started out with heroin. I have my theories on how those drugs got here. They ruined cities like Detroit. The last time I saw David was three years ago. He came to our sister's funeral. Somehow he'd found out about it. Got a suit and everything."

About a half hour later, the jury announced they had reached a verdict. My heart clenched. All morning, I'd felt tremulous and expectant. Adding to the drama, several extra bailiffs had been brought into the courtroom as a standard precautionary show of force in case the defendant or any of the spectators reacted badly to the verdict. Their presence had the effect of making it feel as if an eruption of violence should be considered highly probable.

The jury found Howell guilty of first-degree murder and mutilation of a body. One of Howell's sisters burst into tears and fled into the hallway. Morgan's family also wept. To my surprise, I found myself tearing up as well. I wasn't even sure why. I'd been upset when Coleman's case had been dismissed, even though, logically, I understood the evidence hadn't been there. The prospect of Howell's also walking had been gnawing at my equanimity. But when the foreman read the verdict, the full tragedy of the situation finally hit me—the senselessness of Morgan's death, Howell's own wasted life, the appalling loss afflicted on both families.

Outside, in hamhanded, bathetic fashion, dark storm clouds had been massing over the city, and suddenly it began to pour. Morgan's family emerged from the courthouse shortly after I did. His sister opened a giant Motor City Casino umbrella and together they marched toward a nearby parking structure for the rival Greektown Casino. Farther in the distance, heading in the same direction, I could see Mary Howell's blue windbreaker, as she walked, arms linked, with one of her daughters.

* * *

My ride-along with Lieutenant Rochon coincided with a new initiative by Chief Godbee called "Operation Inside Out," in which the Detroit Police Department's patrol squads would be reinforced by cops who normally worked desk jobs. The Inside officer driving our squad car told me his regular job mostly entailed going to high schools and talking to kids about drugs and crime. As austerity-era public relations, Operation Inside Out had an obvious "more-with-less" appeal, but its efficacy as a policy struck me as dubious. At one point in the evening, we had to race across town to a shooting. The Inside cop, who was driving, kept fumbling with the siren and flashing lights. We also had no GPS and occasionally got turned around. Sometimes less was simply less, no matter what you did with it.

More often, anticrime measures in Detroit did not resemble para-military raids so much as containment policies. A certain degree of crime could be ignored as long as the fulcrum of change in Detroit (downtown, the university district, and the handful of other neigh-borhoods where the city's elite actually live) remained safe and rela-tively unaffected. Short of fundamentally changing the underlying conditions producing such high levels of violence and illegal activity in the first place, policing could do only so much, so the best-case scenario amounted to hoping the criminals stuck to killing one another and kept the collateral damage to a minimum. This approach plays out in the coverage different crimes receive in the local media. For exam-ple, when a random white teenager is carjacked in broad daylight at a suburban fast food restaurant and his dead body turns up a week later in an abandoned home in Detroit—as happened shortly after I moved back to the city, dominating headlines for weeks and even reaching a national prime-time news show—the event amounts to 100 percent collateral damage and elicits corresponding levels of civic and media outrage. On the other hand, one drug dealer killing another or hacking up the body of a crack addict as part of an inane turf war—well, in that case, the collateral damage plummets closer to zero, and the outcome of the ensuing trial barely merits a newspaper blurb.

In fact, the unspoken attitude toward violence in Detroit today isn't radically different from that of Mayor Charles Bowles, who held office during the Purple Gang's heyday. "It is just as well to let these gangsters kill each other off, if they are so minded," he said in 1930, after a murder spree in which twelve bootleggers were shot and killed over the course of eleven days. "You know the scientists employ one set of parasites to destroy another. May not that be the plan of Provi-dence in these killings among the bandits?"

David Morgan Jr. was no bandit, of course. But expand Bowles's sentiment only slightly and even some of the best-intended ideas for reinventing the city begin to take on a disturbing purgative aspect, undertones of a cleansing that leaves no room for the likes of Morgan or Jermaine Overman or Mary Howell. Aside from burned-out buildings and overgrown lots, what's missing from the Tomorrowland renderings of Detroit 2030, with its monorails and Christmas tree farms and office parks and Apple stores? Oh, right: poor people.

* * *

An appeals lawyer approached Howell after the trial and offered to take Kevin's case. "But he wants $4,000 down ASAP, and then he wants $550 a month," Mary Howell told me when I visited. "I can't afford no appeal attorney." She hadn't been able to visit either of her sons in jail since the trial ended, because she had no car and seats on the van service running loved ones out to the prisons got expensive. She figured she'd probably be able to visit once or twice a year, and whenever she could afford to send her boys money orders for phone cards, they could give her a call.

Of the young men close to Kevin Howell, Aaron Coleman remained in jail on EWOP ("entering without permission") charges related to scrapping. After the trial ended, I learned that Coleman's older brother Jason was serving his own prison sentence for the strangulation of his nineteen-year-old girlfriend, Jalona Stafford, on Valentine's Day several years earlier. They'd been at an EconoLodge motel in the suburbs, arguing over a television program. After killing Stafford, Jason Coleman had driven her body back to Upper Chene, dragged it inside an abandoned pickle factory, and set the corpse on fire. Neighbors reported seeing a stray dog running down the street with her leg in its mouth.

Jermaine Overman, meanwhile, had been portrayed throughout the trial by his own friends' attorneys as an unreliable and perhaps even sinister character. The judge made no attempt to feign neutrality on this issue—he did not like Overman—and even Prasad acknowledged the credibility problems of a witness who admitted to having committed crimes with the very two (alleged) crack-dealing sociopaths he hoped to convict. Surprisingly, though, when I approached Overman after his testimony, he agreed to meet up and chat.

I texted him the following week. Within moments, I received a text back reading, cryptically, "Mr Holly Kartel." I didn't understand what this meant, so I just called him. Overman answered. He did not explain the text but said that he remembered me and that we could get together the following day.

Overman lived in a low-income housing complex on Chene Street. When I pulled into the parking lot, he was standing outside, and we drove over to a diner in Eastern Market for a late breakfast. Overman was in a pensive mood. He'd just come from a government office downtown, where he had been sorting out an unspecified problem involving his birth certificate. His parents needed to be present and so he had ended up seeing them for the first time in eight months. "How was that?" I asked. He shrugged and said, "Awkward silence all around. That's like a CD on loop. It's gonna play that way forever. Some people are better at a distance."

Overman was the second-youngest of ten kids. His family had briefly moved to Sacramento when he was five, but money became funny and they'd returned to Detroit a few years later. "I pretty much raised myself, basically," he said. "Both of my parents were in the house, but it was like they *weren't* in the house. That left me as a loner. There'd be times I'd be out of school for weeks, just waiting to go back." School had been Frederick Douglass Academy, which Overman described as "like a motherfucking clubhouse. One teacher good, but he like one finger in a fist. The others just let you lounge around. If they'd balled that fist up, maybe it would've worked." Frederick Douglass closed three years ago. The graffiti-covered building, now missing most of its doors and windows, remained one of the major eyesores of Upper Chene; occasionally, you'd see neighborhood kids tossing basketballs through the rusting, netless hoops on the old court. Overman said he'd scrapped the place but hadn't thought to grab his old locker.

Though Overman almost certainly knew more about the killing of David Morgan Jr. than he was letting on, he didn't come across as a dangerous guy. He spoke in an adenoidal baritone, and snickered at his own jokes, and almost shyly brought up the rap songs he'd write alone, at night. After ordering a western omelet, politely calling the waitress ma'am, he said of his friend Kevin Howell, "I can't imagine him doing that." He wouldn't say much more about his testimony or his thoughts as to what had really happened. Of Coleman, he said, "No matter what we scrapped, what we did, he *always* had money. He was trying to get custody of his kid, so he was always saving. You could hand him a dollar with your signature on it and he'd still have it in a month."

He insisted he had no idea what happened to the gun that accidentally killed Kevin Williams and possibly intentionally killed David Morgan Jr. "I don't fuck with guns," Overman told me. "I don't even know how to load the clip or switch the latch or whatever you call it. And I didn't want that gun in my house. I have a three-year-old daughter." Overman didn't deny scrapping and even acknowledged having "filled in" on the odd occasion for drug-dealing friends, when he was younger, earning seventy bucks or so for a few hours' work. As a kid, he'd always thought he'd be some kind of builder—he loved making things—but now there was no work and cash was tight. Scrapping, you might get two hundred dollars' worth of metal out of a good house, which, even split three ways, wasn't bad money. "It'll keep me maintained as hell," Overman said.

In the middle of our breakfast, Overman's girlfriend called. After speaking with her for a few moments, he grimaced and hung up. It seemed that her friend wanted a ride to Hamtramck and was willing to pay, the main hitch being Overman's girlfriend did not possess a valid driver's license. Overman told her not to do it, but she seemed intent on making the quick cash. "Women don't be wanting to listen!" he muttered, scooping up a forkful of omelet. "They just wanna *drive*. I don't want to sound sexist, but it's true."

We left the restaurant and went for a quick ride around the neighborhood. As we rolled alongside the decimated blocks of Upper Chene, Overman provided a running commentary: "This place used to be a liquor store. It's been burned for about twelve years. It's kinda crazy, because as the fire department was putting the fire out, you had people busting in on the other side taking the liquor out. Black people owned this place here for a minute, but it's already gone. This shit been fucked up forever. Black people owned this clothing store—see the NBA sign?

Didn't work out, though. Location, location. People are looking at us riding down the street. We look like investors, like we coming to rush everybody out. Well, *you* do." He laughed hard at this. "I got chased out of this building right here, with the water tower on top of it? The guy had on a cop badge, but he was security. But all in all it looked the same, so we got out of there. We wasn't doing shit anyway. We was just casing it out to see if there was money to be made. Cool little church right here. Historic buildings, that's what I'm into. I like the architecture, that design and shit. This is where they gave us free lunch, for schoolkids. I really don't hang around with too many people, because too many people bring trouble, as you can see. Now I'm seeing people doing straight cocaine. They call it the rich man's drug. I didn't even think that was our cup of tea. . . .

"I always think about leaving, bro. There ain't shit here. I can't because of finances. If I could, I would move to a farm, something like that. Upper Michigan. This city just fucked up all the way around. If I had a choice, I *would* turn this into a farmland. It's vacant for a reason. I believe that. The city know what they doing. They waiting for it to deteriorate. And it's almost there now. So whoever come up with the best price, they can build whatever they want, bring in the richer white folks, the richer black folks. You know, the bank got henchmen, too. I know a guy who was paid to burn down houses. Crooks is crooks. They come in baggy jeans and shirts and they come in suits and ties."

Overman said he was still scrapping, but he also planned to build a three-wheeled bicycle cart—he's a skilled welder—large enough to carry five hundred bottles of water, which he could sell for a dollar a bottle at some of the free outdoor concerts downtown. As we approached his apartment, Overman pointed to a sign advertising new condominiums "starting in the 150's." He shook his head. "Everyone waiting on a list as long as a scroll to get into low-income housing, and they building these condominiums? It seems to me like they moving the upper class here and the lower class across 8 Mile."

His voice shifting to a skeptical murmur, he read the sign's tagline: "Be Part of Detroit's Revitalization." Then he chuckled. "You *know* they not talking to us." By "us," he wasn't including me, of course.

"Unless that's a hundred and fifty *dollars*," he said. "You feel me?"

Former Detroit mayor Kwame Kilpatrick, handcuffed in court
after violating the terms of his probation.
[Daniel Mears/ *Detroit News*]

II

POLITICS

THE QUESTION PERSISTED, AS yet unresolved: was Dave Bing really the man we wanted behind the wheel of the car metaphor representing Detroit's future? As the nationwide sense of economic doom was hitting Michigan harder than any other state of the union, Detroit not only faced bankruptcy but the threat of a state takeover, made possible by Governor Snyder's emergency management law, dangling like an invisible sword. Was it real, or just that, a threat, meant to stiffen the spines of Detroit's historically feckless political class in their forced marched toward austerity?

Detroit's tawdry and dispiriting political erosion had started at the top, with the undoing of Kwame Kilpatrick, the young, virtuosic, wildly charismatic mayor who'd come into office in 2002 on a wave of promise and left in handcuffs, charged with perjury and obstruction of justice. While Kilpatrick and his administration also stood accused of bribery, kickbacks, embezzlement, blatant cronyism, and running the city like mafia capos, his ultimate downfall proved to be a humiliating sex scandal involving his chief of staff—and most damningly, his agreement to settle a police whistle-blower lawsuit with nearly nine million dollars of taxpayer money in order to prevent a series of suggestive text messages from seeing the light of day. That ploy obviously failed, and so the public was eventually treated to ripe exchanges such as the following:

CB (Christine Beatty, the mayor's chief of staff): I really wanted to give you some good head this morning and i didn't know how to ask you to let me do it. I have wanted to since friday

KK: Next time, just tell me to sit down, shut up and do your thing!

Meanwhile, several members of Detroit's city council managed the improbable concurrent feat of almost equally disgraceful public misbehavior, including mockery of a fellow councilperson's hearing aid (Council President Monica Conyers), involvement in a bar fight with another woman (ditto), threatening to "get a gun if she had to" in order to shoot a mayoral staffer (ditto), skipping important votes to tour in England while casually referring to the council in the UK press as "a second job I have" (ex–Motown star Martha Reeves), and paying an annual sixty-eight dollars in property taxes for years without once questioning the preposterously low, clearly erroneous bill (JoAnn Watson, who insisted the charge had simply led her to "the natural conclusion my house isn't worth much anymore").

In a plot twist too delicious for fiction, Conyers, the wife of long-serving and belovedly liberal Representative John Conyers, eventually pled guilty to a bribery case involving a billion-dollar sewage sludge disposal contract. As of this writing, she is serving a thirty-seven-month prison term. When news of the FBI's investigation into the sewage deal broke, Reeves, asked for comment, claimed to identify a net positive. What she said, exactly, was: "What I think it will do is get a bit more publicity for the council. This is one of the most highly publicized councils in the history of Detroit. They say if you're not doing anything, they're not saying anything about you."

The writer Zev Chafets, in *Devil's Night*, his 1991 book about Detroit, compared the city to a postcolonial African state, despoiled by attendant historical baggage and endemic corruption. It's sort of a great analogy, but also a flawed one. Black Detroiters were not a conquered people; they moved to Detroit to improve their lives—and *did*, building the city alongside the white majority, albeit in drastically disadvantaged and prejudicial circumstances. To me, the power shift in Detroit, and the ensuing hostilities with the suburbs, feels much closer to a cold war satellite-state scenario, in which dueling ideologies play themselves out through largely immaterial pawns. And so in the seventies and eighties, Coleman Young was spoken of by suburbanites in terms reserved, at a national level, for the likes of Fidel Castro or Ayatollah Khomeini. At the invocation of Young's name, many suburbanites easily lapsed into the fanaticism of the anti-Castro Cubans raging from the shores of Miami Beach at the not-so-distant island paradise snatched from them, the rightful owners, by a corrupt demagoguing madman.*

Likewise, for all his outsized flaws, Kilpatrick clearly did himself no favors by being African American and built like a linebacker. Putting his blackness aside, Kilpatrick would have still been a flamboyant, almost Shakespearean character in many ways, but certainly his penchant for wearing diamond-studded earrings and flashy suits and listening to hip-hop abetted his transformation into a cartoonish bogeyman. There was a slightly creepy, Willie Horton aspect to the way the camera lingered on his mug shot on local newscasts and the ease with which it became de rigueur for (generally white) commentators to describe him as a "thug." While still mayor, at the height of the scandals assailing his administration, Kilpatrick made an infamous state of the city address in which he claimed, "In the past thirty days, I've been called a nigger more than any time in my life." Using such inflammatory language so opportunistically, and in so public a forum, drove his critics and even many of his few remaining supporters apoplectic—and yet the pointed, incessant deployment of "thug" as descriptor suggested that perhaps he wasn't exaggerating all that much.

After Kilpatrick's resignation, the president of the city council, Ken Cockrel Jr.—whose late, aggressively Afroed father, a radical civil rights attorney, had served on the council in the seventies as an openly Marxist candidate—automatically became mayor. Prior to his ascension, the bald and somewhat hulking (but quite genial) Cockrel had become an unintentional YouTube sensation thanks to clips of a city council meeting in which Monica Conyers seemed to violate parliamentary procedure by shouting "You not my daddy!" at Cockrel before angrily referring to him as "Shrek."

---

*A better-natured satirical collection of the (admittedly eminently) quotable Young, released in 1991, was printed in the style of Mao's Little Red Book.

Cockrel's reign was short. Within a few months, a special election was held, giving the business community the opportunity to install one of their own, Dave Bing, who had parlayed his NBA stardom into the creation of a successful steel- and auto-parts-supply company. Coming after Kilpatrick, the anointment of the former Detroit Pistons point guard made perfect sense. Bing was the anti-Kwame, a lanky, graying man in his late sixties, bespectacled and mild-mannered. Critics pointed out that Bing had not lived in the city proper for decades, having long ago decamped to the tony suburb of Franklin. But voters didn't care. Bing cut a perfect visual contrast to the gross appetites of the Kilpatrick administration, which had remained on public display for so long. There was an appealing, ascetic quality to the new mayor—something monkish about his gauntness, his quiet dignity, his unself-conscious baldness and drooping silver mustache. He looked like an avuncular praying mantis. Even his eye-glazing ineptitude at public speaking became a plus when compared with the glibness of his quick-tongued predecessor. This guy was not going to cause trouble; this guy wouldn't be *capable* of tricking us. Detroit no longer wanted a visionary—just a ruthlessly competent technocrat in the mold of Michael Bloomberg, someone whose very lack of charisma would be its own mark of authenticity.

* * *

With Bing firmly in place, political observers turned their attention to the city council, a governing body that historically had a contentious relationship with the mayor of Detroit. Considering Bing's age and his vow to serve for a single term, the council might also be the place where the next mayor emerged, a man or woman with the boldness to steer Detroit through this uncharted, transformational moment—once noble, self-sacrificing Bing had taken the hits for implementing tough new policies in the name of rightsizing and budgetary rectitude. The 2009 elections looked to be an exciting race. By summer, 167 candidates had thrown their hats into the primary, all jockeying for only nine seats, and the scandal-weary Detroit electorate seemed prepared to usher in a new slate of leaders: the postprimary field, whittled down to eighteen, had shed both Monica Conyers and Martha Reeves.

One evening that October, I attended the closing candidate debate, which was being held at the grand, domed Charles H. Wright Museum of African American History. Because of their potentially unruly number, the candidates had agreed to multiple, subdivided debates featuring randomly selected participants, so this final meeting would involve only six of the contenders. Still, it was being closely watched because it featured the two front-runners, Charles Pugh, a former TV news personality who also happened to be openly gay, and Gary Brown, an ousted police officer whose whistle-blowing lawsuit had set off the chain of revelations ending with the toppling of Kilpatrick. Pugh's popularity, in particular, was considered surprising, as conventional wisdom had pegged Detroit's predominantly black electorate as socially conservative when it came to issues like homosexuality.

Both men, though, came bearing, "uniquely Detroit" (Pugh's words) backstories. In 1974, when Pugh was three years old, his mother was murdered by her heroin-dealing boyfriend; four years later, his father, depressed after being laid off from Ford, killed himself. Pugh, aged seven and the only other person in the house at the time, discovered the body. Somehow, he not only survived but flourished. Raised by his grandmother, Pugh decided to go to journalism school, with the intention—he mapped out this plan in high school—of starting in local news, moving onto a national broadcast like *The Today Show*, and eventually running for the U.S. Senate. The years of television experience had given Pugh a distinct messaging advantage over most of his opponents. A young-looking thirty-eight-year-old with a highly personable, perpetually empathetic demeanor, Pugh addressed potential constituents with a warm and expertly calibrated sincerity. He had the broadcaster's habit of smiling as he spoke and took an almost childish delight in the pronunciation of every word, as if, rather than speaking, he were nibbling a treat or unwrapping a series of little presents with his mouth.

Meanwhile, Brown, a methodical-minded overachiever, had known he wanted to be a cop by the time he was twelve. By sixteen, he'd finished high school, though before graduating he'd already enrolled in after-school community college courses in criminal justice. On the advice of one of his professors, a judge, he joined the Marine Corps rather than head straight for the police academy, where he was too young to become a cop, anyway. After being stationed at Pearl Harbor, he returned home to Detroit to find his twin brother had become addicted to heroin. Brown, in turn, became an undercover narcotics officer. "I thought this was a way of helping him," Brown told me. "I've raided every drug house in the city. I guess it was me being idealistic." Brown, who helped build complex conspiracy cases against drug gangs like Young Boys Inc. and the Chambers Brothers, would call his brother before certain raids to make sure he wasn't in the targeted dope house. As for his eventual clash with Kilpatrick, there was an almost literary perfection to the asymmetry between the two men, it seeming especially poetic for the ostentatious Goliath of a former mayor to be brought low by someone as unassuming, at least at first glance, as Brown. A trim, preppy guy with glasses, a neat little mustache, and the high, purring voice of a chain-smoking grandmother, Brown was basically Eliot Ness, exuding both military discipline and an upright fixation on investigatory precision.

The auditorium for the debate was packed. I sat beside an unusually tall man wearing an expensive gray suit and a gold Fendi watch. He told me he tried to attend most of the debates in order to stay involved, though he was more of an Eisenhower Republican. Introducing himself as a lawyer "by trade," he said he hoped to one day produce his own low-budget, self-financed movies for a black audience. He also thought one of the keys to Detroit's revival might lie in its rich cultural history, in somehow pivoting on the world's consistent adoration of the Motown sound, and of Detroit artists like Aretha and Eminem, by cultivating a vibrant club district. "New Orleans has a six-block entertainment strip and it attracts two million people a year," my neighbor said. He understood the job would not be easy. His brother, he said, liked to tell a story about leading a blind man into the light. *What's the first thing he does?* his brother asked. *Close his eyes.*

I didn't entirely understand the fable. Detroit was, presumably, meant to be the blind man, recoiling from too much change, even change of a positive nature. But had the blind man actually regained his sight? Or was the point that even his blind eyes were sensitive to bright new surroundings? The lawyer, after delivering the punch line, gave me a gnomic grin. I smiled back and nodded foolishly, as if we'd shared a moment of wisdom. After that, I didn't feel like I could ask what he'd actually meant.

Soon the six candidates filed onstage. Part of the drama of the debate, aside from its finality, surrounded Charles Pugh, who had been forced, just the day before, to make a humiliating disclosure: his $385,000 downtown condominium was about to be foreclosed on, after his default on a second mortgage. Apparently, Pugh was also being sued by his condo association for unpaid dues. As a broadcast personality, Pugh made well over $200,000, a year, but he claimed that leaving his job in order to run for city council full-time had put him in financial jeopardy—a claim undermined when the *Detroit News* reported on the eleven different eviction notices Pugh had received while renting an earlier apartment during a four-year period beginning in 2001. In an effort at damage control, Pugh posted a video on his website. It appeared to have been hastily produced with a cheap webcam. Pugh's large and uncannily egg-shaped head—which, completely shaved, made him look like a colossal baby—had been shot at an unflattering angle and nearly filled the screen as he exhorted viewers to pray for him and vowed to remain "on the grind, asking for your vote." He also insisted that going into foreclosure actually opened a number of "options" for the foreclosee—true, in a sense, if those options were limited to (a) leaving your house or (b) paying back the money you owed.

In his introductory remarks, Pugh assumed an upbeat tone, as if he were anchoring live from a Super Bowl victory party for the Detroit Lions. Explaining his decision to move from journalism to electoral politics, Pugh said, "I'm tired of just reporting what's *wrong*." As for his more immediate problems, he transformed them into an asset—an issue not of irresponsibility but of relatability, pointing out, "Just like many families, I've experienced personal tragedy. And just like many families, I'm facing financial challenges right now."

Aside from his polished delivery, Pugh's performance struck me as terrible. At one point, he told the moderator, straight-faced, "Well, the good thing is, personal finances have nothing to do with how the city is run." He also had the annoying habit of referring to his finances as "my challenges," as if he'd been nobly struggling to overcome some severe disability, like being been born with flipper arms and then deciding, through sheer force of will, to become a professional juggler.

Several of Pugh's opponents provided even greater entertainment value. Kwame Kenyatta, a gaunt fifty-three-year-old sporting a pinstripe jacket, mustard yellow turtleneck, and brown *kofia*, had the best fashion sense of anyone on the stage, a sort of Casual Friday Afro-centric look. That April, Kenyatta and his wife had not only defaulted on the mortgage of their four-bedroom colonial home on Detroit's northwest side but physically abandoned the property, simply walking away from the loan. When confronted with this fact by the moderator, Kenyatta was unapologetic. Flashing a tricky half smile and peering over his podium through permanently hooded eyes that gave him a serpentine quality, Kenyatta insisted he'd made a financial decision, "just like GM made a financial decision to go bankrupt." This line received hardy applause, as did his bit of one-upmanship of candidate James Bennett, an ex-cop who had declared himself "a blue-collar guy," to which Kenyatta responded, "I'm *street* collar, not necessarily blue col-lar. I come from the streets."

Mohammad Okdie, the only non–African American to make the final primary cutoff—Okdie's parents were Lebanese immigrants—mentioned he regularly rode the bus. During his closing remarks, he declared, "I am you, Detroit."

Gary Brown said, "I will not embarrass you."

Kenyatta, delightfully, concluded with a quote: "As the Last Poets said, 'It's down to now.'"

Pugh asked the voters of Detroit for their support of his leader-ship, "flaws and all," then flashed a grin.

On Election Day, the voters—such as they were: turnout was under 25 percent—wound up responding to Pugh's message, and he became the new city council president. Brown, coming in second, became council president pro tem. After his victory, Pugh told the *Free Press* he'd be calling the newly reelected Detroit city clerk to congratulate her and also, more urgently, "ask[ing] her for a certified letter that I was the top vote-getter . . . and the salary that corresponds to the top vote-getter is $85,000 a year. That's officially provable income. And the mortgage company was kind enough to postpone the sheriff's sale.

"I'm on much more solid footing on negotiating," he went on. "It'll be wrapped up before the swearing-in. Hell, it may be wrapped up before December."

* * *

As November approached, stencils began appearing on buildings around town featuring an anachronistic, bearded visage and the words RE-ELECT PINGREE. Elected in 1890, Hazen S. Pingree still reigns, pretty much uncontested, as Detroit's finest mayor. Republican railroad barons thought they had hand-picked an acceptable leader from the capitalist ranks, one who gave (per Robert Conot) "every indication [he] would complaisantly respond to their desires." Pingree, fifty years old, a Civil War veteran and owner of the largest shoe factory west of New England, surprised and infuriated his benefactors by becoming one of most progressive mayors in the country, siding with labor during a streetcar-workers' strike and dramatically revealing the dirty dealings of the public school board (apparently, some things never change) during a surprise appearance at a Board of Education meeting, where he announced to his stunned audience, "You are a bunch of thieves, grafters and rascals! As your names are called, the police will take you into custody."

Other echoes of futures to come: the depression of 1893 had left one-third of Detroiters unemployed. Along with securing money for an ambitious public works program, Pingree pioneered, nearly a century before it became a staple of the bright-new-ideas-for-saving-Detroit trend piece, an urban farming scheme in which more than three thousand families were encouraged (and partially subsidized) to grow vegetables on five-hundred acres' worth of half-acre plots throughout the city. Because the program launched in mid-June, the only crops harvested that first year were turnips, beans, and late potatoes, and the gardens were mocked as "Pingree's potato patches." In the end, though, it became Pingree's signature initiative, ultimately viewed as an ingenious pilot program by copycat mayors in Boston, Minneapolis, and New York.

Pingree eventually became governor of Michigan, a vanguard presence of the coming Progressive Era, admired, and copied by towering figures in the movement like Robert LaFollette and Teddy Roosevelt. In his 1895 account of his battles with the status quo, *Facts and opinion; or, Dangers that beset us*, Pingree wrote that "monopolistic corporations" were to blame for "nearly all the thieving and boodling" besetting us and our cities and wonderfully described the white collar bandits of the late nineteenth century as "a grade of criminals of finished rascality." The book's frontispiece was a photograph of Pingree's dedication of the volume to the "great masses of American people," handwritten on a potato. (A note at the bottom of the page reads, "Photographed from Original Potato.") It was as governor, campaigning against his would-be Democratic replacement in the mayor's office, that he informed a crowd in Detroit that "this town needs somebody to tell the public-utility crowd to kiss something else besides babies."

PHOTOGRAPHED FROM ORIGINAL POTATO.

Frontispiece, *Facts and opinion; or, Dangers that beset us*

The yearning for a duly-elected savior like Pingree was understandable. In recent years, the only Detroit politician who'd come close to the old man's panache—as terrible as it was to admit—was the Hon. Kwame Kilpatrick. From the moment I returned to the city, no matter what Bing or the council happened to be grappling with, a disproportionate amount of news coverage was devoted to the deposed mayor. It was like Nixon being sentenced to house arrest in the Lincoln Bedroom and still being allowed to call the periodic press conference. Kilpatrick had served time, moved his family to an expensive home in suburban Dallas, missed several restitution payments, and was ultimately sent back to jail. Still, his every move, voluntary or otherwise, caused seismic tremors in Detroit—a telling commentary on the power of his charismatic pull, even in exile and disgrace, and especially compared with those who had replaced him. Voters had declared their preference for the dull but steady Bing, Pugh the effervescent anchorman, Brown the crime-fighting Boy Scout—but still, they couldn't tear their eyes from the larger-than-life figure born to command a room.

Part of the reason, of course, had to do with the soap operatic pull of scandal involving sex, all manner of corruption (shakedowns, nepotism, general kleptocratic rot), even murder. (Rumors had circulated about wild parties the mayor had thrown in the Manoogian Mansion, including one in which his wife arrived unexpectedly and allegedly assaulted an exotic dancer named Tamara "Strawberry" Greene. Later, the twenty-seven-year-old dancer was shot and killed at four-thirty in the morning while sitting in her car with her boyfriend on the city's west side, feeding lurid but wholly unfounded conspiracy theories that had Greene snuffed by a mayoral hit man in order to prevent her from speaking publicly about the alleged party incident.) But there was an extra sting to Kilpatrick's downfall precisely because, once upon a time, he truly had struck many as an energetic and even visionary leader who might alter Detroit's trajectory through the sheer strength of his personality.

Kilpatrick came from a politically connected family—his mother, Carolyn Cheeks-Kilpatrick, was a U.S. Representative—and when Kwame was elected in 2001, at the age of thirty-one, he was the youngest mayor in Detroit's history. I spent two days shadowing Kilpatrick in 2002,* when he was celebrating his first year in office with a 75 percent approval rating, having already logged an impressive list of early-term accomplishments that included five thousand new housing starts and balancing the city budget, despite the inheritance of a seventy-five-million dollar deficit. At the time, the comedian Chris Rock gave an interview about preparing for his role as the first black president in the 2003 film *Head of State*; he didn't cite Barack Obama, the obscure state senator from Illinois, as a model for his character, but Kwame Kilpatrick.

---

*For a planned magazine profile, ultimately never published.

"Kwame got it—he was brilliant," Kurt Metzger, Detroit's most respected demographer, told me later, after everything had gone wrong. "He just understood data. Whenever I threw a number at him, he'd know it, and could respond with numbers of his own. And he'd be right!" Metzger smiled sadly. "Unfortunately, he was also a sociopath. But other than that . . ."

Almost immediately, I took to the mayor. Despite his size, he moved with a relaxed, ambling gait. His head looked small atop such a bulky presence, his ears tinier still, with a slightly crushed quality, as if they'd been stuck to either temple as globs of half-baked dough. But Kilpatrick was a handsome man, with an easy, confident smile, and he backed his storied personal magnetism with obvious intelligence and a quick wit. He also possessed the natural charm advantage of the physically imposing, whereby little more than a reassuring nod or welcoming grin from a person twice your size triggers, on some dank evolutionary substrata, an involuntary rush of gratitude. When I heard rumblings about "immaturity" and "arrogance," I was quick to write off the objections as generational, stylistic. Kilpatrick and I were close in age, and when journalists dubbed him "the hip-hop mayor,"* I didn't see it as an epithet, but, rather, a milestone.

Still, the cockiness of his administration—"swagger," in hip-hop terms—was evident. One evening, when I joined Kilpatrick on an Angel's Night patrol, the mayor's press secretary, Jamaine Dickens, casually popped a CD into the stereo of his blue Crown Vic as we drove to meet the mayor. "Do you like Ludacris?" he asked. "This was our unofficial campaign song, just because we spent so much time on the road." The rapper boomed, "You got to MOVE, bitch! Get out the WAY!"

Dickens smiled, flinched, and went on: "You know what? Our real song was 'You Scared.' You know that one?" To refresh my memory, he shout-rapped, in the manner of Lil' Jon, the song's *auteur*, its

---

*Partly, this referred to Kilpatrick's youth and sartorial flair, but Kilpatrick had certainly lived up to his nickname, inviting Biz Markie to spin at his inauguration party and allowing himself to be sampled by the Detroit rap group Black Bottom Collective, on a ten-second track called "Best Not Keep Da Mayor Waitin'," on which he exhorted the group to "'come wit' it Detroit style."

bullying chorus: "You SCARED! You SCARED! Bee-AAAAA bee-AAAAA!" "Bee-AAAAA" was short for "bitch." (The actual title of the song was "Bia Bia," with other choice lines including "Stop acting like a BITCH and get your HANDS up!") Adding clarification, Dickens explained, "That was our song because it seemed like everybody was scared to endorse us."

My exchange with Kilpatrick himself that night felt raw and honest, more so than the majority of interactions I've had with public figures. Earlier in the day, Kilpatrick had addressed a council of Baptist preachers (telling them, "The next wave of the Civil Rights movement is access to capital"); he'd since changed from a suit into brown Timberland boots, grey jeans, and an Angel's Night sweatshirt the safety-orange shade of a deer hunter's anorak. The night was proceeding smoothly and the mayor lapsed into a decided informality between stops. At one point, while a small group of us rode in the back of the black mayoral Suburban, Kilpatrick absently picked up one of the flashlights being passed out to volunteers and announced, "I wanna flash some people." He began shining the light out the window. Then he illuminated his own face, like one of the ill-fated teenagers from the movie *The Blair Witch Project*, only instead of telling a campfire story, he began to imitate a man being hassled by a police officer.

"'What you doin', man?'

"'Well, I'm *blind*, now. Could you take the flashlight out of my face? I ain't going nowhere.'

"'You being smart?'

"'I'm always smart. I went to school, man. I'm just hoping you'll take that flashlight down so we can have a conversation.'"

Shifting back to his own voice, Kilpatrick said, "They used to *hate* me." He meant the cops. After falling silent for a moment, he turned to me and asked drolly, "Mark, have you had positive experiences with police officers?"

I said, "Positive? I don't know. Probably not."

The mayor said, "Heh."

I said I guessed my experiences had been pretty neutral. Then I asked, "What about you?"

"I was getting hassled during the campaign," Kilpatrick said. "The police department was against me. *Vehemently* against me. So that was going on. But I had a real bad experience with a police officer once. I thought he was going to kill me for no reason."

I asked what happened. The mayor went quiet again, and seemed to be considering whether or not to tell the story. When he spoke, his tone had become more serious. "It was about three years ago," he began slowly, "He told me I robbed something. This is Seven Mile here," he said to the driver, before continuing: "I was standing in my driveway. I was trying to tell him that I lived there. A house down the street had been robbed. I was coming outside with my friend and we were about to go to the store and get some food. My wife was going to cook dinner. It was after church, so I was pretty well dressed." The mayor cleared his throat. "The police pulled up and, to make a long story short, he put a nine-millimeter gun to my head, told me to get on the ground, or he was gonna shoot me."

There was a long silence. Finally, I began, "So when he figured out you weren't the guy—"

"No apology," the mayor interrupted. He gazed out the window, shadows flickering across his broad face. "There were like four police cars by that point. Matter of fact, he was yelling, 'I was following procedure, I didn't do nothing wrong!' He was such a bad officer. He'd been cussing at me the whole time. 'I swear to God, you move, I'm gonna kill you.' Another officer grabbed my friend and threw him in the car. I was this calm, talking to him just like this, but with a gun in my face. I said, 'Just put the gun down. My license is in my pocket. This is my house.' It was like three or four in the afternoon. Kids were riding their bikes, skipping up the street." Kilpatrick chuckled mordantly. "It was a *nice* day." Kilpatrick said the reason he didn't get on the ground right away was because his two-year-old twins were standing in the doorway.

Later, of course, I wondered how much of the story had been bullshit.*

---

*Who could say? My friend Stephen Henderson, the editorial page editor at the *Detroit Free Press*, once witnessed a Kilpatrick performance in which the mayor, near tears, convincingly pro-

* * *

I visited Gary Brown one afternoon at his home in Sherwood Forest, a neighborhood of handsome brick estates with its own private security patrol. Brown's political career had been the one thing Kilpatrick had inarguably bequeathed to the city, and the council president pro-tem was certainly the most impressive of the new lot of Detroit politicians. We chatted in a sunny Florida room in the back of the house, where African masks hung on the wall above a Bose stereo system. Brown, dressed like a suburban dad, wore a zippered sweater and a pair of loafers with no socks.

Brown's lawsuit had made him a well-liked public figure in Detroit,[*] and once in office, Brown proved to be the most hard-headed of the new council, training the forensic obsessiveness he'd honed as a narcotics and internal affairs investigator on Detroit's budgetary crime scene. Almost single-handedly, Brown pushed the council to propose far deeper annual spending cuts than the Bing administration—in 2011, $50 million more than Bing had proposed—not out of right-wing austerity-mindedness but because Brown understood the very real threat of a state takeover of Detroit.

By April 2012, when it became clear that Detroit, drowning in $12 billion of debt, would have to accede to some form of state control,

---

claimed his innocence to an assembled group of supposedly jaded *Free Press* editors and writers, Henderson among them, who basically walked away believing him.

As rumors of Kilpatrick's after-hours partying at the mayoral mansion trickled out, I recalled how, at end of our night together, I'd overheard the mayor ask a member of his entourage, "So she's gonna be able to come to the mansion tonight?" It was close to midnight. We'd seen the mayor's wife at an earlier stop, but she had gone home with the children. (The mansion was being renovated, so the Kilpatricks were still living at their personal residence.) Someone noticed me standing there and quickly said, "We just found out a woman who does massages is going to be able to come to the mansion tonight. We go there to work sometimes, and she'll come out if it's been a long day." I nodded, not sure how credulous they expected me to act. I decided to go with "extremely credulous."

*Well, not *universally*: during an interview, a prominent, politically connected local activist turned off my tape recorder and said, "Gary Brown is a *punk bitch*. What happens when you investigate your boss? You get fired. That's what happened. He was serving at the mayor's discretion. Okay, Kwame was a boner. He was a baller. You get to the position where a hundred and fifty women a year are throwing themselves at you, what do you do? You might hit one or two. If it's okay with them and okay with your wife, why is it anyone else's business?"

Brown and Charles Pugh led the council in crafting a responsible compromise "consent agreement" in which a nine-member financial oversight board would oversee budgetary reforms. The consent agreement opened the door to more public-service union concessions and deeper governmental cuts, but also staved off the appointment of an emergency manager, which would have sidelined elected representatives like Bing and the council. Brown and Pugh came off especially well in comparison to Bing, who spent much of the budget crisis either engaging in dubious accounting tricks or seemingly angling to be appointed emergency manager himself, and to longer-serving council members like Kwame Kenyatta and JoAnn Watson, who played to their base with righteous-sounding but ultimately fatuous obstructionism.

At times, Gary Brown and Charles Pugh felt like two sides of the Kilpatrick persona, Brown embodying the wonk, Pugh the great communicator. If Pugh seemed weak discussing specifics of policy— the first time we met, he brought up his idea to bottle and market water from the Detroit River—he nonetheless assembled a smart, young team, and was generally upbeat and forward-looking rather than fixated on the racial and geographical battles of the past. In a city like Detroit, where so many citizens had felt disenfranchished for so long, the ability to clearly and effectively speak to one's constituents, as Pugh could, masterfully, struck me as no superficial tool.

To that end, Pugh spent an hour or two most Friday afternoons riding the city buses and mingling with the electorate. Using public transportation as a means of proving "relatability" has always been an easy PR stunt, but in Detroit, the very act of riding the harrowing, unreliable bus system became a deeply empathetic act of shared sacrifice. One Friday, when Pugh invited me to join him in the field, a woman at the bus stop glanced at us as she wandered by, then came to a full stop. "Hi, Pugh!" she called out. "What you doing out here?"

"Talking to people like you," Pugh said enthusiastically.

When one of Pugh's staffers informed him of the arrival of his bus, a look of concern spread over the woman's face. "You gonna catch the bus, Pugh?"

"I ride the bus every week!" he called over his shoulder.

The woman snorted, seeming both skeptical and anxious for the young man.

On board, the driver recognizing the council president, evinced similar incredulity. Staring back at us in his wide rearview mirror, he shouted, "When was the last time you been on the Iron Pimp?"

Pugh said, "I ride the bus two or three times a month."

"For real?"

Pugh said, "The very first time we rode the bus, it broke down on Woodward! Just so you know." Then he added, "I love it because it keeps us connected."

The driver said, "You about to get connected with some kids in a minute."

Pugh's staff laughed nervously.

We'd started at the central bus terminus, named for Rosa Parks, one of the few examples of ambitious and aesthetically pleasing new architecture to appear in downtown Detroit in the past several decades—most strikingly, the curved white awnings sheltering each bus stop, looking from the street like the billowing sails of a grand seafaring vessel, and appearing from directly below like the underside of a row of dirigibles, docked and awaiting take-off, either conjured image working as a fitting tribute to Parks, hinting as they did of the moment before an epic journey.

Over the course of our two-hour ride, I was the only white passenger, save for a single man with a ponytail and camouflage jacket who boarded for a brief stretch near Highland Park. On the bus, Pugh took a seat near the middle. It was not very crowded yet. One of the first passengers we picked up, a middle-aged man, took a seat in the handicapped area near the front, then spotted Pugh and shouted back a greeting. He told Pugh they'd met once at Eastern Market. Pugh asked if the man shopped there. "No, I *work* there," the man said. When they'd met, he told Pugh, he'd been fixing a broken HiLo (a type of forklift), which seemed to puzzle Pugh.

"Hey, you got a pencil?" the man called out. "Write down this number. I want you to call my mama."

Pugh wrote down the number and promised the man he would call his mother and tell her that he'd met her son on the bus.

As we meandered up Woodward, Pugh occasionally switched seats to chat with other passengers. His team members had spread out, too, distributing flyers with information about the council, including phone numbers and Internet addresses related to various city services and departments. The interactions highlighted, in a pitiless way, the difficulties many in the city faced. Pugh approached a pair of weary looking men and handed them flyers, asking brightly, "Y'all know anybody looking for a job?" The flyers contained information about city employment programs.

"Yeah," one of the guys muttered, barely glancing at Pugh or the flyer. "Everybody."

Another man in a knit Carhart cap took the seat behind Pugh and leaned forward. "I wonder if you can help me," he asked. "I have a felony, fifteen years old, but they discriminate against me now when I'm trying to get work." The man was gaunt, in his fifties, with a toothpick in his mouth and a nasty-looking bruise under his left eye. Pugh chatted with him for a few minutes, then asked if he ever used the Internet. The man said yes and Pugh handed him a flyer and told him to go to his website, where there was an entire section devoted to constituents with criminal records.

And so it went. One teenage boy turned out to be returning from a visit to his lawyer for a charge he didn't want to discuss; he'd also been temporarily expelled from school. A group of high school girls discussed *Raisin in the Sun* with Pugh, who recommended various colleges and argued gently with the one who said she couldn't wait to get out of Detroit. I noticed that one of the staffers, a stocky older man, stuck close to Pugh whenever he moved around, always sure to position himself in a seat nearby, no doubt acting as a sort of bodyguard. I wondered if they thought Pugh was in danger of being mugged while riding a bus in broad daylight.

During a lull, Pugh told me that he hoped to see more regional cooperation with the suburbs, that he would love for the planned lightrail line to connect Detroit with surrounding communities. Most of the constituent interfacing had gone well up to this point. But then an older man sitting behind Pugh perked up and noticed his famous neighbor. The man had an old-fashioned pair of oversized headphones hanging around his neck, and he reeked of booze. Leaning forward, he introduced himself to Pugh, then said, "I have a lot of questions for you. Why are you hiding back here?"

A glimmer of annoyance crept into Pugh's voice, sounding odder because he couldn't turn off its chirpier inflection. "I'm not hiding!" he said. "You just got on. You don't know what I've been doing."

The man nodded and said, "So, in regards to the change issue, I'm wondering, 'What is our destination?' For instance, this dumping right here." The man nodded out the window to his left. On the other side of the street, there was a rubble-strewn lot.

"No, no!" Pugh said. "See, that's not dumping. That was an abandoned building. It was taken down. That's a good thing."

The man considered this response, pursing his lips, then said, "So what you're saying is, I'm not viewing urban blight. I'm viewing urban progress."

Pugh didn't seem to know if he was being messed with or not, but he stuck with his argument about abandoned buildings needing to be demolished.

"I'm part of your constituency," the man interrupted. "And what you're not hearing is, a couple of days ago, I saw trucks illegally dumping. These guys are making sixteen hundred dollars dumping in the city, and they've got no overhead. Man, in this area I'm talking about, you see mounds and mounds and mounds. It's Trumbell and . . . and . . . Well, I'm an old man. I forget."

"Elijah McCoy Drive?" Pugh asked. As the man spoke, Pugh had taken out his BlackBerry and pecked out a memo regarding the dumping location, or at least pretended to. "There are a lot of abandoned fields over there. It's not far from where I grew up."

"Do you remember Maryanne McCaffery?" the old man asked, referring to a beloved city council member from the Coleman Young era, now deceased. He asked Pugh about a specific bill McCaffery had championed. Pugh obviously had no idea what the man was talking about. "See, I read history," the man said. "It's important to know history."

As he spoke, we pulled back into the Rosa Parks Terminal, and Pugh rose abruptly, his patience all used up. "When she was elected,

I was seven years old, dog," he noted sourly. "I wasn't following politics then. Sorry."

* * *

Dave Bing had initially pledged to serve only a single term as mayor. But by December 2009, in a year-end interview with the *Free Press*, the mayor reversed himself, declaring, "I never considered myself a one-term mayor. My nature is to finish what I start. Can I do that in this job? I don't think so. It's a ten-to-twenty-year process. I don't know if I have that kind of time, but I'm not coming to this job saying I'm only going to do it for one term."

The backpedaling was both unsurprising—he was a politician, after all—but also not, as Bing hardly struck anyone as enjoying his job or being particularly engaged with it. The *Detroit News* reported that Bing's workdays rarely extended past 5:00 p.m. As a public speaker, he remained leaden and stultifying, unerringly tone-deaf to the expectations of his audience. Even his storied managerial skills didn't appear to be so hot. He bragged in an early interview about not "believ[ing] in emails," preferring to walk down the hall and look a person in the face, which, while presumably meant to convey old-timey virtue and simplicity, came off rather like a stubborn and bizarrely inefficient personal quirk. And in truth, becoming a wealthy auto-parts supplier in Detroit doesn't necessarily prove any sort of genius-level business acumen, especially when you happen to be a local basketball star potential clients would be eager to meet.*

The Bing administration's tepid rollout of the Detroit Works project in the fall of 2010 did nothing to boost the city's confidence in its mayor. And over the following year, it became increasingly clear that Council President Pugh and Pro Tem Brown recognized Bing's weaknesses. Brown was said to be exploring a senate run. Pugh, meanwhile, found it less and less necessary to mask his own obvious designs

---

*The shameless number of sports analogies used by Bing in speeches and interviews suggests he remains well aware of the power of his former athletic celebrity and has in fact been flexing those muscles for so long it's now second nature. During my own half-hour interview with the mayor, he cited, as an analogy for his deliberative style of governance, how he'd always been someone who "makes layups and free throws, not three-pointers."

on the mayor's office. The first time we'd met, shortly before Pugh's own election, he had tiptoed around his ambition, shifting it over to anecdotal strawmen ("There are people who walk up and say, 'You should have run for mayor.' Not right now. Give me four years, as we downsize and get used to that, the innovations that we bring . . ."), while undermining Bing via backhanded words of support ("He's got a monumental task ahead of him, in downsizing government—and he's the oldest man ever elected mayor in Detroit's history."). By the time of our bus ride, however, Pugh's tone vis-à-vis Bing had shifted to open condescension: "All mayors have some growing pains, and obviously, Dave Bing is the quiet, unassuming type. I just don't think he realizes the power he has. He's *too* quiet. I know I would have done the right-sizing meetings a little different. There needs to be more door-knocking. People need hope. I wish Dave Bing would take the lead."

All of this naturally decreased Bing's incentive to assume a conciliatory tone with the council in general and the council president in particular. In the midst of difficult negotiations over the city budget, for example, Bing's press office coolly announced that seventy-seven public parks would close for the summer because of the council's fiscal outrageousness—a move that ultimately forced the council to blink and restore nearly $18 million of budget cuts they'd previously overridden a Bing veto to preserve. By most other metrics, though, Bing had few wins after three years in office: crime was up, the most elementary public services (the bus system, the lighting department) remained miserable failures, and a head-turning number of high-profile city hall departures left the impression of an administration in disarray.

While Detroit's leadership had bickered, venture capitalist Rick Snyder had settled into the governor's mansion in Lansing. Even more overtly than Bing, Snyder made much of his stiffness as a public speaker, proudly describing himself as a "nerd" in his campaign ads—he injected six million dollars of his own money into the campaign, outspending his Democratic opponent four to one—and trading on the public's stereotypical association of nerdiness with a high I.Q. and a certain level of uptightness, which Snyder implied would act as twin virtues when it came to the governance of a state in desperate need of rebuilding.

Immediately after taking office, Snyder embraced supply-side economic solutions to address Michigan's fiscal problems—basically, cutting taxes on most businesses while raising taxes on just about everyone else, in hopes of attracting new private-sector investment in the state. (Specifically, Snyder lowered corporate taxes by more than $1.5 billion a year, making up some of the difference by cutting state aid to colleges and universities by 15 percent, reducing K–12 education funding by $430 per pupil, and raising taxes on pensions.) More alarming still was the adoption of the Emergency Financial Manager law. As critics noted, the bill passed at a time when Michigan still had one of the country's highest unemployment rates, which in turn was having a steep attritive effect on the state's population (along with its tax base), the result being that dozens of local government leaders finding themselves staring down potential bankruptcy unless they enacted draconian cuts in basic city services and the unionized civic employees who provided them. At the same time, the federal government, and now the state government under Snyder, was actually reducing local aid.

Detroit was the fattest prize, for someone willing to take the most cynical, Machiavellian view of the Snyder administration, of Republicans foaming at the mouth to snatch the city back from the liberals—a racially coded word here—who'd run it into the ground. So, as Bing and Pugh spent a few weeks arguing over control of a city-run public access cable channel (really), others worried that such machinations were soon to become wholly irrelevant. In the end, the city-state consent agreement reached was infinitely preferable to emergency management: the mayor and council would retain their power, though their budgets would now be subject to final approval by the nine-person financial oversight board. Mayor and council would solely or jointly appoint five of the board's members; the board would not have an emergency manager's power to discard union contracts completely. Still, the city was basically agreeing to work with the state to slash payroll, sell off city assets, and outsource departments. Though Detroit's elected leadership remained in place, it felt less relevant than ever; its powers, in the face of unworkable math, had basically come down to managed decline.

Gary Brown, ever the realist, was quick to declare the consent agreement a "great deal"—if, as he pointed out, "you look at the fact that we don't have anything to bargain with, we don't have anything to negotiate with, we're down to the ninth hour, we don't have any cash and we don't have any leverage."

Steve and Dorota Coy, the Hygienic Dress League, in Detroit's Brush Park.
[Steve and Dorota Coy]

12

LET US PAINT YOUR
FACTORY MAGENTA

ONE OCTOBER MORNING, TWO hundred members of the art world elite gathered for a catered buffet brunch in the Great Hall of the Detroit Institute of Arts. The museum, a Beaux-Arts temple built in 1927, when Detroit's auto barons had money to spare for such conspicuous cultural displays, had been chosen as the starting point of an epic performance by the contemporary art superstar Matthew Barney, best known for his series of visually ravishing and fanatically art-directed *Cremaster* films, and also for being the longtime companion of the Icelandic singer Björk. The event was invitation-only; of the guests, most had flown in from New York and Los Angeles, and the list included curators from the Museum of Modern Art and the Whitney, auctioneers from Sotheby's, directors of the Warhol Foundation, PS1, and the Dia Foundation, along with various other artists, gallery owners, wealthy and well-connected patrons, and Björk herself.

The Barney performance, titled *Khu*, would be part of his first major effort since the *Cremaster* films, in which the handsome ex-jock had cast himself as a grotesque, unrecognizably made-up satyr figure (*Cremaster 4*) or as the murderer Gary Gilmore (*Cremaster 2*), often spending interminable chunks of screen time doing things like (say) squeezing through a narrow tunnel lubricated with what appeared to be Vaseline. Barney's latest project was a planned seven-chapter adaptation of the Norman Mailer novel *Ancient Evenings*, which concerned classical Egyptian notions of the seven stages of death and rebirth. Though Mailer's book had been a decidedly minor late-period work, the choice, at least topic-wise, seemed fitting for Barney, whose own films, like allegorical paintings made animate, arrived coded with enough multilayered references and fraught symbolism as to conjure their own mythology. Unlike *Cremaster*, this new piece consisted of a series of live, site-specific, one-time-only performances, all to be filmed for some edited future use.

Part of the reason for the setting of *Khu* had to do with the local connections of two of Barney's personal heroes, who were referenced in the production: the performance artist James Lee Byars, who was born in Detroit and died, appropriately enough, in Cairo, and Harry Houdini, who died in Detroit* and whom Barney clearly considered a sort of proto–performance artist, so much so that the great magician and escapist (played by Norman Mailer!) had already made an appearance in *Cremaster 2*. Barney had earlier spent time in the city filming a prologue to *Ancient Evenings*, which culminated with a Pontiac Trans Am driving off the Belle Isle Bridge, an homage to a Houdini stunt, performed in 1906, in which he leapt from the bridge while shackled with handcuffs. The Trans Am was supposed to be a reincarnation of the 1967 Chrysler Crown Imperial used in the smashup derby in *Cremaster 3*.

At the brunch, I ate some fresh fruit and a made-to-order omelet. While I was standing in line for the fruit, a Detroit artist told me how, while taking Björk on a tour of his neighborhood the day before, he'd pointed out a foreclosed home he hoped to buy, with plans of transforming the yard into a skateboarder's half-pipe. Björk, misunderstanding, had cried, delighted, "You're turning the houses into *pipe organs*? What a great idea!"

After brunch, we filed onto the tour buses that would shuttle us to the first act of the performance. The buses embarked upon a leisurely caravan through the city, pausing in front of the abandoned train station and cruising past the more mundane ruins scarring every other block. A chic British gallerist in her sixties sat beside me for the tour. She said she'd been one of the earliest champions of Barney's work.

---

*Though (in flagrant disregard of cultural stereotyping) the infamous appendix-rupturing sucker punch meant to test Houdini's iron gut came from a Canadian, not a Detroiter, at the previous tour stop in Montreal.

When we passed the fourteen-story Wurlitzer Building—built in 1926, empty since 1982—her eyes lit up. She told me the Wurlitzers were old family friends. Turning to one of her traveling companions, a young, long-haired artist who looked like a guitar tech for a heavy metal band, she exclaimed, "Neville! We should buy one of these buildings for a dollar!" Everyone around us laughed.

Eventually our buses parked on a residential street a mile or so west of downtown. A couple of guys in hooded sweatshirts watched from the front lawn of their dilapidated apartment complex as we exited the tour buses and were directed into a moldering two-story glue factory, where folding chairs had been set up on the main floor, along with standing-room spots on a second-level loft. We entered the scene in medias res: a group of assembly line workers toiled at a long bench, meticulously assembling about a dozen junkyard viols. The workers, for the most part burly men with walrus mustaches, ponytails, and UAW Local 600 T-shirts, looked authentically working class, and the "set," likewise, felt "real," from the foreboding hook dangling from the ceiling to the defunct heavy machinery crowding the perimeter. It was unclear which (if any) elements of the set had been found and which had been constructed by Barney, who was known for his fastidious attention to the tiniest sculptural details. I didn't find it impossible to imagine a team of art interns distressing freshly painted walls with specially designed dust applicators and hand flakers. Barney himself was nowhere to be seen; I was told that he was directing the scene from an undisclosed location.

On the assembly line, the workers were employing Fordist manufacturing techniques, each applying himself to a single, specific task, from drawing strings along the necks of the instruments to soldering their bodies into place. As each viol was completed, a musician appeared from the wings and began to play a tuneless dirge, the size and cacophony of the band growing with every finished instrument. The workers, meanwhile, remained bent to their individual jobs, proceeding at a punishingly unhurried pace. This continued for at least a half hour, giving viewers plenty of time to absorb every sarcophagal detail of the decaying factory space.

I wondered if the screeching hideousness of the tune was distracting to the instrument makers, and how it must feel for an hourly worker in

Detroit to playact his or her trade in a performance with a reputed budget of five million dollars for an audience of the cultural elite. I noticed that the actor James Franco had fallen asleep in the front row. Maybe one day the only factory work left in Detroit would be stylized performance art—manufacturing as historical reenactment!

Upon leaving the glue factory, we marched on a gangplank, single file, onto a two-hundred-foot barge that took us on a journey down the Rouge River, through the heart of Detroit's industrial history—not only past the Rouge plant but under Gothic drawbridges and alongside factory smokestacks spewing actual flame, until it began to feel as if we were traveling back in time to some extinct era. Which, of course, we sort of were. It was a cold and wet afternoon, and the grey midwestern sky looked especially vast and portentous. Aside from Björk, who, being from Iceland, had dressed appropriately for the weather (in a warm-looking parka and headwrap), many of us shivered on the open-air deck, occasionally taking seats on a tiered row of damp girders lining the starboard of the barge like bleachers, while helicopters buzzed overhead to film the forensic investigation of the drowned Trans Am, fished from the water with a massive crane and deposited on the deck. A smaller motorized boat circled in our wake, a horn section on its own deck serenading us with blasts of free jazz. Later, while a pair of male twins sang threatening operatic arias, the remains of the Trans Am were removed from the barge and melted in the furnaces of a gargantuan multistory foundry, as several dozen other laborers swarmed like ants in a yawning quarry. The rain and wind pounded out such a squall by the end that most of us fled to the tour buses, missing the coda, the release of a live vulture.

At the after-party, in line at the open bar, I ran into one of the curators and asked how Barney's location scouts had chosen the foundry. "Oh," she explained, "actually, none of the foundries they looked at were the right size. He built that one."

Later, I discovered the blue-collar workers toiling on the viol assembly line were not, in fact, blue-collar workers but art-world types who had helped with the shoot, news that had the effect of making me slightly more depressed.

* * *

By the standard of media-friendliness, the only serious competitor to urban farming as a saving-Detroit story was the arrival of the artists: they were scooping up houses for a hundred bucks; they were repurposing defunct Albert Kahn plants as miles of studio space; they came to Detroit from Brooklyn, because Detroit was the new Brooklyn; they came to Detroit from Europe, because Detroit was the next Berlin. Artists froze a vacant house solid and David Byrne showed up at a Mike Kelly opening (and blogged about how much he'd loved cycling around town), and the crème de la crème of single-named street artists (Swoon! Banksy! Retna!) made pilgrimages to tag our aging factory walls. During a talk at Cooper Union, Patti Smith advised young artists in the audience to move to Detroit. (She also mentioned Poughkeepsie, so perhaps she'd just been listing places cheaper than New York. In any case, she said Detroit first.)

Serious people—most vociferously, urbanist Richard Florida—had long been making the case for the ways in which discarded Rust Belt cities like Detroit and Pittsburgh might obtain tangible economic benefits, could *possibly save themselves*, by becoming more like Austin and San Francisco. His theory of the so-called creative class linked the success of modern cities to their ability to attract a specific genre of person, not necessarily artists and musicians but tech entrepreneurs, gays, bartenders who happened to dress stylishly or use Apple products— basically anyone who could plausibly be described as being "with it."

If there was a syllogism at work here—dynamic and prosperous cities tend to be attractive to urbane creative types who like dynamic and prosperous cities—nobody seemed to care. Quantifiable proof that the "creative class" brought job growth to moribund economies was hard to come by, discounting the job created for one specific person, Richard Florida, who was living in Pittsburgh at the time and who, after the success of his 2001 book, *The Rise of the Creative Class*, became a highly paid consultant and motivational speaker in cities desperate to soak up the talent and lucre that, according to Florida, inevitably followed the arrival of a critical mass of people who could hum at least three LCD Soundsystem songs.* In Michigan, then

---

*In 2011, Florida conceded that some of the postindustrial cities he'd cited as ripe for creative-class reengineering might, in the wake of the crash, be pretty much screwed. He'd come up with

Governor Jennifer Granholm had unveiled a "Cool Cities" initiative promising grants to Michigan towns, Detroit included, for rebranding efforts. On the state's website, someone helpfully posed the possibilities. What is a cool city? the writer asked rhetorically:

> Is it a leafy, green park and an inviting public square? Or is it a sidewalk bistro and an internet café? Maybe it's a jazz club or a coffee house that invites office workers to linger in your downtown well past 5:00 p.m. Maybe it's nothing more extravagant—or more important—than a quality neighborhood school, a job within walking distance and a safe path for getting to both. Whatever your vision of a cool city, we are working to make that vision a reality.

"Cool" is an amorphous term, but stretching its definition to include "public education," "employment," and "not being murdered on the way to work" struck me as—how would a cool person put this?—"diluting the brand, dude."

By 2009, however, Detroit's reputation as a bohemian paradise was beginning to gain cultural traction, along with, increasingly, a burgeoning film scene. Cheap rent and no rules attracted the artists and musicians. The presence of the film industry, on the other hand, had come as a result of a top-down, managed economic undertaking, with the state offering preposterously large tax incentives (a 40 percent rebate of all money spent on a particular production) to filmmakers willing to shoot in Michigan. And so the appeal of Detroit for Matthew Barney—and others shooting movies in and around the city, including the makers of *Transformers 3*, *Scream 4*, *A Very Harold & Kumar Christmas*, and the Miley Cyrus vehicle *LOL: Laughing Out Loud*—was not merely aesthetic but also financial.

People debated whether doling out such a considerable wad of incentive to Hollywood made sense for a state as revenue-poor as Michigan. Proponents portrayed cash lost in the short term as a necessary investment in exactly the sort of new industry Detroit so sorely

---

a solution for those who stuck around, though: high-speed rail! Trains would soon be so fleet, Detroit "could be repositioned as a suburb of sorts for Chicago and potentially even Toronto," and the creative class would now seek gainful employment as a commuter class.

needed; the opposition contended the public and its legislators had been dazzled by the glamour of a fickle industry that would bolt as soon as American Samoa managed to slap together an even more generous package of tax breaks.

Still, the bill passed with bipartisan support, after which over a hundred film and television productions came to the state, with spending by film companies ballooning from $2 million to $224 million in just two years. The $1.6 million Maxsar Digital Studios opened in a retrofitted 60,000-square-foot factory in the west side suburb of Livonia. Pontiac, another suburb—so broke it had outsourced its police and fire departments and announced it would be selling city hall, the library, and two cemeteries—became home to Raleigh Studios, a $120 million facility on twenty-two acres of land, encompassing a vacant GM office building that once housed three thousand engineers, with investors including the William Morris talent agency. A senior vice president at the Motion Picture Association of America called Raleigh, which has one of the largest sound stages in the world, "the premiere studio facility in the U.S." The place was to become, in the words of the *Detroit Free Press*, a "destination campus" where "laid-off autoworkers . . . would undergo training for production jobs."

Hollywood's response to the tax credits had been immediate and high-profile. Celebrity sightings, the lights and equipment and union crew bustle—the spectacle of so many people visibly working in town, often right in the middle of the street—had even the most cynical wondering: "Detroit as the Hollywood of the Midwest: *Why not?*"

* * *

The most lavishly budgeted, surreally conspicuous of all the productions staking out beachheads in the area involved Tom Cruise—more specifically, Tom Cruise's son, who would be making his screen acting debut in a remake of the 1980s action movie *Red Dawn*. The original version of the film, a Reagan-era triumphalist fantasia in which a band of American teenagers take up arms in resistance to a surprise invasion by the Soviets, had famously received funding from the National Rifle

Association. The remake, which had no connection to the NRA, swapped out the Russians for Red Chinese.*

The shoot took months, and its evidence was everywhere. One night, I stumbled across a couple of tanks parked in the middle of Fort Street, along with a Cultural Revolution–style tribunal stage and propaganda posters tacked across buildings in varying states of decline. The posters, evoking the empty sloganeering of a totalitarian leader, hailed a regime at work:

Repairing Your Economy
Fighting Corporate Corruption
Restoring Your Country
Helping You Back on Your Feet

It all felt very meta—any of the posters could have applied to the current state of the U.S. economy—but also oddly cruel, moving somewhere beyond irony, Detroit being, after all, not merely a set designed to resemble a ruined American city but an actual ruined American city.

Parts of the filming were scheduled to take place at my alma mater, Notre Dame, an all-boys' Catholic high school. In 2005, in the face of declining enrollment, Notre Dame had embarked upon a familiar migration, away from Detroit to the farther-flung suburbs—in this case, from Harper Woods, sandwiched between the city proper and St. Clair Shores, all the way out to Pontiac, about thirty miles north. Harper Woods had been declining for years: there was a higher foreclosure rate in the tiny suburb than in Detroit, and the papers reported an alarming increase in home invasions and daylight carjackings. The sign outside the school, which had once alerted passersby that Notre Dame was "Home of the Fightin' Irish," now read "99K Sq Ft School On 1.5 Acres," along with the number of a realtor.

The producers of *Red Dawn* did not want reporters around during filming and refused access to the set, but one night I snuck onto the school property, disguised in jeans and a hooded sweatshirt as a member of the crew. Inside, my old high school cafeteria, virtually unchanged since I'd been a student, had been repurposed as a catering hall for the

---

*In postproduction, the filmmakers changed the ethnicity of the invaders, making the attacking country North Korea (reportedly in an effort to appeal to the growing Chinese film market).

cast and crew. Chinese actors wearing military fatigues chatted at long tables alongside "Americans" in orange prison jumpsuits. A disco ball still hung at one end of the ceiling, a last vestige of high school dances.

Outside, the football field had become an internment camp. Earlier in the production, they'd filmed a football game; presumably tonight's shoot would be the "after" scene, taking place later in the film, in the wake of the Chinese invasion. Semi-truck trailers, the kind used as temporary housing by FEMA, only here painted red with Communist stars, had been positioned on the field. They'd also erected a guard tower, something out of a prison yard; the American flag fluttering atop the tower had been defaced with a giant red star. The football scoreboard had been covered over with a sign, reading, in marquee-sized black lettering:

YOU
DESERVE
TO BE HERE

I climbed into the bleachers to watch for a bit. It happened to be Friday, but tonight the lights bathing the football field captured a group of Chinese soldiers with automatic weapons marching American prisoners along the forty-yard line. Someone said the guard tower was going to be blown up, but probably not for several hours. A crew guy from Los Angeles began telling me how much he loved filming in Detroit. I expected him to offer some platitudes about how friendly the locals were, but instead he gushed, "We were setting off *major explosions* in the middle of downtown! Seriously, man, there's nowhere else in the country they'd let you do something like this."

Setting up each shot took forever, and eventually, I headed back to Service Street, where I bumped into Holice, my neighbor, who proceeded to get me very high. Afterward, I couldn't fall asleep, and suddenly, very badly, I wanted to see my old high school consumed by a Hollywood fireball. I lay on my bed, contemplating driving all the way back to Harper Woods; with no traffic, it would be about twenty minutes via freeway. But in the end, I wasn't feeling all that reckless, and glumly accepted the fact that I'd be missing the pyrotechnics. When I finally dozed off, my bed felt adrift on choppy waters, and I had visions of Notre Dame lit up by a string of fiery squibs.

The next morning, I woke up very early—around 6:30—and decided, before even having coffee, to race over to the school, in hopes that maybe the explosion hadn't happened yet. By the time I arrived, though, the cast and crew had packed up and left. All that remained were a couple of lighting trucks. The only other sign that any moviemaking had taken place was the watchtower, still standing at the edge of the football field, but in the charred, burst-headed state of a detonated firecracker. The American flag desecrated by our Chinese conquerors no longer fluttered in the wind; now, it hung limply from what was left of the tower's roof, black and in tatters.

* * *

In 2011, Governor Snyder announced that the state would no longer be in the business of "picking winners" when it came to wooing job creators—all job creators would be equally welcome, which meant a phasing out of targeted tax incentives for the film industry. The invisible hand of the market responded swiftly, yanking the brakes on nearly all of the planned film shoots in Michigan. Raleigh Studios managed to stay afloat with a 3-D Disney remake of *The Wizard of Oz*, but by 2012 the company had defaulted on more than $600,000 in interest payments and retained a staff of only twenty. Since Governor Snyder ended the tax credits, just one other film with a budget of more than $15 million (a comedy starring Jason Segel and Emily Blunt) was attracted to the state. A report by Ernst & Young claimed that every dollar Michigan issued in tax credits generated six times the amount of economic activity (via subsidiary businesses like hotels and catering); the governor's office countered that each dollar spent brought in only twenty-eight cents.

The visual arts scene continued to attract attention, though. The *New York Times*, for example, declared Detroit "a Midwestern TriBeCa" in a front-page Fashion & Style section story illustrated entirely with photos of young white people. This was followed by a visit from Tony Goldman, the developer responsible for the gentrification of SoHo and South Beach, who came to Detroit for the first time to give a talk on how the city could become the next SoHo or South Beach.

Goldman's standing-room-only discussion happened to take place on Service Street, at the old Butcher & Packer shop, which had been tranformed into an arts and performance space by a guy from Brooklyn after the owners finally decided to throw in the towel and move their operation out to Madison Heights. Since settling on the block, I'd stopped into Butcher & Packer a couple of times to pick up spices for my dad and uncle, who'd gone on a sausage-making bender in the wake of their mutual retirements, and the end of the business felt like a real loss. But the new owners had done a beautiful job with the redesign: clearing out the shelving, stripping the wood floor, even—and I really didn't think this would be possible—exorcising the overpowering spice-rack odor of the place. The first event in the new space had been an avant-garde classical music performance on a trio of microtonal pianos.

Goldman was introduced by Phil Cooley, a bearded ex-model who owned a successful barbecue restaurant and had since become the unofficial mayor of white Detroit hipsterdom. Cooley had also been charged with giving Goldman a tour of the city, and he told the audience Goldman had been "respectful" to "the community," unlike a number of other "people from the outside" he'd shown around. Goldman himself was dressed casually, but in clothes so obviously expensive their very casualness became another unobtainable luxury; you might one day find yourself wearing an outfit this loose-fitting yet perfectly comfortable, but it was deeply unlikely. He told us how South Beach had been a shithole (I'm paraphrasing) the first time he'd visited, but he'd had the foresight to envision "an American Riviera." He called the oft-cited forty square miles of empty land in Detroit "scary" then added, "But what a canvas!" He also warned, ominously, of "greedy bastards" who liked to swoop into burgeoning art scenes like Detroit's, and called his own version of gentrification "gentle-fication."

Goldman's talk was necessarily facile (he'd only spent forty-eight hours familiarizing himself with the city) and riddled with empty self-help exhortations ("If you don't have an Art Basel, make one!"). Still, people in the audience took notes. During the question-and-answer session, an earnest young man asked for book recommendations on the subject of city transformation and was directed toward an author Goldman had "heard about" but never read—Jane Jacobs.* Goldman's

---

*In *The Death and Life of Great American Cities* Jacobs described Detroit as "dispirited and dull" and "largely composed . . . of seemingly endless square miles of low-density failure."

most concrete proposal was offered during an audience with Mayor Bing, whom he'd advised to give free housing to 100,000 artists.

And yet, self-interested hype aside, Goldman did have a track record for sniffing out and cannily perceiving ways to monetize distressed neighborhoods on the cusp of gaining cultural capital. In Detroit, beyond the anecdotal evidence, empirical indicators of change began to materialize. The 2010 census, for example, revealed a head-turning spike in the number of college-educated Detroiters under the age of thirty-five—up 59 percent in a census when the overall population of the city dropped by 25 percent. By 2012, Midtown, the university district popular with young white newcomers to the city, was actually experiencing a scarcity of rental properties, with 96 percent of units occupied. Cooley's barbecue restaurant, in nearby Corktown, did $1.8 million in sales in its first year of business and had become the anchor of a Brooklynized block of prime real estate that included a single-origin coffee shop, an artisanal cocktail bar, and a miniature boutique hotel. A youth hostel opened down the street to accomodate all the visitors from Europe and hip North American cities like Montreal and Portland. (When a friend started renting out apartments on the website Airbnb, he quickly became overbooked and started turning people away.) An arts group in the Netherlands now sponsored nine-week arts residencies in Detroit; during a single visit to another arts space in Corktown (a 30,000-square-foot warehouse purchased by Cooley), I met a boat builder from Maine, a video game architect from Copenhagen, an industrial designer from San Francisco, a Los Angeles choreographer, a Detroiter who made coats for homeless people that could be turned into sleeping bags, and an American graffiti artist who'd come to Detroit via Paris.

The economic benefits endowed a city by various arts and cultural institutions can be tricky to calculate with anything approaching precision. In its heyday, Detroit's other great twentieth-century cultural assembly line, Berry Gordy's Motown Records, was the largest black-owned business in the country, the aspirational nature of the music* contributing as much to the city's aura as the stylized, evocatively named cars rolling from the factory lots. Today, the Heidelberg Project

---

*The very first Motown hit, written by Gordy himself, was Barrett Strong's "Money (That's What I Want)."

alone draws an estimated 50,000 visitors annually, and art collectors and curators are beginning to pay serious attention to Detroit's art output. In an interview, Jay Sanders, the cocurator of the 2012 Whitney Biennial, specifically highlighted a trip to Detroit as "having a big impact" on the emerging vision of the show, ultimately resulting in the inclusion of three Detroit artists,* more than from any other city beyond New York and Los Angeles.

That said, any potential Detroit arts renaissance remains in its earliest phase of development, more about insane real estate opportunities and the romantic vision of a crumbling heartland Berlin—basically, vicarious wish fulfillment by coastal arts types living in long-gentrified cities—than an overarching homegrown aesthetic. The rise of a new infrastructure catering to the incoming "creatives" in neighborhoods like Midtown and Corktown, such as the planned Whole Foods, had an undeniable tangibility. But the changes felt miniscule in comparison with the problems facing the rest of the city.

Derrick May, my neighbor on Service Street, had a unique perspective on cultural bubble economies, having been a prime instigator behind another of Detroit's stabs at an arts-driven reinvention. At that time—the late eighties and early nineties—Detroit was becoming known internationally for techno music. May and two of the acknowledged cocreators of the genre, Juan Atkins and Kevin Saunderson, had actually grown up in the semirural town of Belleville (much closer to Ann Arbor than to Detroit), where they'd bonded as African Americans in a predominantly white high school. Later, they'd moved into the city and helped to colonize Service Street, artsy black gentrifiers interested less in Motown than in Kraftwerk, the reclusive German electronic music duo portrayed in their press and album photographs as robotic mannequins.

In Detroit, a local disc jockey called the Electrifying Mojo played Kraftwerk's 1981 album, *Computer World*, in its entirety nearly every night when it was released. The group's biggest (really, only) hit in the United States, "Autobahn," a Teutonic celebration of the open road—minimalist, repetitive, with a synthesized electronic pulse and the

---

*If you include the late Detroit native Mike Kelly, whose showstopping Biennial piece, a film of an exact replica of his childhood home being driven around the city on the back of a flatbed trailer, was commissioned by Detroit's Museum of Contemporary Art.

stray cyborg vocal effect—presages techno from a compositional stand-point, to be sure, but also on the pure level of vibe: Detroit techno was driving music, created in the Motor City and tailored perfectly to the city's endless highways and boulevards. Wildly cinematic, the songs unspooled perfectly alongside the scenes flashing across one's windshield—all of that empty space, punctuated by the dark shapes of unlit buildings, shadowy figures, strobed bursts of color from the occasional working streetlamp.*

And for a brief moment it seemed as if this weird microgenre might have a shot at commercial success. The May-produced compilation *Techno! The New Dance Sound of Detroit*, its title an obvious play on Motown's old slogan "The Sound of Young America," came out just as rave culture was beginning to explode in the United Kingdom. Back in the day, May told me, there would be dozens of guys hanging out in front of the studios on Service Street, waiting to drop off demos. Detroit suddenly had new cachet, the city itself becoming a key aspect of the mystique of techno music and its mysterious, faceless creators.

"We never thought of this music as anything other than our own," May told me one evening. "The same question I always get asked, in Europe or Asia or wherever I'm traveling, is basically, and it's never phrased exactly this way, but it's, 'How did three black guys from Detroit'—from this shithole of a city—'make this music?' They don't mean it in the way you'd imagine: 'How did three dumb-ass black niggers do this?' They sincerely want to know how this music came from us. From this place."

But after the initial hype in Europe, which resulted in Saunder-son scoring Top Ten hits with his group Inner City and May turning down a chance to appear on *Top of the Pops*, techno, in the States, and even in its birthplace, Detroit, settled back into its natural place as a

---

*Others have pointed out that, at the moment of ascension of that most verbal of African American popular music forms, hip-hop, these three kids in Detroit were moving in the opposite direction, recording largely instrumental rhythm tracks. Techno was dance music in the most avant-garde sense of the term, the imaginary sound track to a science fiction movie: *Alphaville*, maybe, or one of those Last Man on Earth pictures, only set in present-day Detroit, its creators understanding that the city of the future required appropriately forward-looking music. Juan Atkins, who coined the term *techno* and produced some of its most enduring tracks under various pseudonyms (Cybotron, Model 500), once said, "Today the automobile plants use robots and computers to make their cars. I'm more interested in Ford's robots than Gordy's music."

decidedly underground phenomenon. While techno has added to the city's mythic image abroad, it provided little in the way of lasting transformative effects. In past interviews, May would say things like, "If this [techno] happened in New York, everyone responsible would be considered geniuses. But it happened in Detroit, so we get nothing."

Today, May no longer seems bitter. He makes a healthy living flying to Europe or Asia nearly every weekend, DJing at some club where nostalgic fans freak out the same way baby boomers would if Eric Clapton showed up to play a local rock bar in Scranton. "What's happening in Detroit today is almost like Barack Obama being elected president," May told me. "I love Barack Obama. But he's only president because George Bush was an absolute fuck-up. In my book, the same level of desperation is happening in Detroit. The powers that be have tried everything else, and they don't know what to do, so now what they're doing is nothing. And in the process of doing nothing, the creative class is finally being let free to roam the city for the first time since I was a young kid.

"I want to try to be optimistic, like everyone else," he went on. "But the fight here has just begun. A couple of blocks of commerce in Corktown is in no way the resurgence of a city. Detroit is the next Brooklyn? That's just a false sense of romanticism. That person has not driven here much. Let's see how these people feel after a couple of winters or when they start having kids—let's see if they can still hang then."

May had invited me to his place to watch the sunset. I'd figured he must have had a rooftop deck I'd somehow never noticed before, but when I arrived, May and his friends were sitting on folding chairs on the sidewalk in front of his building, sipping cava from plastic cups. Only in Detroit, I thought, would twilight at the edge of an eight-lane boulevard strike anyone as a relaxing proposition.

Behind the warehouses of Eastern Market, though, the sky had gone a lovely, cool shade of pink. Occasionally, a single car would seem to float past on Gratiot, otherwise deserted. The tires, isolated from regular traffic noise, created a soothing tidal sound.

May told me foreign interviewers, once they got through asking him how techno could possibly have come out of a place like Detroit, always had a second question: So, why didn't you ever leave?

The roof of the abandoned Packard automotive plant, winter 2009. The artist Scott Hocking, who created the television installation, is on the left; the author is second from left. [Corine Vermeulen]

13

FABULOUS RUIN

DURING THE FATEFUL SUMMER of 1967, a Chilean electrical engineering student at the University of Notre Dame named Camilo José Vergara read an article in *Time* about Gary, Indiana, a debased steel town about an hour west of South Bend (and home of rising Motown stars the Jackson Five). Fascinated, to an immediate and unseemly degree, by the salacious descriptions of the lawless-sounding "paradise" (*Time*'s word) for vice-seeking Chicago businessmen (Chicago's brothels and illegal gambling dens having been largely shuttered by the first Mayor Daley), Vergara quickly made the drive with a friend, arriving on an uncomfortably sweltering summer afternoon. A foul odor hung over the city—exhaust from the steel plants, which burned Vergara's eyes. Years later, though, he would recall the day as "one of the most memorable" of his college experience. Eventually returning to Gary "perhaps a hundred times," in his own estimation, Vergara began to photograph largely ignored sections of the ghetto—fortresslike public housing projects, numbingly decaying storefronts, churches and train stations fallen into ruin—his very alienness (not African American, not even *North* American) becoming an asset to his sociological observations, to which he bore an untainted curiosity, the willingness of the freshly disembarked to brazenly stare, especially in directions natives no longer bothered to look.

Vergara spent the next decades photographing on Chicago's South

Side, in South Central Los Angeles, in Harlem and the South Bronx, Camden and Newark, dubbing the growing body of work his "Smithsonian of Decline." In 1987, he made his first photographs of Detroit, but only added the city to his "collection" six years later, when he began documenting its grand ruins in earnest. His focus remained on the awesome collection of prewar skyscrapers clustered in the city center, most of which now stood hauntingly empty. At night, Vergara noticed how different they looked from historical photographs, when the high-rises were still occupied and lights ornamented their long shafts. By the time he arrived, the only sources of illumination came from street lamps, and maybe, on clear evenings, the moon, casting the towers in a shadowy, enigmatic chiaroscuro, as if dramatically lit for an old film noir.

In 1995, in a deadpan, deliberatively provocative essay, Vergara proposed the city "place a moratorium on the razing of skyscrapers, our most sublime ruins, and instead . . . stabilize them," setting aside a dozen or so downtown blocks as an "urban Monument Valley" that would act as a "memorial of our throwaway cities," an "American Acropolis":

> Midwestern prairie would be allowed to invade from the north. Trees, vines, and wildflowers would grow on roofs and out of windows; wild animals, goats, squirrels, possum, bats, owls, ravens, snakes, insects, and perhaps even an occasional bear would live in the empty behemoths, adding their calls, hoots, and screeches to the smell of rotten leaves and animal droppings.

Acknowledging the Swiftian nature of his essay, Vergara called it "an immodest proposal." At the time, Detroiters were predictably outraged. John Slater, the head of Detroit's Planning Commission, insisted, "For [Vergara] to suggest that this is an empty ghost town is bizarre." *The New York Times* managed to find an actual Greek, Constantine Roumel, to say—even better: "sputter"—"American Acropolis! It's an insult to America, to what America stands for. It's an insult to the classical Greeks." Roumel was one of the owners of the David Stott Building, a gorgeous thirty-seven-story art deco tower built in 1929 and taking its cues from Eliel Saarinen's famous second-place proposal for

Chicago's Tribune Tower; at the time, Roumel was attempting to lure tenants with office rents as low as ten dollars per square foot. "For a city to set itself as the world's symbolic ruin—that is not going to attract tourists from Peoria, Illinois," Michael Goodin, a writer at *Crain's Detroit Business*, told Vergara. "The Romans, that is a dead civilization. Americans [sic] are not a dead civilization."

* * *

For decades, a succession of city officials had struggled mightily to rebrand Detroit's battered image. Their schemes had included casino gambling, an Eighties festival mall, new ballparks, hosting a Grand Prix, hosting a Super Bowl, even commissioning (this was Mayor Young, in 1984) Motown Records founder Berry Gordy (who had fled Detroit for Los Angeles in the early 1970s, taking the entire Motown operation with him) to write a theme song for the city modeled after Frank Sinatra's "Theme from New York, New York," which had been a hit a few years earlier. It being Detroit, a blacker member of the Rat Pack, Sammy Davis Jr., was conscripted to handle the vocals, but sadly, Gordy's song, "Hello, Detroit," failed to burn up the charts. (Except in Belgium, where, inexplicably, it reached number one.)*

But now much of the attention being showered on Detroit from the trendiest quarters came in no small measure thanks to the city's blight. Detroit's brand had become authenticity, and a key component of this authenticity had to do with the way the city looked.

Would fixing the very real problems faced by Detroiters, I began to wonder, mean inevitably robbing Detroit of some part of its essential Detroitness?

This is not exactly a question of gentrification: when your city has seventy thousand abandoned buildings, it will not be gentrified anytime soon. Rather, it's one of aesthetics. The Quicken Loans CEO Dan Gilbert had been an active proponent of finding uses for the very buildings Vergara had suggested turning into a homegrown Acropolis,

---

*To be fair to Gordy, his assignment was a vexing one, as the inherent jauntiness of the city-song genre was bound to grate against the necessity of acknowledging Detroit's troubles. At no point in, say, "I Love Paris" did Cole Porter feel as if he had to plead for divine intervention on the city's behalf, whereas one of the couplets of "Hello, Detroit" rhymes "I will always be there for you" with "I will say a little prayer for you."

but most of the other big-money developers in Detroit (such as they were) had brought with them a suburban vision, made manifest in the dated mall architecture of the new Compuware Headquarters or the MotorCity Casino's Reno *manqué* attempts at high roller gaudiness. The latter complex, seventeen stories tall, with green and purple and pink bands of neon slashing its girth, throbbed every night on the nonexistent skyline like an epic, failed art installation, maybe something by Donald Judd's cousin from South Beach. The MotorCity Casino was owned by the Ilitch family, the local Little Caesars Pizza tycoons, who had also bought and beautifully restored downtown's grand Fox Theatre—while, at the same time, leveling countless other historic buildings (like the old Motown Headquarters) to make more parking lots for their baseball and hockey arenas. (The Ilitches owned both the Tigers and the Red Wings.)

In Detroit, you can't talk aesthetics without talking ruin porn, a term that had recently begun circulating in the city. Detroiters, understandably, could get quite touchy about the way descriptions and photographs of ruined buildings had become the favorite Midwestern souvenirs of visiting reporters. *Dateline: NBC* had devoted large portions of a particularly derided hour-long special on the city to sweeping aerial shots of ravaged neighborhoods. Even my own *Rolling Stone* story on the auto industry had opened with a two-page photo spread, the uppermost panel depicting an antique postcard image of Ford's Highland Park plant in 1916 (identical rows of open-topped Model T Fords spread across the lot, the gold-tinted steering wheels looking like the raised shields of a brutally disciplined chariot army maintaining tight formation), while below, a row of junked, snow-covered cars foregrounded a present-day shot of the same plant from the same angle.

Ruin porn was generally assessed the same way as the other kind, with you-know-it-when-you-see-it subjectivity. Everyone seemed to agree that Camilo Vergara's work was not ruin pornography, though he'd arguably been the Hefner of the genre. Likewise, the local artist Lowell Boileau, who, around the same time Vergara proposed his American Acropolis, began posting his own photographs on a website called the Fabulous Ruins of Detroit, also received a pass, perhaps because he approached his subject from a native's perspective, and with unabashed nostalgia. Photojournalists, on the other hand, were almost universally considered creeps pandering to a sticky-fingered Internet slide-show demographic. To some extent the critique had been just: as with stories about misbehaving teenage starlets, editorial love of Detroit came with obvious exploitative commercial reward: a link to a titillating shot of Detroit's architectural dishabille could always be counted to rise to the top of your website's "most emailed" lists, which was, of course, the bottom line.

At the same time, it wasn't fair to automatically condemn all such photography. As often as portraits of the city's ruins might be distorted and sensationalized, blanket condemnations felt equally disingenuous. Ignoring the blight altogether would have been reportorial malpractice akin to writing a travel piece about Malibu and failing to mention the Pacific Ocean.

Far more noxious, to my mind, than the commercial carpetbaggers were the hobbyists. One of the more fascinating Internet-age curiosities marking the rise of ruin-as-aesthetic-object were the number of websites dedicated to the so-called "urban explorer," or "urbexer" for short. Urbexers snuck into abandoned urban structures (or shopping malls, or subway tunnels) and took photographs of what they found, the use of the term "explorer" being especially telling: like the gentlemen explorers of yore (Stanley and Fawcett and Livingstone, or their fictional counterparts Allan Quatermain and Indiana Jones), who braved the darker continents for untold riches, the urbexers tended to be white and (at least the ones I met) from relatively privileged socioeconomic backgrounds. Unlike their predecessors, though, the only treasures the urbexers hoped to bring back to civilization were high-res digital camera images to post on Flickr streams and anonymous message boards as proof of their spectacular stealth missions, often presented with startling incuriosity as to the human history of the places being explored, if not outright ghoulish glee.

One group of urbexers began calling themselves the Survival Crackas, after they discovered an old can of Civil Defense "Survival Crackers" in the ruins of the Packard plant; they posted videos of themselves smashing through abandoned housing complexes, theaters, even psychiatric hospitals and prisons, all set to aggressive heavy metal and hip-hop sound tracks. Another white urbexer in his twenties once regaled me with the story of the time he'd been startled by a homeless man passed out in a room of a long-vacant high-rise apartment. Only later, he noted coolly, did he think to wonder if the guy might have been dead.

For all of the local complaints about ruin porn, outsiders were not alone in their fascination. Among my circle of friends and acquaintances, Phil staged secret, multi-course gourmet meals, prepared by well-known chefs from local restaurants, in abandoned buildings like the old train station. John and his buddies played ice hockey on the frozen floors of decrepit factories, and occasionally watched Tigers games from the roofs of empty skyscrapers nearby. (Well, they listened to the games on the radio. From such a distance, the players, they said, looked like little moving dots.) Travis was hired to shoot suburban wedding photographs in the ruins of the Packard plant and a woman who had moved to Detroit from Brooklyn began to take nude photographs of herself in wrecked spaces (thrusting the concept of ruin porn to a less metaphorical level). The Cupcake Girls, a coed arts collective originally from Portland, or maybe it was San Francisco, arranged an installation of little cupcake statues in the window of a long-shuttered bakery in Upper Chene. A few days later, someone firebombed the place. People debated whether or not this was a coincidence.

* * *

One afternoon, I tagged along on a tour of the Packard plant with Scott Hocking, an artist who had been exploring Detroit's ruins for years, and who had been asked to show around a young visiting scholar from Denmark. The scholar had striking, pale-blue eyes and a bird's face. Her thesis focused on creative ways the residents of cities like Detroit attempted to reclaim their postindustrial detritus. Scott, precisely the sort of person she had in mind, built wild installations in abandoned buildings, using only material found onsite.*

---

*Europeans—particularly from Germany, Scandinavia, and the Netherlands—love a ruined American city. Every Detroiter I know who has ever photographed an abandoned building and possesses any kind of Web presence has been contacted by strangers from Copenhagen, Rotterdam, Paris, or Berlin, asking about the best way to sneak into the old train station or offering to pay for a local tour.

Scott had recently assembled a new piece in the Packard. We walked over there with Corine Vermeulen, the photographer who had taken me to the Zone, and Faina Lerman, a Latvian performance artist whose family had moved to Detroit in 1980. It was December, so we all wore puffy winter coats as we marched down the middle of the street, our boots crunching the surface of a deeply impacted layer of snow and ice. We eventually reached the train tracks that had once carried freight directly in and out of the sprawling complex. Scott made a joke about finding a dead body, a nod to the movie *Stand By Me*, but none of the foreign-born members of our party seemed to get the reference.

The factory, five stories, stretching across two sides of a major road, seemed to have no end. Scott said you could get lost inside, and that even he hadn't explored every corner. Huge chunks of wall had collapsed to reveal the gray innards of the place, and gangly, stoop-backed trees hugged the walls like ivy. For years after it ceased operation, the Packard had been used as a storage facility. Scott's new installation made use of a bunch of antique television sets he'd discovered in one of the storage sheds, and had involved his painstakingly hauling the bulky frames to a partially collapsed section of the roof.

Now he led us through an open bay door. As if in preparation for a public burning, someone had unloaded a dense thicket of tree branches just inside the space, otherwise cavernous and empty. A section of brick had been removed from the base of a far wall, forming a tiny crawlspace. Cartoonish, illegible blue graffiti tagged the circumference of the hole. Crouching so low he practically knelt, Scott led us through the passageway. I wondered if the person who'd cut it had been thinking of Lewis Carroll, or maybe *Stalker*.

On the other side of the hole, we entered a stairwell. The stairs had no railing and each step had a coarse, treacherous dusting of rubble. We climbed past broken windows overlooking a snowy graveyard, eventually coming to the top floor, where a huge portion of the roof had collapsed, flooding that end of the space with afternoon light. The covered portion of the floor remained dim and shadowy, though, only enhancing the spotlit quality of Scott's installation. In the place where the roof had caved, he had arranged his empty television boxes on top of a number of the exposed columns, which looked like the remains of some Doric temple. It was a spectacular vision. Some of the columns had toppled over; others remained stoically upright, surrounded by boulder-sized chunks of concrete and gnarled fingers of rebar.

We climbed up to the roof for a better look, Scott deriving a perverse pleasure from pointing out the places he suspected would soon collapse, explaining how various support pillars would buckle and the angles at which they might come to ground.* Corine set up her tripod and took our picture as we peered over the edge. The roof was covered with snow, and in the photo, it looks as if we're standing on a wintry plain, at the edge of a cliff, but in fact the building had been abandoned for so long that scrub grass and little trees had begun to grow on the roof and now poked up through the layer of whiteness. The post-apocalyptic grandeur of the scene momentarily silenced us, as if we were in the presence of something demanding respectful meditation—but what, exactly? If you manage to slip inside certain Detroit ruins, you are sometimes struck by their sacred aura; like cathedrals, they can feel beautiful and tragic at the same time, monuments to flawed human aspiration that, in an unintentional way, begin to approach the holy.

It was freezing. Our fingers went numb taking notes and pictures. Faina said if the place were turned into a museum, you could fix up a little space in the corner and put in a café, make that part warm. We could hear scrappers in another part of the plant, the clattering of their equipment. Back inside, we came across another section of the building where an industrious type had dragged a couple of car seats to a scenic overlook. We saw very fresh footprints in the snow near a window.

On one wall, someone had spray-painted a blue Krishna figure, over which someone else had written FUCK YOU BUDA.

As we were leaving, a carload of teenage boys pulled up, looking for a way in.

---

*Sure enough, by the following summer, much of the section of roof we stood upon had collapsed entirely.

* * *

Meditation on ruin is part of a long and noble tradition. In Renaissance Italy, antiquarians such as Leon Battista Alberti and Poggio Bracciolini began to promote the study and preservation of Roman ruins, which, to that point, had been unsystematically pushed aside as the city expanded. In some instances, great marble statues and magnificent columns were quarried and tossed into kilns, where they were burned to make lime.

There was a contemplative aspect to the antiquarians' work—Bracciolini's best-known essay on the topic was called "On Vicissitudes of Fortune"—but, according to Alberti's biographer, Anthony Grafton, they also "made fun of those who became too depressed" about the ruins, like poor, over-sensitive Cyriac of Ancona, who "seemed to mourn the fall of Rome with excessive emotion," and who was compared by Renaissance humanist Antonio Loschi to "the man at Milan who began to cry when he heard a *cantastorie*, or public storyteller, sing 'of the death of Roland, who perished seven hundred years ago in battle,' went home still in tears, and was still weeping inconsolably at dinnertime because 'Roland, the only defender of the Christians, is dead.'"

My grandfather Alberti, who traced our family origins back to Florence, insisted that we were related to Leon Battista Alberti, also a Florentine, and one of the great polymaths of his day, the prototypical Renaissance Man: playwright, poet, architect, painter, mathematician, "father of Western cryptography,"* astronomer, lawyer, and prize-winning horseman, so physically fit that he was able, according to his own possibly unreliable autobiography, *Vita Anonyma*, to leap over the head of another man from a standing position. Thanks to the efforts of protopreservationists like cousin Alberti, many later generations of painters and poets continued to meditate on the transitory nature of man's greatest achievements (and their inherent folly) in the shadow of once-majestic edifices like the Baths of Caracalla, built in the early third century by the Roman emperor of the same name (well, nickname—a "caracalla" is thought to be an early form of hooded cloak

---

*David Kahn, in *The Code Breakers*, writes of the incredibly still-in-use "Alberti cipher" being one of the first polyalphabetic codes.

that the emperor brought into fashion, which makes him sound like a rather likable tastemaker, though in fact he's widely regarded as one of the worst emperors—Edward Gibbon describes him as "the common enemy of mankind," despicable enough to be murdered by a member of his own entourage while stopping by the side of the road to urinate) and pretty much entirely destroyed by the sacking Ostrogoths approximately three hundred years later.

The baths inspired paintings by Giovanni Paolo Panini, for one, who imagined, in his "Statues in a Ruined Arcade" (1738), the ruins of Caracalla with enough gaping holes for small forests to poke through, the classical statues lining both sides of the walk dwarfing the humans wandering past with their dogs and lovers (Panini's "Ruins of a Triumphal Arch," part of the collection at the Detroit Institute of Arts, works a similar theme); as well as etchings by Panini's younger contemporary Giovanni Paolo Piranesi, who depicted the baths in a far more advanced state of decomposition, trees growing from mossy columns and a trio of stave-wielding goatherds leading their tiny flock past toppled statuary and the remains of walls; and Percy Bysshe Shelley's *Prometheus Unbound* (1820)—Shelley acknowledged that the poem-in-dramatic-form "was chiefly written upon the mountainous ruins of the Baths of Caracalla," and in her own notes on the play, Mary Shelley described her husband wandering "among the ruins made one with Nature in their decay."

Perhaps not incidentally, Michigan Central Station, the best-known Detroit ruin—the Parthenon of Vergara's American Acropolis, a towering eighteen-story Beaux-Arts train station with a lavish waiting room of marble floors and a fifty-foot ceiling—was modeled after the Baths of Caracalla. Michigan Central was built in 1913 by the same architectural firms that designed New York's Grand Central, and it does seem perversely fitting that Detroit's grandest husk could be interpreted as a public memorial celebrating the irrelevancy of train travel in the age of the automobile. After the station closed in 1988, a developer talked about turning the building into a casino; the current owner, Manuel "Matty" Moroun, had discussed the possibility, with Mayor Kilpatrick's administration, of selling the station to the city as part of a scheme to turn the place into a combination police headquarters and law enforcement museum.

Mostly, though, Moroun has allowed the station to steadily molder.* Sitting nearly a mile and a half from the high-rises of downtown, Michigan Central looms like a Gothic castle over its humbler neighbors on Michigan Avenue. There's a gray, sepulchral quality to the place. Standing before a ruin as monolithic as the station, it's hard not to think of other epic-scale disasters that seemed engineered from above to illustrate man's folly—as if the Titanic, after sinking, had washed ashore and been permanently beached as a warning. The ornate ground floor, with its soaring arches—this is the part of the building modeled on the baths—juts from the base of the brick tower, which, up close, draws your eyes along its facade of tightly gridded windows, nearly all broken now, giving the structure an odd, insubstantial affect, that of meshwork, or a scrim, in contrast with its dominating physical presence. In fact, the most striking thing about the train station might be the fact that, approaching from a certain angle, you can actually see right through the building. Trees have begun growing inside the tower, and in the summer, green leaves shimmer in the uppermost windows, their branches flapping so like arms my notebook read after one visit, "Suggested graffiti: *Don't Jump!*"

In the Detroit essay in *Yoga for People Who Can't Be Bothered to Do*

---

*In a city weak enough to be routinely pushed around by wealthy power players, Moroun has managed the impressive feat of reigning, undisputed, as the most reviled member of the local oligarchy. A reclusive octogenarian billionaire, Moroun also owns the nearby Ambassador Bridge, which spans the Detroit River to connect the city with Windsor, Ontario, thereby controlling an unbelievably lucrative international border crossing. A quarter of the annual $400 billion in trade between the U.S. and Canada travels across this single bridge. Moroun is estimated to earn $60 million annually in tolls alone, and he has spent the past decade stymying efforts by the U.S. and Canada to build a second, jointly owned public bridge two miles down the river, necessary in part because the Ambassador Bridge is over seventy-five years old and sorely in need of refurbishment, and in part because of the outrageousness of the fact that a single private individual owns the busiest international border crossing in North America. Moroun's counterproposal—that he will build *his own* second bridge, right next to the current bridge—has been given a cold reception by everyone but the Republican-controlled Michigan Senate, this despite the Canadian government's offer to pay up front for the broke state of Michigan's share of a second bridge. In the meantime, Moroun has gobbled up properties in both Detroit and Windsor, near the sites of both proposed bridges, most of which are maintained as lovingly as Michigan Central. The son of a Lebanese gas station owner who eventually bought a small trucking company, Moroun took over the family business in the seventies and has been widely despised ever since. An article about him in *Forbes* was titled "The Troll Under the Bridge." (Moroun is also very short.)

It, Geoff Dyer visits Michigan Central Station and runs into some tourists photographing the place. In a funny exchange prompted by one of the tourists remarking on how bustling the train station must have been at the height of Detroit's production, Dyer disagrees, arguing:

> Ruins don't encourage you to dwell on what they were like in their heyday, before they were ruins. The Coliseum in Rome or the amphitheater at Leptis Magna has never been anything but ruins. They're eternal ruins. It's the same here. This building could never have looked more magnificent than it does now, surrounded by its own silence. Ruins don't make you think of the past, they direct you towards the future. The effect is almost prophetic. This is what the future will end up like. This is what the future has always ended up looking like.

It's true, while vacationing in Rome, after I'd spent about a year back in Detroit, I certainly didn't find myself mentally restoring the Senate or the various temples or filling out the scene with centurions and charioteers and vestal virgins. But the past was nonetheless on my mind—the past of Keats and Shelley, when a consumptive poet might wander the same sites without security guards and throngs of German tourists, without seeing a single camera, a time when the ruins were still ruins, but desolate, abandoned, free of caretakers, not so *horribly crowded*. That was the heyday I dwelt upon, and I found myself feeling strangely grateful that I'd been able to experience Detroit's ruins in their unmediated state, before someone in power wised up and appointed Vergara Minister of Tourism.

I'm joking, but not. If the Packard, Michigan Central, and a few other iconic structures were stabilized enough for safety purposes, official guided tours would immediately become one of the most popular tourist activities in the city. Of course, there is a greater likelihood of Ford announcing, tomorrow, that the company has been pouring all of its F-150 profits into a top-secret program to develop a zero-carbon flying car, which will be built in the Packard plant and ready for market by the first quarter of 2014. Surely, though, such preservation could be managed tastefully and in a way that didn't exploit.

Beyond the stark appeal of the ruins themselves, the passing of the industrial Midwest—or at least of a certain version of the industrial Midwest, if we're not prepared to concede its wholesale demise—is undeniably of deep historic significance. As Francis Grunow of the Detroit Vacant Property Campaign told me, "I don't see the ruins as a negative. I've never been to Rome or Athens. But the only thing I know about Rome is the Forum and the Coliseum and the only thing I know about Athens is the Acropolis. Could some of the buildings in Detroit become sculptural—say, lit at night? But it's a tough argument here. This is the city where we invented the mechanism by which history has no meaning, where last year's model has no value."

Detroiters themselves would likely be split over such a proposition, along racial and generational fault lines. Anecdotally, though, I suspect this might hold up if actual ruin-related polling were conducted, black Detroiters tend toward the unsentimental when it comes to the old buildings and battles to save them. University of Michigan professor Angela Dillard, a black Detroiter in her forties, once told me, "When people come to town, I won't do the ruins tour anymore. I'm an advocate for tearing that stuff down. That old Packard building? That could come down in an afternoon. I think they ought to mail the train station to some Scandinavian country, if they love it so much."

But the tours go on, in an unofficial capacity. One afternoon at the Packard plant, I ran into a family from Paris. The daughter said she'd read about the building in *Lonely Planet*; her father had a camcorder hanging around his neck. Their previous stop has been Michigan Central. Another time, while conducting my own tour for an out-of-town guest, a group of German college students drove up. When queried as to the appeal of Detroit, one of them gleefully exclaimed, "I came to see the end of the world!"

* * *

One evening, I went to hear a talk on the ruins of Detroit taking place in a warehouse and occasional performance space in Eastern Market. The speaker, Jim Griffoein, authored the thoughtful local blog Sweet Juniper. His writing centered on life as a stay-at-home-dad in Detroit. Prior to moving back to Michigan, where he'd grown up (in Kalamazoo), he'd worked as a lawyer in the Bay Area, but he had quit his job to write and take care of his children. His wife still practiced law, and on the blog, he described his family as "just two more yuppies raising their kids in the most dangerous city in America." Close to two hundred guests packed the warehouse, most seated on folding chairs. Griffoein, a thirty-something white guy with a scruffy beard dressed casually in jeans and a T-shirt, was introduced by the academic who had organized the event, a statuesque blond woman from Germany.

On Sweet Juniper, Griffoein had posted a number of ruin shots: "feral" houses almost completely overgrown with vegetation, a decommissioned public school book depository in which trees had begun growing out of the piles of rotting textbooks. But he apparently possessed a special license to publish such images, as he spent much of his talk denouncing lazy out-of-town journalists who use Detroit's ruins as a convenient recession-year symbol for the end of the American Dream. (In fact, Griffoein might have been the one to coin the term "ruin porn," in an interview with *Vice* magazine.) The lecture included a funny story about a call Griffoein had received from a Hollywood producer regarding an idea for a television pilot (in which a group of Canadian autoworkers win $38 million in a lottery and decide to buy Detroit) and a discussion of the fact that Germans actually have a specific word for the love of ruins, *ruinenwert*.* Griffoein could also be exasperatingly self-congratulatory, as when he exhorted the crowd to "take ownership of these ruins," adding, "We're not gonna let New York City reporters come here and define us!"

During the question-and-answer period, a stylishly dressed African American woman in her fifties stood up to make a contrarian point: that devotees of the ruined buildings should be aware of the way in which the objects of their affection left "retinal scars" on the children of Detroit, contributing to a "significant part of the psychological trauma" inflicted on them on a daily basis. "I appreciate the humility with which you approach this topic," she told Griffoein, but then added, "It's one thing to romanticize this level of destruction. But to live with it is very psychically traumatic." Glancing around the lily-white

---

*The term originated with Albert Speer, whose *Die Ruinenwerttheorie* ("Theory of Ruin Value") proposed an architecture worthy of the thousand-year Reich—in other words, buildings that would eventually make cool-looking ruins.

audience—there were four other black people in the room—she went on, "I don't want to insult anybody. But when you talk about how 'we' need to take this city back, I look at this room, and I'm not sure what 'we' you're talking about."

After the talk, I introduced myself to the woman, whose name was Marsha Cusic. It turned out we were practically neighbors: she lived in one of the Lafayette Park townhouses. Cusic wore round, chunky framed glasses and a colorful wrap, and her hair spilled out in long, thin locks from under a matching head scarf. She'd grown up in Highland Park, but her father, the late Joe Von Battle, had been in the music business in Detroit, running a much-loved record shop on Hastings Street. John Lee Hooker, as an aspiring bluesman, had frequented Von Battle's shop, where Von Battle made the first recording of a young Aretha Franklin, as well as a number of sermons by her father, the Reverend C. L. Franklin, and records by Hooker, Jackie Wilson, and Sonny Boy Williamson, among others. Cusic, who worked as an executive assistant to a Detroit judge, was writing her own book about her father, so she was reluctant to say more on the topic, but she agreed to take me on a driving tour of the Detroit of her youth.

We met up on a Sunday afternoon. Cusic drove us by the location of her father's original store—roughly on a stretch of Interstate 75 that runs through the former Black Bottom neighborhood. En route to the site of his second store on Rosa Parks Boulevard (12th Street in Von Battle's day), we passed the house (now museum) on West Grand Boulevard where Berry Gordy founded Motown Records, "Hitsville U.S.A." still scrawled in cursive on its white frame.

"My father hated that shit," Cusic said. "We would drive past here every time I came to work with him. I'd try to play the Supremes. He'd tell me to turn it down, that they couldn't sing. Same kind of things I say when I hear rap music."

We turned onto Rosa Parks. Cusic pointed out the vacant lots on both sides of the boulevard. "At the time, all of this was stores and businesses," she said. "There would have basically been another whole row of buildings between us and those houses back there." She pointed to a row of residential homes set far back from the street. "All burned. It's missing an entire layer of history."

The intersection of 12th Street and Clairmount had been the epicenter of the 1967 civic unrest, the location of the blind pig raided by police on the night of July 23. Cusic's father's record store was just a few blocks south. Cusic said that the morning after the riot began, you could see the smoke in Highland Park, three miles away. "It started up past that light," she said, pointing north. We had pulled over at Euclid, near where her father's store had stood. "And then it started moving this way. My father came down with his gun, but the National Guard eventually moved him out. He assumed the guards would be protecting his store. And it wasn't burned. But it was completely trashed and destroyed. There was lots of water damage from the fire hoses, because there were so many other burning buildings nearby. He'd written 'Soul Brother' on the window, which was discomfiting." Cusic paused, then said, "I felt embarrassed for him, that he felt like he had to do that. He was older. He hated all of that black nationalism. I was thirteen at the time, and I was already getting into it. But if he saw Muhammad Ali on TV, he'd say, 'I'm not calling him that—it's Cassius Clay!'"

"Everyone likes to point to the riot as the moment everything went wrong in Detroit," Cusic went on. "But you have to understand the idea of a nodal point. It's the same way a tea kettle heats up and heats up and only at the very end does it whistle. It's easy to look at the riot as that nodal point, but really, you're ignoring all of the heat that came before."

Over forty years later, there was still a row of torched storefronts on one of the corners of 12th and Clairmount, though nothing remained on the corner where the blind pig had stood.

Cusic wanted to make sure we saw some handsomer neighborhoods, so we continued up through Palmer Park and Boston-Edison, with their mansion-sized homes the equal of anything in Grosse Pointe. We also detoured into Highland Park, and even there she turned up a handful of attractive residential streets lined with immaculate bungalows. This was where Cusic had grown up. When her family had first moved in, she said, the area had been almost entirely white, primarily automobile executives.

She pulled to a stop at the corner of California and John R, where a two-story wood-framed home was boarded-up and severely burned.

"This was my house," she said. Cusic hadn't mentioned that we would be driving by her childhood home, or that it had burned. She had actually been living there until fairly recently, with her husband at the time, after her mother had become ill. The place had been damaged in an electrical fire. Luckily, no one had been home.

"I still have books in there," Cusic said. She'd begun removing things, but her brother had made her stop. Too dangerous. Part of the roof had already collapsed. Cusic pointed out her bedroom, on the second floor, overlooking the backyard, once lush with trees. "Oh my Lord," she said, tearing up. After the fire, she'd signed the deed of the house over to a man who lived down the street, wanting to wash her hands of the place. It was too painful to deal with, and this guy had just fixed up another house nearby, so she'd trusted him to do the right thing. But he'd left the house to rot, and since then she'd heard he was moving away. A realtor's sign hung in one of the windows. She jotted down the number, and then we drove on.

Eventually, we ended up in Corktown, the formerly Irish neighborhood adjacent to the old train station, which has become a tiny pocket of gentrification. Cusic pointed out a chicken coop in an urban farmer's backyard. "Chickens in Corktown," she said. "Some of these neighborhoods, they're turning back into what people left behind in the South." We passed a couple of young white guys with beards standing on a corner, waiting for a light to change. "Some of the people coming here bring a sort of bacchanal spirit—like they're out on the frontier and they can do anything," Cusic said. I agreed that certain of the new residents carried a degree of arrogance. "There's a word for it," Cusic said. "'White supremacy.' I don't care if it's young people. It's the same thing. They do it, too." I brought up urbexing, though did not use that word. "People don't understand how offensive that is to us. Just the arrogance of it. What do you think would happen if four black kids went into one of those buildings?" Cusic asked. "They'd be arrested. White kids? 'All right, go home, son.' *Freezing houses.* Detroit isn't some kind of abstract art project. It's real for people. These are real memories. Every one of these houses has a story."

We stopped for lunch at a little French bistro. Cusic told me she had a grown son who moved to Los Angeles for work, and a sister in

Atlanta. Cusic still hadn't visited her sister, and had even been reluctant to go out west to see her son. She worried she wouldn't want to come back.

* * *

Professional photographers, post-Vergara, have continued to follow his lead. The year after the economic crash, the *New York Times T Magazine*, which covers fashion and design, published a brief article (together with an online sideshow) titled "Ruin With a View" about a pair of Detroit-themed photography books: Andrew Moore's *Detroit Disassembled* and Yves Marchand and Romain Meffre's *The Ruins of Detroit*. In his afterword to *Detroit Disassembled*, which begins with the unfortunate sentence, "My initial visit to Detroit started with a dinner in Paris," Moore touches on all of the familiar tropes of the ruin tourist: old carpets turned to moss, pheasants flying from the fields behind crumbling Brush Park mansions. He describes Detroit as a city "whose decomposition is barely comprehensible," a place that has moved "beyond decay into a surreal landscape, where the past is receding so quickly that time itself seems to be distorted."

While this line is a nice reference to one of the most famous images in Moore's book, a close-up of a clock hanging on the peeling wall of the long-abandoned Cass Technical High School, its face half-melted in a real-life imitation of a Dali painting, it also rings false. Detroit, if anything, is a place where the past cannot be shook loose. It hangs on, tenaciously, creeping over the city like a slow-growing mold, until— this begins to seem inevitable, if you get into a certain mood—the entire place will be nothing but past. For Moore, who, according to his afterword, ended up spending "nearly three months" in Detroit over the two-year period following his Parisian dinner, perhaps it seemed as if the decay had happened at some accelerated pace, stealing into the city overnight—when in fact, it's been an ongoing process for a half-century or more, only the layers of dust getting thicker with each passing year.

I do love that Dali clock, though. The face is some sort of plastic overlay, with the melting taking place in the upper left and right quadrants, leaving only the latest hours visible. The twelve has been stretched into what now looks like Arabic lettering, or a child's drawing of a long-barreled gun, and the remainder of the plastic has shriveled and curled, hanging loosely over the hour and minute hands, which are frozen at about seven of four. It's the color of plaque on teeth or Caucasian skin of a certain shading, a comparison the looseness, the way the face ("face"!) droops, also calls to mind.

The final image in Moore's book remains my other favorite. It's the old Cooper Elementary building, the school where Corine and I took refuge in the Zone, shot by Moore as a distant shell on the horizon, gray clouds amassed above and a marshy field of tall grass and flora blanketing the landscape in every other direction, the building's gaping, two-tiered windows suggesting columned Senatorial antiquity. Most of the flowers, Corine had told me that afternoon, were wild, but if you walked around in warmer months, she said, you could still find remnants of once-tended gardens. One afternoon, Corine had even stumbled across a patch of tulips. Being Dutch, she plucked them; they reminded her of home.

The following spring, I returned to the Zone. I was crossing a field when I heard what, later, I realized must have been the sound of water running into a sewer drain covered by grass. Just for a moment, though, I found myself looking around and thinking, "Wow, there must be a stream nearby. Someone should really get a picture of that."

CONCLUSION

THE WRITERS, THE BUILDERS, the hydroponic farmers—we all came to see the future, but three years later, none of use could say which version of the city would win the day, which Detroit would prove the more useful harbinger. With the shortfalls of capitalism on garish display around the world, logging datelines in, well, close your eyes and spin the globe like a roulette wheel, it doesn't matter—Athens, Cairo, Montreal, Santiago, Stockton, Jefferson County, Zuccotti Park—I knew the obvious choice: Detroit the cautionary tale; Detroit the forsaken; Detroit the city of outlaws and eviction and perpetual fire.

But as the recession ground on, I noticed a fascinating reversal of fortune taking place. As the country felt increasingly shrouded by a dark, pessimistic mood, Detroit had begun to receive its best press in decades. President Obama, quite understandably, had decided to make the auto-industry bailout a centerpiece of his reelection campaign. (When Obama made an appearance at Chrysler's Jefferson Avenue assembly plant, I watched from the press scrum, wondering when they would be unfurling the MISSION ACCOMPLISHED banner.) But the Detroit comeback narrative was proving infectious, even if people who lived here knew better. Americans, it turned out, wanted uplifting stories now, stories of the Horatio Alger variety. We craved miracles: Ford inventing the twentieth century in a backwater called Highland Park, a kid from the Brewster Projects figuring out a way to make black music the Sound of Young America, Houdini emerging from the frozen Detroit River long after he should have drowned.*

The notion of a Detroit rebound became *Chicken Soup for the Post-American Soul.* And it made a kind of sense; upon receipt of a cancer diagnosis, one yearns to hear about the woman who not only licked it but ran a marathon the following spring, the guy whose doctor informed him he had six months to live twelve years ago. Advertising copywriters, our savviest modern myth-makers, understood this. It was no coincidence the most praised and widely dissected commercials during the Super Bowl, for two years running, cannily played upon the Detroit comeback theme. Handsome Chrysler automobiles made cameos in both spots, along with Eminem and Clint Eastwood, but what the ads really meant to pitch us had far less to do with cars than an elemental, nearly lost sense of American optimism. People who once might have looked condescendingly upon the Paleolithic "Buy American" manufacturing sector of the U.S. economy suddenly found themselves becoming misty-eyed and patriotic as Coach Eastwood (it was the Super Bowl, remember) ordered us to get out there and give 110 percent, just like Detroit had done.

My favorite example of the comeback narrative run amok arrived in the fall of 2011, when the Detroit Lions, a team that, only three short years earlier, had played the worst season of any National Foot-

---

*Much of the symbolism of the Matthew Barney performance hinged on Egyptian notions of death and resurrection, perfectly suited (thematically speaking) for a city like Detroit. But later, I found myself dwelling on the Houdini Belle Isle Bridge stunt, so inspirational to the piece. It had been Houdini's first-ever bridge jump, and in subsequent retellings of the day's events, he'd embellished the story, claiming the Detroit River had frozen, forcing him to plunge through a hole cut into the ice, and that after unshackling himself from the handcuffs, he'd been swept downstream by the current and spent eight minutes floundering in the frigid river while he searched for the lost opening, snatching breaths from the ribbon of air between the surface of the water and the underside of the ice.

In *Houdini,* the 1953 biopic starring Tony Curtis as the escape artist, the stunned crowd eventually begins to disperse, assuming the Handcuff King is dead; meanwhile, hidden from the spectators, we see Houdini paddling frantically along the bottom of the ice, his face a sputtering periscope. Not necessarily the metaphor I'd have consciously chosen to represent the struggles of Detroit. But I couldn't seem to shake it.

Curtis's lips, in the movie, come so close to the jagged underbelly of the ice, it looks as if he's preparing to kiss some hallowed ground where a miracle had once occurred.

ball League franchise since World War II, losing all sixteen of its regular season games, managed to rebound all the way to the playoffs. The Lions' losing streak had taken place during the season of the contentious auto-bailout hearings and thus had served as useful symbolism for Detroit's larger socioeconomic hard-luck story. Now, the boys were winning again. Coincidence?

Clearly, yes! But that didn't prevent an embarassing number of journalists from marshalling the victories on Ford Field, along with the Detroit Tigers' concurrent trip to the American League Championship Series, as bullet points for a trend piece: "Lions, Tigers and Cars: Detroit on the Rebound?" to quote an actual blog headline. Or, as a CNN columnist wrote, "History has shown that when the city's sports teams start doing well, it's a sign of healing in Detroit."

And really, who wanted to be the one to splash cold water on such magical thinking? I, for one, no longer felt above accepting signs. Even if the upswing had begun as media hype, it no longer mattered, because the rest of the country had bought the story. Friends from other towns had always promised to visit me in Detroit but rarely followed through. As my time in the city came to an end, though, people emailed to ask: Should I consider moving there? Justin was thinking about opening a bakery; Coco, of launching a newspaper written entirely by underprivileged high school kids; Eric, of rehabbing an old dive bar and living upstairs. Why *not* in Detroit?

* * *

Yet three years on, the local headlines still failed to reflect the new, inspirational national narrative.

By the end of February 2012, the newspapers reported, there had been one murder every day of the year, including a six-year-old (shot by a pair of fifteen-year-old would-be carjackers) and a nine-month-old baby. It had taken the 911 dispatcher nearly a half-hour to get an ambulance out to the nine-month-old's house, after the place had been shot up with an AK-47 assault rifle.

That same spring, Council President Pugh's $385,000 Brush Park condo went into foreclosure for the third time in five years. This time, Pugh decided to walk away from the mortgage. "These are the tough choices Detroiters make every day," he wrote his supporters in an email, "and I am no different." Shortly thereafter, he announced that he would not be running for a second City Council term, but that he would be weighing a mayoral bid. Mayor Bing, meanwhile, proposed a budget that would cut the city workforce by 2,500 (one-quarter of its employees) along with a 10 percent across-the-board cut in wages for those remaining on the payroll.

On the day when former Detroit police chief Stanley Knox was robbed while mowing his lawn, a pair of teenagers shot and killed an 84-year-old security guard in the parking lot of a church where a Bible study group was taking place. One week later, it was reported that Pastor Marvin Wayans, of the famous gospel-singing Wayans family, was beaten and carjacked while pumping gas at a Detroit Citgo station on a Wednesday afternoon, the assailants not only stealing Wayans's luxury Infiniti sports utility vehicle, but also a $15,000 Rolex watch.

Details regarding the Detroit Works plan had still failed to materialize, but the *Detroit Free Press* reported on the Bing administration's stealth attempts at coerced shrinkage, by quietly denying the most distressed neighborhoods basic services (new streetlights, home improvement grants, tax breaks for developers, abandoned-property demolitions, road repair) in order to entice those residents to decamp to more stable locations. "There are some areas where we are not going to invest," Mayor Bing told the newspaper. "It makes little sense . . ." According to the report, developers were being informed that if they chose to build new properties in certain neighborhoods, "the city will not provide sewer lines, sidewalks, lighting or any other amenities."

In other words, the bold reinvention of the city had devolved into an austerity plan that would impose sanctions on its poorest citizens. I did notice one major new construction project, just down Gratiot Avenue from my apartment, striking because you basically never saw cranes in the city proper, only wrecking balls. But upon closer examination, it turned out to be a new jail, an upgrading of the old one, right across the street.

* * *

And yet, secretly, surprisingly? It didn't make rational sense, I knew, but I found myself edging over to the side of the optimists. I couldn't say why; it happened gradually, on the level of anecdote: I caught myself noticing and relishing slight indicators that in aggregate (or perhaps viewed through lenses with the proper tinting) couldn't help but make you feel like Detroit's luck, despite such unimaginable obstacles, might still turn.

One evening, I stopped by the Highland Park firehouse. Everything looked the same: guys like Marvin and Lt. Hollowell cooling out in their folding chairs in the mouth of the loading door, chain-smoking and drinking coffee. But when Sergeant Irwin emerged, he struck me as . . . happy. Apparently, a group called Michigan Arson Prevention, backed by insurance companies, had begun paying the salaries of a prosecutor and multiple investigators to focus on insurance fraud. Irwin had obtained his license and become a qualified fire investigator, and Michigan Arson Prevention had awarded him a grant for tools the city of Highland Park could never otherwise afford, including a special camera and the best fingerprint equipment on the market.

Since then, Irwin had four cases accepted by the prosecutor's office, unprecedented for Highland Park. The city had also received grant money to subsidize aggressive demolitions of vacant houses. All of these factors had conspired to make for a drop in the number of fires over the past summer. Irwin smiled shyly and shrugged, unsure if he should believe it himself. "I'm actually feeling good about things here," he admitted.

Even bad news contained some reason for optimism. The Detroit public school system had been making national newscasts since Roy Roberts, a former vice president at General Motors, had been appointed to replace Bob Bobb as emergency manager. His variation on Bobb's efforts to privatize a number of Detroit schools was sounding like a public-sector version of the auto bailout—specifically, of the structured, private-equity-style bankruptcies foisted upon Chrysler and General Motors, in which the most toxic, irredeemable portions of the respective companies were split off into their own separate holdings, effectively quarantined. As applied to a school system, such a plan meant removing forty or so of the 137 schools in the regular (failing) district and converting them to charters. This new, all-charter district would receive the per-pupil funding of whichever students migrated over from DPS, while DPS's budget would shrink accordingly—but "legacy costs," like old debt and money owed to pensioners, would not be carried over to the new "clean slate" district, so it was easy to foresee a scenario in which the best DPS schools would bleed students and money as the charters pressed their advantages.

More immediately distressing, one of the schools slated for closing in the fall of 2011 was the Catherine Ferguson Academy. Several students, including Tiffini Baldwin, had been arrested after refusing to leave the school during a sit-in protest, and the image of pregnant black teenagers being led away by cops while handcuffed wound up replayed endlessly on *The Rachel Maddow Show*. A final rally was scheduled to take place on the front lawn of the school on the last day of class.

But then, that very morning, as activists gathered in the street facing the school, a dramatic reversal occurred: Roberts, apparently sensing the public relations disaster on his hands, announced that Catherine Ferguson Academy would remain open as a charter school, with its current curriculum and administration, including Principal Andrews, intact.

Detroit hadn't been treated to many happy endings, eleventh-hour or otherwise, as unqualified as this one, not in recent memory. The rally still took place, but it went from being an angry wake to a raucous celebration. By the time I arrived, the school's hay-covered tractor bed had been converted into a stage. The actor and liberal activist Danny Glover showed up to give his support. Standing atop the wagon, he hugged Principal Andrews, who was beaming happily and wearing a giant pink carnation, and declared the caving of Roberts "a significant victory in a long war."

A marching band from another school made its way to the center of the gathering. Several of the female band members had doctored their yellow band shirts to reveal brassieres and pierced navels, and their dances incorporated pelvis-thrusting striptease grinds. I wondered if staging this performance at a school for pregnant teenagers constituted a mixed message. But the rally's collective mood would not be dimmed by such concerns.

I ran into Tiffini. Her hair looked wilder than before, and she was furiously snapping photos for a website. She told me she was going to Henry Ford Community College, taking her pre-reqs for a physical therapy major. She said, "When I heard the news this morning, and it was official"—and then, instead of finishing her sentence, she touched her heart.

UAW workers in vests reading "Fight the Attack on the Middle Class" cheered alongside a hipster with a waxed mustache and an old bearded man in overalls. I spotted Rich Feldman from the Boggs Foundation and his son Micah, and my neighbor on Service Street, Ron Scott, the local Black Panther founder, took the stage and announced, "I'm gonna start this speech with what we used to finish up with long ago: Power to the People!" Everyone raised their fists in support. A stray dog wandered through the crowd, some kind of husky, it looked like. One of the UAW guys made a tongue-clicking noise, but the dog ignored him and kept moving.

* * *

Not long after that, I found myself on the rooftop of a Detroit apartment complex, gazing over downtown, recalling the wintery afternoon when I'd scaled the crumbling Metropolitan Building with Detroitblogger John. Now, though, I looked upon signs of positive momentum. Quicken Loans had moved four thousand employees downtown and the company's owner, Detroit loyalist Dan Gilbert, had been purchasing a number of long-vacant buildings, including the Madison Theatre, the planned fulcrum of his "Detroit 2.0" initiative to rebrand the city as a Midwestern hub of tech-savvy entrepreneurial start-ups. New tenants at the Madison (which, in an ill-advised moment of nineties nostalgia, Gilbert had renamed the M@dison) included a graphic design firm, a designer of iPhone apps and a local Twitter office; Chrysler had also announced seventy employees would be migrating downtown from the suburbs. Nearby, the thirty-four story Broderick Tower, vacant since the mid-eighties, was finally in the process of being renovated, thanks to fifty-million dollars' worth of federal tax credits and private investments. Plans for the building included retail, office, and residential spaces. Another group of investors had picked up the GAR Building, the castle with the boardedup turrets originally built for Union veterans of the Civil War, for $200,000. After a three-million-dollar rehabilitation, the place would house a media production company.

The particular rooftop upon which I stood happened to be the communal area of a lovely riverside apartment building on Jefferson. I'd stopped to visit a pair of young senior staffers who worked for Council President Pugh: Quan Tez Pressley, Pugh's director of communications, and Bryan Barnhill, his policy director. We'd met during Pugh's campaign and had stayed in touch. Both only twenty-four years old, Pressley and Barnhill been best friends since attending Renaissance High School, an academically excellent magnet school in Detroit, and had independently returned to the city after graduating from Morehouse and Harvard, respectively. Now they also shared an apartment.

Barnhill was smooth-faced, handsome, and a dapper dresser; he spoke in long, intricate sentences ready for a position paper. The first night we met, over beers and pizza, he said things like, "That's a typical conservative-behaviorist/ liberal-institutionalist argument. In reality, both are wrong. Complexity demands simultaneous convergence of truths" and "My particular environment and background garrisoned me with a lot of tools that made me a very formidable competitor." Barnhill's father was a truck driver and his mother was a registered nurse. "Honestly, I'm from the hood," he said politely. "I can remember frequent shootings outside my house. A crack house on the block. Abandoned buildings. Some people in my family were involved in these sorts of activities. But there's a dual story: positive instruction, and positive instruction by contrast. I could see what I didn't want to be." His mother used to make him work on textbooks two years ahead of his grade. When Detroit's African American history museum built its slave ship exhibit, Barnhill, as a boy, was selected to be one of the models. They covered him with plaster squares and made a cast of his body. Today, Barnhill's ten-year-old self remains in the museum's permanent collection, perpetually embarking on the doomed voyage.

Pressley, taller and skinnier, comes from an auto family: his father worked at Chrysler for thirty-five years. Going back only a single generation, his father's brother was murdered and his mother's brother was beaten to death in a case of mistaken identity. Pressley's parents wouldn't allow him to spend the night at his grandmother's house because she was an alcoholic. At Morehouse, he majored in political science and religion. He'd begun preaching at age four; by six, his mother had given him his pastor's anniversary.

"My message at that point," Pressley, blinking from behind chunky, stylish glasses, told me, "was—"

"Wait till you hear what it is," Barnhill interrupted.

Pressley: "'You may be going up, but you might not be getting in.'"

After leaving for college, they'd both missed Detroit. Barnhill's background seemed so unusual at Harvard, he was profiled in the *Crimson* on three separate occasions. For Pressley, Atlanta was "a city void of obstacles." He said that while he loved Morehouse, it also "felt false, like a false sense of security. Like I didn't have to try hard."

Pressley had been thinking of joining the Peace Corps and working in Jordan; Barnhill, of moving to New York and working for an investment bank. But after the financial collapse, with various job offers rescinded, they both ended up back in their hometown, unemployed and sleeping in their childhood bedrooms. Pressley admitted, "There was a point where our parents were questioning our decisions."

Barnhill's girlfriend brought up fresh lemonade; strangely, the roof was carpeted with green AstroTurf. Barnhill said he'd come out here the night before, around three in the morning, just to think and pray. Today, the river shimmered in the light of a bright autumn afternoon, and from this distance, it was impossible to tell which of the buildings in the downtown core were occupied or vacant, or slightly less vacant than when I'd first returned.

Despite my reservations about their boss, Barnhill and Pressley both struck me as youthful embodiments of the possibility for positive change in the city. I wondered if their time on the job had curdled their idealism. They admitted to having been disappointed more than once, when that idealism met realpolitik; in a city like Detroit, the council has limited power.

"We created Charles's platform, essentially," Barnhill said. "We had all these grandiose ideas. But," he paused, quoting educator Geoffrey Canada, "we were confronted by the system." For the local government's senior staffers, Pressley noted that "new ideas were an affront to their authority. But Charles gave us room."

Recently, Barnhill helped Pugh craft Detroit's amended consent agreement with the state and has also been working on moving up the city's threat-level status when it comes to possible terrorist attacks, which would mean more federal homeland security money. (Detroit is a border town, and amazingly, Barnhill claimed, no one had requested additional funds before.) "Some people thought us sticking around Detroit would be a gamble on our future, a gamble on the fate of the city," he said. "But it's allowed us to experience a fructifying or manifestation of our talent. Young people are coming to Detroit because they want to be part of a movement. I just came from a meeting with the governor. We are some of the most influential people in this city, in terms of how things get done."

I wasn't sure if this was true, but the possibility comforted me.

"I didn't grow up with that post-nineteen-fifties drop to compare everything to, so from my perspective, Detroit has always been improving," Pressley told me. That said, he went on, smiling, "If you come to Detroit, you're probably someone who likes challenges."

* * *

Even Service Street was changing. The building next door to mine, uninhabited the entire time I'd lived there, had been purchased by a Brooklyn artist. Three of the haggard storefront facades overlooking Gratiot were in the process of being restored. And Steve and Dorota Coy, the Hygienic Dress League, had moved from their studio to a foreclosed loft in Brush Park, the depopulated neighborhood of robber baron mansions just off Woodward. A few of the mansions had been meticulously restored; others clung to verticality in assorted states of collapse. The Coys had bought their loft, over twice the size of my Manhattan apartment, for the cost of about eight months' rent on that same apartment.

Now I recall my Detroit home with no small tint of nostalgia. Mostly, I remember the late nights spent listening to music and staring out of my huge front windows. Gratiot always lay empty and dark, except in winter, when steam from the manholes would swirl cinematically outside the glass, as thick as mist in a Gothic novel. The neon sign of the meat market across the street backlit the septic fog, giving it an otherworldly glow. Occasionally a car would drive by, but otherwise, in the downtown of a major American city, I felt totally alone.

Of course, it would be easy to end this book on a different note. Any number of the city's grisly headlines could be plucked and highlighted, and not unrepresentatively, either. But if I did that, it would only be to make sure you understand I'm not a soft touch. The truth is, my optimism was proving tenacious. I couldn't say why.

And even when it faltered, all I had to do was turn to the bulging Detroit section of my bookshelf and pluck out something old—say, *All About Detroit: An Illustrated Guide, Map and Historical Souvenir, with Local Stories*, a handbook to the city written in 1899 by the historian Silas Farmer. Once upon a time, I would have thrilled at the cheap ironies therein, especially in the endlessly quotable section Farmer titled "Dictionary of Detroit." The very first entry, "Advantages," reads, in full: "Because of our location on the Detroit River, our advantages are many and exceptional."

I could go on, almost at random: "'Homes, Attractive': Are very numerous in all parts of Detroit . . .

"'Air and atmosphere': Our skies are as fair as those of Italy . . .

"'Geographical Position': The position of Detroit is favorable for constant growth . . .

"'Floods': We have none. Our river never overflows nor dries up. Residents along the margins of other streams should make a note of this fact . . ."

It's difficult to stop. "'Shady streets': We have an unusual number . . .

"'Morals': Of Detroit will compare very favorably with any city of its size . . .

"'Burial caskets': Are produced in large quantities . . ."

Okay, I'll stop. Well, one last personal favorite: "'Italians': Judging by the frequency with which we hear their street cries, our Italian friends are not at all an insignificant portion of our population. That cry of 'Banan, nicey banan' is heard in every part of the city and their two-wheeled, flat-topped carts laden with the fruit are pushed energetically into the way of probable purchasers."

But something changed in me, somewhere along the way, and Farmer's sentiments no longer felt worthy of mockery. *All About Detroit* had been published two full years before Henry Ford scraped together enough capital to start the Ford Motor Company. Yet Farmer, a laughable booster, had already been indulging his readers with bigger dreams. His book read like that of a naif, yet he'd engaged in a touching and prescient leap of faith, one that had paid out far beyond any odds he or his contemporaries might have ever thought to set. So, who knows? Why not again?

Now, I'm struck by the way certain passages jump out like lines of verse—reminders of how long people had been wanting to believe this city was blessed, and of the poignant distance between that need and our reality, and I feel like I could be reading about Detroit at the turn of the twentieth century, or about any number of cities at the cusp of their grandest hours—Paris, Beijing, New Orleans, Buenos Aires, Bombay, Addis Ababa, St. Clair Shores, Madonna di Campiglio, Manhattan—or maybe even about your town, right now; about cities of memory and cities of desire, trading cities and hidden cities and cities of the dead, lost forever; about Detroit tomorrow, and about everything we allow ourselves to dream our places could become.

> The city is really remarkable in this respect.
> Unusually numerous and beautiful.
> Admittedly the most attractive city on the northern continent.
> First class the year around.
> Not excelled by any other city.
> Visitors cannot fail to notice the beautiful complexions.
> Never a menace.
> Always a joy and blessing.
> Our skies are as fair as those of Italy.
> Progress is manifest.

SELECTED BIBLIOGRAPHY

Adler, William M., *Land of Opportunity: One Family's Quest for the American Dream in the Age of Crack* (New York: The Atlantic Monthly Press, 1995).

Bergmann, Luke, *Getting Ghost: Two Young Lives and the Struggle for the Soul of an American City* (New York: The New Press, 2008).

Bingay, Malcolm, *Detroit Is My Own Home Town* (New York: The Bobs Merrill Company, 1946).

Bjorn, Lars, and Gallert, Jim, *Before Motown: A History of Jazz in Detroit, 1920-60* (Ann Arbor: University of Michigan Press, 2001).

Boyle, Kevin, *Arc of Justice* (New York: Henry Holt and Company, 2004).

Burton, Clarence, *The City of Detroit, Michigan, 1701–1922* (Ann Arbor: University of Michigan Library, 2005).

Carlisle, John, *313: Life in the Motor City* (Charleston, S.C.: The History Press, 2011).

Chafets, Zev, *Devil's Night: And Other True Tales of Detroit* (New York: Random House, 1990).

Conot, Robert E., *American Odyssey* (New York: Morrow, 1974).

Downs, Linda Bank, *Diego Rivera: The Detroit Industry Murals* (New York: W. W. Norton & Company, 1999).

Dunnigan, Brian Leigh, *Frontier Metropolis: Picturing Early Detroit, 1701–1838* (Great Lakes Books, 2001).

Farmer, Silas, *All About Detroit: An Illustrated Guide, Map and Historical Souvenir, with Local Stories* (Detroit: Silas Farmer & Co., 1899).

Farmer, Silas, *The History of Detroit and Michigan* (Detroit: Silas Farmer & Co., 1884).

Fine, Sidney, *Violence in the Model City: The Cavanagh Administration, Race Relations, and the Detroit Riot of 1967* (Ann Arbor: University of Michigan Press, 1989).

Gallagher, John, *Reimagining Detroit* (Wayne State University Press, 2010).

Gavrilovich, Peter, and McGraw, Bill, *The Detroit Almanac* (Detroit: Detroit Free Press, 2006).

Georgakas, Dan, *Detroit: I Do Mind Dying* (New York: St. Martin's Press, 1975).

Halberstam, David, *The Reckoning* (New York: William Morrow & Co, 1986).

Hersey, John, *The Algiers Motel Incident* (New York: Bantam Books, 1969).

Jones, Butch, *Y.B.I.: The Autobiography of Butch Jones* (Detroit: H Publications, 1996).

Lichtenstein, Nelson, *Walter Reuther: The Most Dangerous Man in Detroit* (New York: Basic Books, 1995).

Moore, Andrew, *Detroit Disassembled* (Damiani/Akron Art Museum, 2010).

Parkman, Francis, *The Oregon Trail/The Conspiracy of Pontiac* (New York: The Library of America, 1991).

Sicko, Dan, *Techno Rebels: The Renegades of Electronic Funk* (New York: Billboard Books, 1999).

Smith, Suzanne E., *Dancing in the Street: Motown and the Cultural Politics of Detroit* (Cambridge: Harvard University Press, 2001).

Sugrue, Thomas J., *The Origins of the Urban Crisis: Race and Inequality in Postwar Detroit* (Princeton: Princeton University Press, revised edition, 2005).

Taylor, Carl S., *Dangerous Society* (Ann Arbor: Michigan State University Press, 1990).

Vergara, Camilo José, *American Ruins* (New York: The Monacelli Press, 1999).

Vergara, Camilo José, *The New American Ghetto* (Piscataway, N.J.: Rutgers University Press, 1995).

Watts, Steven, *The People's Tycoon: Henry Ford and the American Century* (New York: Alfred A. Knopf, 2005).

Widick, B. J., *Detroit: City of Race and Class Violence* (Chicago: Quadrangle Books, 1972).

Young, Coleman, *Hard Stuff* (New York: Viking, 1994).

ACKNOWLEDGMENTS

Mom, dad, paul, julie.

My Detroit players: Corine Vermeulen (urbex! techno! *vacano!*), Steve and Dorota Coy (and Bob, and that kid in the XXL "Made in Detroit" T-shirt), Courtney Smith, John Carlisle, Brian Merkel, Holice P. Wood, Ara Howrani, Marvin Vaughn, Bertram Ferrell, Brandon Walley, Djallo Djakate, Scott Hocking, Chef Las.

Jim Rutman. Riva Hocherman. The best.

Jason Fine and Will Dana, my great friends and fabulous long-time editors at *Rolling Stone* (and now *Men's Journal*), and assigners of the original story that became this book.

Jann Wenner, Sean Woods, Eric Bates, Nathan Brackett, Mark Healy, Coco McPherson (and the entire research crew), Tom Walsh (ditto for copy), Marielle Anas, Alison Weinflash.

Jessica Lamb-Shapiro (off-season innkeeper *par excellence*), Julia Holmes and E. Tyler Lindvall (together forever on "Islands in the Stream," L. J.'s Lounge, Halloween 2010), Dinaw Mengestu (scholar, gentleman, confidant, midnight chef, procurer of birthday Ocean), Jonathan Ringen (one of the five great *colocataires* of Western history! [along with Stendahl, Proust, Flaubert, and Brad Pitt]), Bill McIntyre (former Governor Engler wants his sign back), Jonathan Hickman (I concede the married lawyer might also have been a grifter), Mac McClelland (R.I.P. Giant Cat Binelli), Steve Dollar, Chad Post,

Caroline Shepard (Massapequa in the house!), Esther Haynes, Kira Henehan, Alex Mar, Wells Tower, Diane Dragon, John Brumer.

The MacDowell Colony. The Corporation of Yaddo.

Detroit, again: John Adamo Jr., Matt Allen, Asenath Andrews, General Baker, Tiffini Baldwin, Bryan Barnhill, Pete Barrow, Dave Bing, the Blackman, Greg Bowens, Michael Brady, Gary Brown, Rev. David Bullock, Eric Campbell, Dan Carlisle, Shance Carlisle, Kenneth Cockerel Jr., Phil Cooley, Mark Covington, Marsha Cusic, Jai-Lee Dearing, Carlie Dennis, Angela Dillard, Rick Ector, Bishop Charles Ellis, Judy Endelman, Duke Fakir, Andrew Farah, Rich Feldman, Geoffrey Fieger, Vanessa Denha Garmo, Geoff George, John George, Dan Gilbert, Ralph Gilles, Ralph Godbee, Kevin and Val Gross, Francis Grunow, Elena Herrada, Steve Henderson, Eric Hollowell, Greg Holm, Mary Howell, Nate Irwin, Annie Janusch, Saunteel Jenkins, Raphael Johnson, Joseph Kassab, Kwame Kilpatrick, Christine Kloostra, Matt Lee, Kathy Leisen, Caesar Lorenzetti, Derrick May, Toni McIlwain, Kurt Metzger, Toni Moceri, John Mogk, Larry Mongo, Eric Novak, Jermaine Overman, the Pettaway family, QuanTez Pressley, Charles Pugh, Sir Mack Rice, Harold Rochon, Ron Scott, Malik Shabazz, John Sinclair, Edwin St. Aubin, Larry Stone, Jay Thunderbolt, Pastor Steve Upshur, Jerome Vaughn, John Zimmick.

The MacDowell crew, especially Scott Ingram, Rosecrans Baldwin, Feliz Molina, Emma Schwarcz, John Haskell, and Missy Mazzoli.

The Atlantic, Keith Gessen and *n+1*, the Inn at the Oaks, the New Politeness, Cafe 1923, Motor City Brewery, Sara Bershtel, Will Sulkin, Rob Levine, Jim Gill, Deckerville, the Park Bar, the Original House of Pancakes (Grosse Pointe Woods, mom's paying), the Old Miami, Service Street (2009–2012), the YesFarm, and why are those electroclash zombies carrying a moonshine jug?

INDEX

ABOUT THE AUTHOR

MARK BINELLI is the author of the novel *Sacco and Vanzetti Must Die!* and a contributing editor at *Rolling Stone* and *Men's Journal.* Born and raised in the Detroit area, he now lives in New York City.